Drip Irrigation
For Every Landscape and All Climates

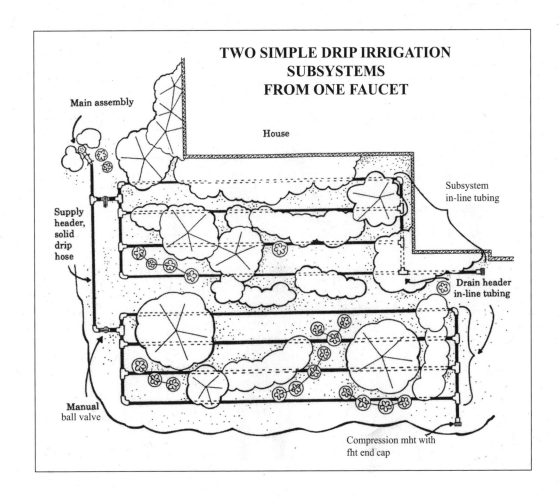

TWO SIMPLE DRIP IRRIGATION
SUBSYSTEMS
FROM ONE FAUCET

Main assembly

House

Supply
header,
solid
drip
hose

Subsystem
in-line tubing

Drain header
in-line tubing

Manual
ball valve

Compression mht with
fht end cap

Helping Your Garden Flourish While Conserving Water!
Outwit Droughts with Expert Guidance

Robert Kourik

Metamorphic Press

Front cover: An edible landscape designed and photographed by the author for the Preston Vineyards and Winery, Healdsburg, CA. Except for the small lawn "piazza," the entire landscape is irrigated with in-line drip tubing. This edible, ornamental landscape was planned and planted by zones of differing water use. With an automatic timer, each zone receives a different amount of water. As this photograph shows, drip irrigation offers the benefit of being virtually invisible.

Front and back cover photographs copyrighted by the author. Line drawings by Sandy Farkas, Pages, Illustration #s: 21 #7, 22 #8, 23 #10, 24 #12,13 , 24 #14, 25 #16, 28 #18 & #19, 30 #21, 32 #24, 74 #56, 87 #62, 90 #64, 100 #67, 101 #68, 102 #70, 103 #71, 111 #74, 117 #76, 125 #8 .
All others by Heidi Schmidt.

Library of Congress Control Number:
2008944362
ISBN 978-0-9615848-4-9 (pbk.)

Distributed by:
Chelsea Green Publications
P.O. Box 428, 85 N. Main St., Suite 120
White River Jct., VT 05001
Orders: 800-639-4099, Phone: 802-295-6300, Fax: 802-295-6444
www.chelseagreen.com
(Wholesale and retail sales.)

FSC
Recycled
Supporting responsible use
of forest resources
www.fsc.org Cert no. SW-COC-002283
© 1996 Forest Stewardship Council
100%

Printed in the United States of America on paper made from 100% renewable mixed-sources paper. Cruelty-free, not tested on animals. Vegan paper. Recyclable. Totally groovy.

10 9 8 7 6 5 4 3 2 1

Dedicated to:

John W. Kourik

My Dad, who has stuck with me through thick and thin.

Acknowledgments

As with the creation of any book, there are many people who have offered personal and professional support. Most books are produced with the help of a veritable social web of friends, associates, and technical authorities—and this book is no exception. Many books are dedicated to a single person. Other than my Dad, I'd like to further dedicate this book to all those listed below and to the greater domain of widespread friendship that makes self-publishing possible. The following alphabetical listing is meant to be fairly complete. But if there's anyone who feels left out, please accept my apologies and thanks.

Chester Aaron—[Occidental, CA] A good buddy and steadfast friend with whom I can commiserate on the difficulties and injustices in the publishing world.

Russell Ackerman—[Santa Monica, CA] Provided much information about Weather-Based Irrigation Controllers and Smart Controllers. Connected me with Bob Galbreath. See Chapter 11.

Angie Albini and Tom Danaher—Harmony Farm Supply [Sebastopol, CA] for providing technical assistance.

Margo Baldwin—[White River Junction., VT] For her faith in my book and valuable assistance with curious inner workings of both the self-publishing and distribution networks.

Bob Galbreath—[Santa Monica, CA] Provided much information about Weather-Based Irrigation Controllers. See Chapter 11.

Lynda [not a typo] Banks—[Novato, CA] The designer who made my Web site look so wonderful.

Elvin Bishop—[Marin County, CA] A great blues guitarist and fantastic year-round gardener. His R&B has nursed me though many tough publishing troubles. Also for teachin' me how to land a few fish.

Paula Blaydes—[Santa Rosa, CA] Who convinced me to revise this book and for her support during its production.

Sandy Farkas—[Forestville, CA] The accomplished artist who designed the front and back covers of the book. Someone who was professional and understanding throughout the production of my "edible" and drip books and gladly returned to work on this book.

Anne Hiaring, Esq.—[San Anselmo, CA] Provided valuable legal guidance.

Dennis Hanson—[Sausalito, CA] Provided important details of subsurface drip irrigation. See Appendix #2.

Pamela Glasscock—[Freestone, CA] Helped with the final proofing of the book.

Patty Holden—[Sebastopol, CA] The computer wizard who helps Sandy and me through the tortuous world of InDesign computer graphics.

Robert Kourik—[Occidental, CA] Laid out the book using InDesign with the help of Patty Holden and Lynda [not a typo!] Banks. Any mistakes are mine alone. Well… and the evil spirit of dyslexia.

John Kourik—[St. Louis, MO] My dad has been unwavering in his support during this project. His financial and emotional support has much to do with this book being born back in the 90s. Plus, it's fun when I visit him in St. Louis, MO.

Wendy Krupnick—[Santa Rosa, CA] A steadfast friend who teaches me a lot about horticulture.

Avis Licht—[Woodacre, CA] Thanks for reviewing my chapter on cisterns.

Marshia [not a typo] Loar —[Crescent City, CA] The patient and understanding landlord for my home, office, and "warehouse." The care of her property sometimes languishes as I become embroiled in final-production obligations. Without her support for "one of the small guys" in publishing, I don't think I could continue to publish.

Mimi Luebbermann—[Petaluma, CA] For her unwavering support over the years. [Decades!] and for all her valuable horticulture and free-lance writing advice.

Linda Parker—[Sebastopol, CA] The most painterly bookkeeper I know. She helps to keep me solvent during bookkeeping madness.

Marty Roberts—[Sebastopol, CA] Thanks for helping organize, build, and manage my Web site: www.robertkourik.com

Scott Sauer—[Sebastopol, CA] For turning me on to the Orbit pre- constucted manifold unit. [And a genius horticulturist as well.]

Ellen Sharron—[Sebastopol, CA] The wonderful and patient indexer who made this book so easy to access.

Betsy Timm and Don Ketman—[Santa Rosa, CA] The dearest friends who have been there for me at all times—for 30 years! [Plus she's a great cook for our Sunday get togethers.]

Laine Velinsky—[Novato, CA] Guided me through the up-and-downs of this self-inflicted self- publishing adventure.

Margie Wilson—[Graton, CA] The editor who looked over the manuscript with an eagle-eye's attention to detail of both the words an all the placement of the illustrations. Any typos are because I missed her notations.

Michael Weaver—Santa Cruz, CA] He provided welcomed advice on marketing this book. And did a great job in keeping in contact with his retail accounts.

ಹಿ Table of Contents ಲ

Foreword

In 1992, I originally wrote a book on drip irrigation for four reasons: Because no other book in good ol' common English had been published about this water-conserving approach to irrigation. Because I was tired of hearing that drip irrigation is just a way to barely keep plants alive in drought-riddled gardens [although it can be used to help plants survive extreme droughts] when my experience is that plants grow better with drip irrigation systems than with any other watering method. Because I was fed up with the countless articles about drip irrigation as a tool only for the arid West when I know good-and-well it's a cost- and time-effective tool for watering in any climate. Lastly, the need for water conservation was becoming a national concern and a permanent part of our future—but our gardens needn't suffer; they can actually be more beautiful and more abundant.

I've revised the book for four reasons:

• Because there is still no other book that makes drip irrigation fun to read.

• Because much of what I wrote in 1992 is only now begun to take hold and I want to continue to reach new readers with the complete scoop on the easiest way to install the highest quality parts.

• Because there are some new widgets and plenty of new timers (aka controllers) to talk about and illustrate.

• Because each manufacturer's product line has one or more bogus parts and I show you how to select the best hardware from a number of sources—I'm not beholden to any one company. [Probably cuts me out of being the "Drip Guy" for one company, but that's the price I'm willing to pay.]

Many of the pamphlets stuffed into the boxes of those drip irrigation kits found in "big box" stores read as if they were first written in Arabic, translated into French, and then transcribed into English. Even do-it-yourself car-care manuals are easier to read. Seems to me, it's time there is a drip irrigation guidebook that isn't cloaked in overly-technical jargon or befuddled by incoherent English. [Luckily some of this has changed since 1992, especially with the instruction booklets for certain timers. That's reserved for Chapter 11.] So, while I won't skirt plumbing terminology, this book is meant to carefully and gradually guide you through every piece of a complete drip irrigation system, what it's called, [how a plumber would write the part down on her parts list] and how to assemble it with the next part. Every part you'll need appears in an illustration.

Drip irrigation does conserve plenty of water; estimates and studies range from 50% to 70% savings. Conserving precious fresh water supplies has become a national issue. Water conservation is no longer the concern of just a few isolated, drought-stricken communities in the West. While water may not always be scarce, everywhere in the country, a supply of fresh, clean water is no longer a given. You needn't be a strident environmentalist to conserve water. Making good use of what water our landscapes and gardens soak up is just being thrifty and wise. The savings are more far-reaching than just the water that dribbles ever so gently out of your drip irrigation system, for water is closely linked to energy. In most cases, virtually every step of the recovery, purification, and distribution of water consumes fuel. To conserve water is to preserve fossil fuels and their effect on global climate change.

For the home gardener, the bottom line is the health of the landscape and garden. Here, drip irrigation's value shines far above all other watering methods. It's a less well-known fact that drip-irrigated plants usually grow better than those sprayed by hand or sprinklers. Trees grow faster, with wider trunks. Shrubs and perennial flowers bloom more profoundly. Vegetables and fruit and nut trees yield more abundantly. And all this with less fungal disease, mildews, or rusts, due to the drier foliage of the drip-irrigated plant.

This is not an encyclopedia of drip irrigation hardware and design. I write best about what I do. And boy, do I also know what not to do! Over the years, I've made every mistake mentioned in this book—and more. And I've manifested every one of Pop Murphy's Laws of Plumbing—some more than once. [See page 9.] So, this book focuses on what has worked the best for me and those designs that make my plants the happiest. All this has come about after years of learning by trial and error. If this book saves you from the expense and frustration of even 10% of what I've gone through, then your money has been well-spent. If, after reading this book, you still feel drip irrigation is not for you, then you've saved a fortune in aspirin alone.

Everybody operates differently. I'm a hands-on kind of guy. When writing about plumbing and drip irrigation, I need to have the parts strewn about my desk to make sure I keep everything straight. And I have a very hard time remembering the "trade" name for many of the parts. I just go to the plumbing store, rummage through the shelves for what I need, and grab some stuff. So, if you're like me, don't be intimidated by the drawings and names of the parts in this book. Just take the book to your local plumbing or hardware store and select a bunch of parts to match the drawings. Then, keep those parts handy while reading the book and finger-fit the various parts together as they're mentioned in the text. Play with your parts. See how many ways you can fit them together. Get familiar with the parts before you're bent over on a hot June afternoon with salty sweat dribbling into your eyes and your sciatica begins to electrify nerve endings you never knew existed. Do your homework before you literally get in the trenches.

No matter what seems to be going wrong, laugh. Or call a plumber. But first check the equity in your house! Remember: What does a plumber charge when one of the pipes you threaded together spouts a major leak, it's three o'clock in the morning and your wife is going into labor? Anything she wants!

But seriously folks, you'll master drip plumbing and watch the benefits grow right before your eyes. Then you can proudly award yourself a Degree in Dripology as found in the Appendix.

Robert Kourik

2009, Occidental, CA

Introduction

Somewhere out there, perhaps, is a garden that wouldn't benefit from drip irrigation. In this garden, the rains come with absolute regularity, just when the soil is beginning to dry, and never too far apart. For real gardens, however, watering between irregular rains or during protracted droughts is a fact of life.

Although drip systems are initially somewhat more complicated than dragging a hose around with an attached oscillating sprinkler, the benefits from drip irrigation, in any climate, far outweigh the hassles.

Is Drip for You?

Drip irrigation isn't for everybody or every situation. No technology or tool is appropriate for universal application, and like any gardening tool, drip irrigation has various benefits and certain limitations. Before you decide to design and install your own system, consider the following pros and cons of drip irrigation. In reading through them, you may find that the drawbacks outweigh the advantages for your garden, in which case an extensive drip system probably isn't for you. Most gardeners, however, will find that drip irrigation may be appropriate for a portion, if not all, of their ornamental plantings and at least some of their edible crops.

The Benefits of Drip Irrigation

The advantages of drip irrigation can be summarized as follows:

• **Uses water efficiently.** Sprinklers waste a lot of water as a result of wind-scattered spray, sun-powered evaporation, runoff, the evaporation of accumulated puddles, or deep leaching. Various studies have documented a savings—when compared to furrow irrigation—of 30% to 70%, depending on the crop, climate, and use of mulch [or no mulch].

• **Provides precise water control.** Every part of a drip irrigation system can be constructed with an exact flow rate. It is very easy to calculate what the total flow of the system amounts to and to match this with the plants' needs. You'll know exactly how much water you're applying and will be able to control the amount down to the ounce.

• **Increases yields.** Drip irrigation can be used for the slow, gradual application of tiny amounts of water on a frequent, or daily, basis. This maintains an ideal soil moisture level, promoting more abundant foliage, greater bloom, and higher yields (by actual comparison) of produce, fruits, and nuts than those produced by any other approach to irrigation.

Research in many different climates and states invariably supports the benefits and cost-effectiveness of drip irrigation. Art Gaus, an extension horticulture specialist with the University of Missouri at Columbia, MO, has had a drip system in his personal garden for nine years. One summer, his bush watermelons with plastic mulch and a drip system produced 32 pounds in a four-by-four-foot area, compared with 9–16 pounds in the same area with conventional irrigation. He reckons a well-timed drip system "could mean a 100% increase in yields; during the droughts of 1980, '83, and '84, it meant the difference between having a crop or no crop at all."

In a study of established pecan trees in Georgia, trees with drip irrigation added had a 51% increase in yields.

Michigan State University has documented

a 30% yield increase in vegetable crops with drip irrigation, even in its humid, summer-rain climate.

A study in Sri Laka, in 2002, found that with chilies, water use was down 34%–50%, while production was up 33%–48%. The researchers attributed this to irrigation that kept the soil moist, not too dry.

A study in New Mexico found amazing differences in yields compared to [respectively] furrow and drip irrigation: 18 pounds versus 30 pounds with cucumbers, 69 to 156 pounds growing Swiss chard, and 64 versus 166 pounds with green beans—to quote a bit of the study. [It is interesting to note that broccoli, Brussels sprouts, and carrots didn't have any greater yields in these drip irrigation plots. Yet, a study at Oregon State University found a 20% increase in carrots compared to plots with sprinklers.]

• **Provides better control of saline water.** Sprinklers apply water to the foliage; if your water is saline, this can cause leaf burn. Drip irrigation applies water only to the soil, and frequent applications with drip irrigation help to keep the salts in solution so they don't affect the roots adversely. [Any salt crust buildup at the margins of the moist area can be leached away with an occasional deep irrigation.]

• **Improves fertilization.** With a device called a fertilizer injector (or proportioner), you can easily apply dissolved or liquid fertilizers with accuracy and without leaching the fertilizer beyond desired root zones. The liquid fertilizers can be applied with each irrigation or only when required.

• **Encourages fewer weeds in dry–summer climates.** The small moist spot around each emitter, where the water slowly dribbles out, covers only a fraction of the soil's surface. The larger dry areas between emitters remain too dry for weed seeds to sprout.

[NOTE: This benefit is lost in areas with summer rains.]

• **Saves time and labor.** Drip irrigation systems eliminate tedious and inefficient hand watering. Automatic drip systems add the convenience of not even having to remember to turn valves on and off by hand. [The initial installation of such a system, however, will take more time and effort than all other forms of irrigation except permanent sprinkler systems.]

• **Reduces disease problems.** Without the mist produced by a sprinkler, drip-irrigated plants are less likely to develop water-stimulated diseases such as powdery mildew, leaf spot, anthracnose, shothole fungus, fireblight, and scab. Furthermore, careful placement of emitters away from the trunks of trees, shrubs, perennials, and vegetables will keep the crown of the root system dry and minimize such root problems as crown rot, root rot, collar rot, and armillaria root rot.

• **Provides better water distribution on slopes.** Sprinklers often create wasteful runoff when set to water the upper slopes of hills or berms. Drip emitters can apply the water slowly enough to allow all the moisture to soak into the soil. Some emitters, known as pressure-compensating emitters, are designed to regulate the water flow so that all emitters in the system put out the same gentle flow, regardless of slope.

• **Promotes better soil structure.** Heavy sprinkler irrigation can produce puddles, causing clay particles to stick together, and increase soil compaction. Drip-applied water gradually soaks into the ground and maintains a healthy aerobic soil, that retains its loamy structure.

• **Conserves energy.** Because of the low-pressure requirements of a drip irrigation system, the pumping costs, whether from municipal water supplies or from your own well, are lower.

- **Uses low-flow rates.** The low-volume application rate of drip emitters permits larger areas to be watered at the same time than is possible with sprinkler systems.

- **Is more economical than permanent sprinkler systems.** While more costly than a hose with an oscillating or hand-held sprinkler, drip irrigation systems usually cost less than fixed sprinkler systems.

The Limitations of Drip Irrigation

Some drawbacks of drip irrigation include the following:

- **Initial costs are high.** A garden hose with a simple oscillating sprinkler will always be cheaper than drip irrigation, but it doesn't offer the same measure of control and water conservation. A well-designed drip system will more than repay the cost of installation in reduced effort, fewer irrigation chores, and greater yields.

- **Can clog.** This is really a limitation of older and outdated emitters. Many early models of emitters were more prone to clogging and gave the industry a bad reputation. All this has changed; with adequate filtration, the emitters featured in this book have performed successfully with city water, well water, and water with dissolved iron and calcium. Some types, such as the noncompensating in-line emitter tubing, even function reliably with filtered grey water systems.

- **May restrict root development.** Early and outmoded designs for drip systems called for only one or two emitters per plant. This led to very restricted root growth around the few points of moisture and thus to stunted plant growth. One major goal of this book is to show how the emitters should be placed to cover the entire area of natural root growth. With the proper placement of emitters, root growth will be uniform, expansive, and healthy.

- **Rodents can eat the tubing.** There are a number of drip irrigation systems that can be buried in the soil, but if your garden has gophers, you'll just be offering them an easier way to drink. Occasionally, even mice and wood rats will hear the running water in the drip hose, especially in dry summer climates, and chew through for a swig of *aqueous delecti.*

- **Isn't compatible with green manure and cover crops.** The growth of a green manure crop gets all tangled up with the drip tubing, thus prohibiting the usual "tilling under" of the plants. Cover crops are usually grazed or mown, both of which would damage a surface drip system. And both buried and surface drip systems would leave too much of the surface dry for adequate germination of cover crop or green manure seeds.

- **Weeding can be difficult.** Unmulched drip irrigation systems will stimulate some weeds around each emitter, and care must be taken not to damage the drip system while weeding. A protective and attractive layer of mulch will greatly reduce, if not eliminate, this problem.

- **Requires greater maintenance.** Very little can go wrong with your typical hose-and-oscillating-sprinkler setup. Drip irrigation requires more routine maintenance to sustain its high level of efficiency, but such maintenance is relatively simple.

- **Eliminates soothing hand watering.** For some gardeners, the act of standing out in the garden near sunset and watching the moon rise, listening to the mockingbird warble, and rhythmically swaying back and forth with a hand-held sprinkler is more valuable than any form of therapy or meditation. For these people, drip irrigation may be counterproductive.

- **Doesn't cleanse the foliage.** In arid climates, some plants, such as lettuce and other leafy greens, prefer periodic sprinkling of leaves to wash off accumulated dust, grit, and/or air pollution. These plants need to receive an occasional sprinkling or be grown with low-flow sprinklers.

- **Doesn't create humidity.** Many plants, most notably humidity-loving perennials from England, the muggy Tropics, and northern Europe, like a moist atmosphere. When these plants are grown outside their natural environment, sprinklers and misters are perhaps the better irrigation devices. [For many other plants, a drip system's lack of additional humidity is a bonus, inhibiting fungal and bacterial diseases.]

- **You can't see the system working.** With a well-mulched drip system, the emitters quietly go about their work hidden from view. For some gardeners, this is the beauty of the system. For others, not being able to watch the watering is slightly unsettling. In a poorly designed system, a clogged emitter goes unnoticed until drought stress affects the plant visibly. This is a serious problem only with poor quality emitters and the old-fashioned concept of placing only one or two emitters next to each plant. The design approach in this book protects the plants from any stress as a result of clogging.

Simple, but Not Easy

People have good cause to be leery about drip irrigation. At first, it seems so darn complicated. Yet, over and over, the phrase "simple, but not easy" comes to my mind.

I got this description from Warren Schultz, when he was working as editor-in-chief for *National Gardening* magazine. We were lamenting the journalistic difficulties of explaining drip irrigation. I like his "simple-but-not-easy" concept because it capsulizes the fact that the basics of drip irrigation really aren't that difficult to understand

or implement—provided you take the time to do a little homework.

There are, however, a number of initial stumbling blocks that prevent many people from even considering messing with this complicated-looking drip business.

Unless it's done with planning, a sense of craftsmanship, and a desire to achieve that elusive look of affordable elegance, a drip irrigation system can be just more garden clutter, and ugly to boot, with black plastic spaghetti tangles running from plant to plant. It seems to "breed" into a veritable mess.

After years of experimenting, my approach to drip irrigation is to use the least number of different parts for the most efficient system. This book is about how to put in a drip irrigation system that's simple to install, efficient, and virtually invisible to the eye.

This approach is beginning to catch on. I've seen the parallel rows of in-line emitter tubing in: a shopping center in Santa Rosa, CA; outside an Olive Garden restaurant in St. Louis, MO; a Wal-Mart on the Big Island, Hawaii; and the Musée du Quai Branly in Paris, France. [I'd like to think someone in Paris was reading my book, no French editions that I know of.]

Gizmophobia

Drip irrigation equipment is pretty weird looking. With gadgets, tubing, dials, buttons, and digital-readout displays, it's enough to send a simple gardener scuttling back to the nineteenth century.

If you're intimidated by any device more complicated than a hand-operated can opener, rest assured that drip irrigation is nowhere near as bad as it seems. Think of all those put-'em-together parts as toys for grown-ups. Harken back to days gone by, the many happy hours spent playing with Lincoln Logs™, Erector Sets™, Legos™ or Tinker Toys™. If you can put yourself in that same carefree frame of mind out in your landscape, drip parts may not seem so intimidating.

Fear of Plumbing

Many homeowners are possessed by a phobia more overpowering than the repulsiveness of spiders or the apprehension caused by visiting in-laws: they have a deep-seated fear of plumbing. This syndrome usually begins when young children are allowed to watch their parents turn pale upon the receipt of their first bill from a union plumber.

While designing and installing an efficient and effective plumbing system for an entire house is a complicated job and often requires professional skills, the plumbing required for landscaping is well within the means and skills of most gardeners. Anyone can learn the relatively simple craft of garden plumbing. Whatever mistakes you make in plumbing a drip system are easily rectified and virtually harmless, as long as you have correctly installed a backflow preventer [described in detail on pages 20 & 65] to protect the purity of your home's drinking water.

The Truth About *%&#$ Plumbing

One important plumbing skill is the well-hurled curse, whether unspoken or thunderously roared. Anyone who proposes to instruct you in trouble-free drip irrigation installation and assures a carefree, routine process is either a liar or a terminal optimist, for they are forgetting the most persistent and perhaps most awesome force in the universe—Pop Murphy's Laws of Plumbing.

Pop Murphy's Laws of Plumbing

Most books describe pipes as if they were just inanimate objects. The truth is that pipes answer to a greater force, the one described on some heretofore lost tablets recently discovered buried beneath a mountain of plumbing parts at a local hardware store. The universal truth is that it's nearly impossible to do any plumbing job without something going awry.

Pop Murphy's Laws of Plumbing are numbered to enable you to refer to each one easily throughout the book. The only antidote known for *Pop Murphy's Laws of Plumbing* is laughter—so apply this important remedy with carefree abandon. But, don't forget...Pop Murphy never sleeps!

The Official List of Pop Murphy's Laws of Plumbing (PMLP)

[These are real. I know! Most have happened to me!]

Numero Uno—No matter how small the job, you will be missing one part—but only when the hardware store is closed.

#2. The thought, "Just one more twist," instantly produces a cracked pipe or leaky thread.

#3. Whenever a job calls for two pipe wrenches,

only one is to be found.

#4. Leaks will always wait for the most inopportune times—like just after you've put on your tux.

#5. When you drop a threaded metal pipe, the pipe always manages to turn around in midair and land directly on the threads—damaging them beyond use.

#6. With any part that has an arrow clearly marking the direction of the flow of water, you will install it backwards at least once.

#7. Even though you know PVC glue is toxic and should not touch skin, you will decide to "skip the gloves just this once and be extra careful." Before you finish the word "careful," a dribble of glue will already be drying on your ungloved hand.

#8. Pipe dope is the only correctly named plumbing part.

#9. When a plastic pipe breaks, it will always break where the threads meet an expensive fitting so that the fitting is rendered useless.

#10. Pipes are just the *Titanic* and water turned inside out. [Think about it!]

#11. Be forewarned: Pop Murphy is, at this very moment, perfecting a gopher capable of gnawing through plastic PVC pipe; metal-chewing gophers will take a bit longer.

#12. Pop Murphy was temporarily diverted from plumbing devices with consulting on the start-up of numerous wars. But now that he has trained the Pentagon in all his best management techniques, he has returned to designing the all-digital, all-confusing, microchipped, maxi-priced irrigation timers and controlling devices.

There's a copy of all of Pop's rules in the back of the book so you can cut it out to refer to while reading the book. Enjoy!

Reality-Based Plumbing

Having 30 years of grubby hands-on experience on which to draw, I have distilled into this book what I've learned from hundreds of hours of self-inflicted mistakes. Instead of explaining a number of different ways to design a drip system for each portion of your garden, I will outline the systems I've come to rely upon after years of messing around with many brands and types of gizmos and widgets. If this book helps you skip even 40% of the learning curve that I went through, I will feel it's worthwhile. No book can solve every irrigation question because all gardens don't match the book's examples. My intent is to explain the basic principles of design, familiarize you with the names of the best parts to use, provide a simple set of design guidelines, and explain some tricks of the trade.

But, ah! The rewards awaiting the persistent budding student of "dripology!" Upon finishing this book, you'll have a working drip irrigation system, and you can endow yourself with an honorary Degree in Dripology [see page 187] from that prestigious school of higher education—the School of Hard Knocks.

A Grounded Beginning

How long, how much, and how widely and deeply you plan to water greatly affects the nuts and bolts of a drip system. Before you can begin to design your own system, it is important to know something about the soil in which you'll be planting and to understand some important principles about irrigation. While the following little discourse on soils and irrigation may seem like a digression, please bear with me and read through it before getting into the nitty-gritty of parts and gizmos.

CHAPTER 1

Why Drip Irrigation Works — Anywhere

To understand how drip irrigation works, you need to know how your garden's soil affects the flow of water from the emitters, how roots absorb moisture and nutrients, and how plants respond to wet and dry cycles.

The emitters release water very slowly and form a wet spot, mostly beneath the soil's surface. The shape of the moist area is affected differently by each type of garden soil and ranges from long and carrot-like to squat and beet-shaped. Knowing how your garden's soil affects an emitter's flow is important to planning your drip irrigation system.

Get to Know Your Soil

To test your soil, buy a single emitter, use an emitter punch (which cuts a tiny circular hole) to pierce a hole near the bottom of an empty plastic one-gallon milk jug, and insert the emitter's barb. [See Figure 1.] Fill the jug with water and place it on a dry spot in the garden. After the milk jug is empty (which may take twenty-four hours or more because it's not under pressure), dig a small trench next to the emitter to see the shape of the wet spot in your soil. This is the most graphic way to understand how the water from each emitter you install will move laterally and vertically in your soil. Put the jug in several places in the garden to see how different soils

affect the shape of the moist spot. Naturally, the width and depth of the wet spot and the degree of moistness will also depend upon the flow rate of the emitter and the length of watering time. Emitters with a higher rating, such as two or four gallons per hour [gph], will cause the wet spot to be wider than 1/2- or 1-gph emitters.

Notice how the surface soil around the emitter is moist but not puddled, as the soil would be with the use of an oscillating sprinkler for the same amount of time. Also note that the wet spot

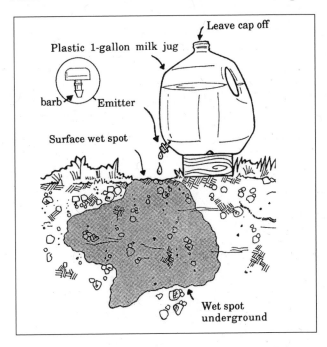

Figure 1 Use an emitter inserted into a plastic milk jug to learn about the flow of water in your soil. The wet spot will be larger when the emitter is pressurized by a complete drip irrigation system.

you've exposed in the trench's wall is also moist but not soggy. It is this moist-but-not-too-wet spot that is the key to drip irrigation's superiority over all other forms of irrigation. With proper timing, a drip irrigation system provides moisture to the soil with little puddling and without overly saturating the pore space in the soil. The labyrinth of minute pore spaces helps the soil breathe. When a fairly aerobic condition in the soil is maintained by drip irrigation, the roots don't drown, the soil's beneficial bacteria can continue to release valuable nutrients, and harmful anaerobic fungi don't easily proliferate.

The dry surface between the emitters' wet spots discourages weeds because dormant seeds don't have enough moisture to germinate. However, although reduced weeding is often touted as an important benefit of drip irrigation, this pertains only to arid climates. Any periodic summer rain will negate the effect of dry spots between plants by providing enough moisture to sprout weed seeds. Mulch, which is routinely used to hide a drip irrigation system, can be used to suppress many weeds that might germinate.

Where Roots Drink and Eat

It seems logical to many gardeners to water plants deeply, with infrequent but lengthy irrigations. Drip irrigation can be used for this kind of irrigation, but the roots of many plants, it turns out, don't really get most of their water and nutrients from the deep regions of the soil. In all the studies I've been able to find, the usual conclusion is that for the sake of quality growth, as opposed to sheer survival, the upper one or two feet of the soil accounts for over 50% of all the water a plant absorbs. [See Figures 2 & 3.] While many plants have roots deeper than two

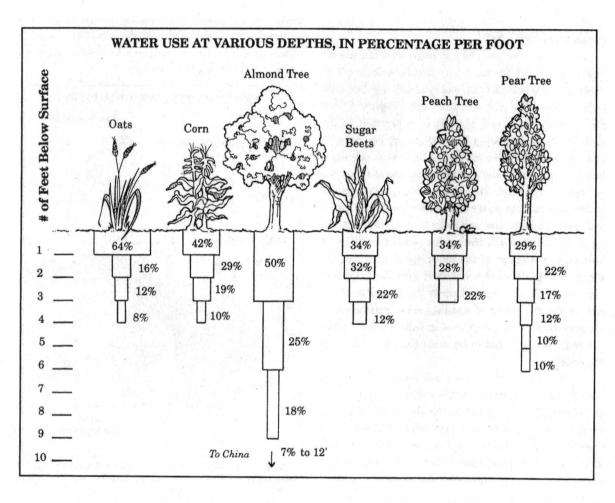

Figure 2 Plants absorb most of their water and nutrients from the upper one to two feet of the soil. Each example is from a different, independent study. Most root "maps" are for economic crops due to their agricultural value. See the Appendix for illustrations of more roots and some native-plant root systems.

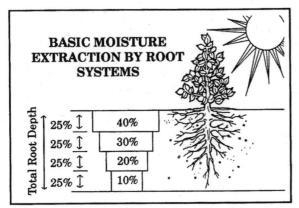

Figure 3 The roots of plants get a majority of their water and nutrition for good growth and high yields from the upper 50% of their root zone. This illustration represents the average absorption by root depth.

feet, these deeper roots exist mostly to stabilize the plant, absorb some micronutrients, and help the plant survive droughts rather than to support an abundance of growth.

The biology behind this phenomenon is quite interesting. The upper layers of the soil are the most aerobic, with the highest population of air-loving bacteria and soil flora. As seen in Figure 4, the top three inches of the soil has nearly four-and-a-half times more bacteria, almost eight-and-a-half times more actinomycetes [tiny aerobic organisms that help decompose dead plant tissue], more than twice as many fungi, and five times the algae of soil found eight to ten inches deep. These bacteria and flora are responsible for the decomposition of organic matter and the liberation of mineralized [unavailable] nutrients into a soluble form that the plant can absorb. They live near the soil's surface because they must have plenty of oxygen to fuel their activity.

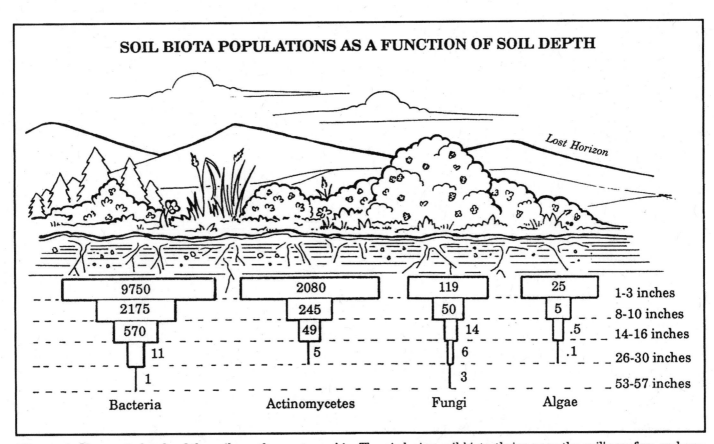

Figure 4 The upper levels of the soil are the most aerobic. The air-loving soil biota thrive near the soil's surface and are greatly responsible for the high availability of nutrients in the upper layers of the soil. (Numbers indicate individuals per zone.)

The Wet and Dry Cycles of Plant Growth

A plant can absorb nutrients only in a water solution, and only when the soil is moist—not too wet or too dry. If the soil is too dry, nutrient uptake is inhibited because the soil life can't thrive, and what little water is in the ground becomes tightly bound to the soil particles. Allowing the upper soil to dry out between infrequent irrigations means that nutrient uptake also "dries up." Then, when plenty of water is again supplied, the soil is saturated to the point that roots and air-loving soil life may be stressed or killed from too much water. Thus, nutrient uptake is inhibited by the lack of air. It also takes some time for the air-loving bacteria to repopulate a soil that is either too wet or too dry, so at either extreme there is a biological lag before the roots get their best meals. Infrequent, deep irrigations tend to produce two points in the watering cycle where the soil life is damaged enough to reduce or prevent growth—during the drying stage and when the soil is too wet.

Soils Often Aren't Very Deep

Another hidden assumption about deep watering concerns the depth of the fertile soil. There are places in the world where glacially deposited topsoil extends down for dozens of feet, but these are more the exception than the rule. If you have such a deep, loamy soil, then rejoice, but remember that the majority of moisture and nutrient absorption still happens in the top two feet. Typically, most suburban yards have a very shallow layer of topsoil, if there's any left at all after construction. If, for example, there is a continuous layer of rich orange clay some 18 inches under the ground, then the 18-inch layer of topsoil is, for all practical purposes, the only place where the plant's roots will be feeding.

Most heavy clays, whatever the color—and dark-blue or white to pale-gray are the worst—are relatively worthless to feeding roots. While clayey soil may have plenty of nutrients, their availability is locked up in its tight, anaerobic structure and strong chemical bonds.

Frequent, Shallow Watering Is Best

For the sake of real growth and the absorption of moisture and nutrients, the loamy upper horizon is the important place to concentrate irrigation and fertilizers. Frequent waterings, if done in a way that avoids puddling or flooding of the soil, produce the best growth. In rainy areas, if watered just enough between periodic storms to maintain a moist-but-not-wet soil, your garden will produce higher vegetable yields or lush ornamental foliage. And the best tool for frequent, gentle watering is drip irrigation.

This is not to suggest that drip irrigation can't be used for infrequent watering of plants hardened to a regimen of drought stress and minimal irrigation. Where water is very limited, drip irrigation is still the most efficient way to apply this precious resource. I live on a parcel of land where the normal summer drought has always been a problem. The fractured geology of the area makes it hard to find underground water, and most wells are poor producers.

To conserve my water supply for essentials, I used to water portions of my landscape only three or four times during the entire six-month dry season. Now, I've figured out how to plant in the fall, water once, mulch, and I never have to irrigate again.

Drip Irrigation Improves Yields and Growth—Everywhere

Research in many different climates and states invariably supports the benefits and cost-effectiveness of drip irrigation. See the examples described in the Introduction.

In dry summer climates, I would prefer frequent watering with small amounts of water, sort of like "topping off the tank." After the winter rains are over and the soil has reached an ideal moisture level, not too anaerobically wet and not too dry, the goal is to replace, as often as daily, exactly the amount of moisture lost due to evaporation from the soil and transpiration from the plant's leaves [called the evapotranspiration rate, or ET], plus an amount that represents enough extra water for gorgeous growth. *Arboriculture*, the preeminent text on growing and caring for trees, recommends frequent irrigation: "In contrast to other systems, drip irrigation must be frequent; waterings should occur daily or every two days during the main growing season…the amount of water applied should equal water lost through evapotranspiration." [As mentioned earlier, I can't do this.]

This is just an introductory look at the basics of soil and watering. Later, in the Chapter 4, titled "When and How Long to Irrigate," I'll talk more about the specifics of the ET rate and timing. And in Chapter 6, the chapter titled "Drip Irrigation for Containers," more detailed guidelines for healthy watering will be discussed.

Now it's time to get into the hardware of drip irrigation—the gizmos, widgets, and gadgets. If drip irrigation seems like a huge ugly bull, it's time, in the words of W.C. Fields, to "grab the bull by the tail and face the situation!" Most people's fears of drip irrigation gadgetry stem from a mild case of "gizmophobia." With a gentle introduction, some time to become familiar with the various parts, and a little practice, most overcome their initial hesitations.

CHAPTER 2

Basic Drip Irrigation Stuff

To paraphrase the late, great comedian George Carlin, "People love their 'stuff.' The more 'stuff' the better. But where are they gonna put all their 'stuff?' " Well, drip irrigation can add a lot more "stuff" to your yard. A poorly designed system can clutter your garden with cheap, breakable "stuff." A well-designed system keeps clutter to a minimum by maximizing the effectiveness of whatever bits and pieces you use and hiding much of the system with an attractive mulch.

So, under the heading of absolutely necessary "stuff" for a good basic drip irrigation system are a backflow preventer to keep water in the hosing from siphoning back into your home's pipes; a fine-mesh filter so the small orifices in the emitters don't clog, a pressure regulator to keep the easily assembled fittings from blowing apart, and carefully placed lengths of black or brown hosing with emitters to control the flow of water. Important "stuff," but not too much.

The Main Assembly

At the beginning of any drip irrigation system, right where you attach it to your garden faucet, is the main assembly that consists of the backflow preventer, filter, and pressure regulator. The main assembly services the drip irrigation hose and a number of branched lines of drip irrigation hose called laterals or subsystems. [See Figure 5.]

The easiest way to begin installing a drip irrigation system is to use the existing garden faucet closest to your plantings. If you must add a faucet to the garden, be sure to use a solid brass one, not one of those shiny fake-chrome or plastic versions, which can so easily split.

All drip irrigation systems require the three above-mentioned parts of the main assembly in order to work effectively and safely. But many discounted drip irrigation kits, as featured at hardware and "big box" stores, either don't include all these parts or offer only cheap, easily broken versions of one or more of the items. For good success and long-term performance, I recommend spending a bit more to get quality parts for a more reliable, longer-lasting system. In this way, you may be able to get one up on Pop Murphy. [See pages 9 and 139.] I've broken and thrown away dozens of cheap parts over the years, so what follows is a list of my very specific recommendations based upon the successes and failures of years of installing drip irrigation systems for clients and in my own garden.

The Backflow Preventer

A backflow preventer [see Figure 6] is essential for the health of your family. Turning off any irrigation system can start a slight back-pressure suction, which can create a reverse siphon of water into the house's plumbing. This reverse siphon can suck dirt, mulch, bacteria, fungus, pesticides, herbicides, manure, or fertilizer through the emitters, into the drip hose, and back into your home's drinking water supply. It is important that a backflow preventer be installed at every garden faucet—whether a drip system is attached to that particular faucet or not.

There are two types of inexpensive backflow preventers—an atmospheric vacuum breaker and a check valve. The atmospheric breaker creates an air gap to prevent the water in the garden

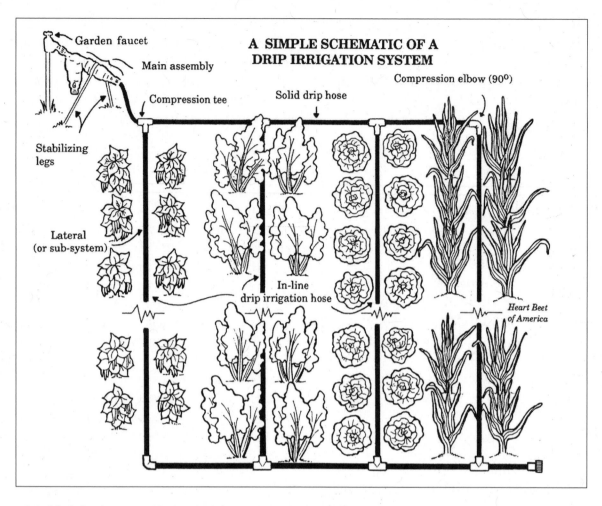

Figure 5 A drip irrigation assembly attached to an existing faucet in the garden. Solid irrigation hose acts as the main water supply line to the vegetable garden. [You could use in-line tubing instead.] Lines of in-line tubing form the laterals along each row of vegetables. Then the laterals are connected to what is called a drain-down header with an end cap. [bottom lower right].

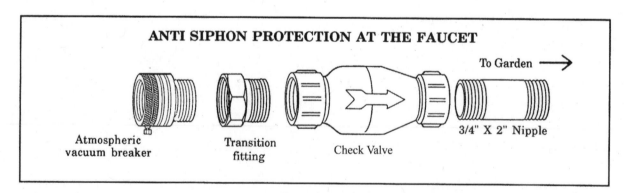

Figure 6 The combination of an atmospheric vacuum breaker and a check valve is one way to protect your family from dirty water back-siphoning into the home's water supply. Be sure to point the arrow on the check valve away from the faucet and toward your garden. Make sure these two parts are at least 12 inches above the highest part of the drip system. Join all the laterals to one series of fittings as a flushing line so you don't have to look for too many endings with each lateral.

hose or drip system from siphoning back into the drinking water. Because of the safety of the air gap, the atmospheric vacuum breaker is becoming the preferred code-required device for anti-siphon protection at all garden faucets.

The check valve has a spring-loaded, gasket-rimmed plunger that quickly seals against a circular seat when the water flow reverses. A check valve shuts off quickly and doesn't waste water [compared with an atmospheric vacuum breaker], but pieces of organic matter, bits of dirt, or a buildup of algae slime, sand, or tiny pebbles can keep the plunger from fully sealing. Thus, cautious gardeners and enforcers of plumbing and building codes will not allow a check valve alone as an anti-siphon device.

The best inexpensive backflow prevention for a faucet assembly combines both an atmospheric vacuum breaker and a check valve to get the advantages of both. [See Figure 6.] A good-quality metal [brass] atmospheric vacuum breaker costs between five and ten dollars. Don't go cheap and use a plastic one, as plastic can't take the stress of the rest of the main assembly hanging off the faucet. The atmospheric vacuum breaker comes with hose threads and is threaded directly onto the faucet before an all-metal hose Y-valve, which has two small ball valves. The cost for a metal one is twice that of the plastic version, but $8 won't set you back too far. [See Figure 8.]

The Y-valve allows both a drip irrigation main assembly and a spare hose for occasional watering tasks to be attached to the same faucet. The atmospheric vacuum breaker will also keep the garden hose from siphoning water back into the house. A check valve costs less than $20, and it should be added in sequence after the atmospheric vacuum breaker. Use a check valve that has a spring rated at one-half pound, so it will close quickly with any reverse flow. Be sure to note the arrow embossed on the check valve's body or printed on the label. Don't forget Pop Murphy's Law of Plumbing [PMLP] #6. The check valve must be installed with the arrow pointing away from the faucet, toward the drip irrigation hose. If you use a check valve with a plastic body, don't tighten it too hard, as cracks may develop. Paint all plastic parts with an outdoor latex paint to shelter them from harmful UV rays which will deteriorate the plastic and shorten its structural integrity.

NOTE: Make sure these two devices are at least 12 inches or higher than any part of the drip irrigation system. If the supply tubing from the faucet travels uphill, the atmospheric vacuum breaker and check valve must be installed 12 or more inches higher than the highest portion of the tubing. See Chapter 5, for setups when the irrigation tubing is higher than 12 inches above the main assembly.

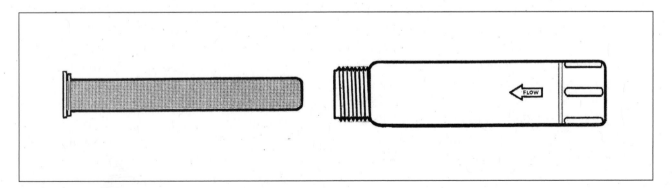

Figure 7 The in-line tube filter comes with a stainless steel 200 mesh filter. At $12 or so, it is cheaper than a $17 Spin Clean Filter™ as shown in Figure 9 on the next page. The difficulty is that these are tedious to take apart and clean. You have to un-thread both ends to remove the casing. Consequently, gardeners are less likely to clean the screen.

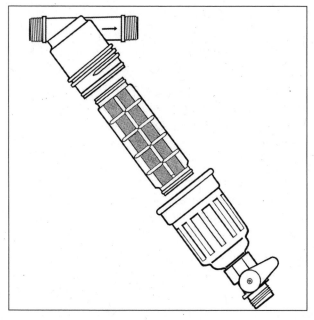

Figure 8 Use the Amiad™ filter because it can take a high psi without splitting. [If something should go wrong with the supply's pressure.] The ball valve allows for easy and rapid flushing without having to disassemble the filter. Still, scrub the wire filter once each year or more with a tooth brush or wire brush and a ten-percent soluton of bleach.

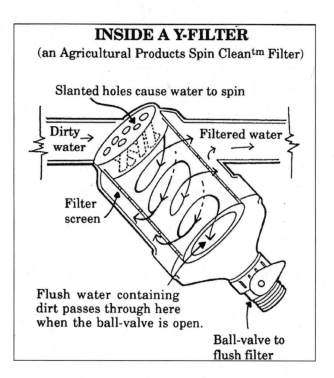

Figure 9 The swirling votex of this filter helps to carry dirt and sediments to the bottom of the filter. Open the ball valve to flush the filter. You still need to scrub the filter at least once a year in the spring and as needed through the summer.

The Filter

Without a good filter, the emitters can clog, rendering your investment of time and money useless. The filter can also be the Achilles heel of a drip irrigation system. Routine cleaning of the filter is essential to a properly functioning drip irrigation system. Filters which have to be taken apart to be cleaned are often ignored and forgotten. A quality filter which is easy to clean can guarantee easy, long-term maintenance. Therefore, for city water my money, the only filter worth getting is a Y-filter with a ball valve at the end of the filter chamber for easy flushing [See Figures 8 & 9.] Priced from about $20 to $30, a Y-filter is more expensive than an eight-dollar tube-type [InLine™] filter and is much easier to clean.

The diagram of a Y-filter in Figure 9 shows how one model lets water pass from the inside of the screen cylinder to the screen's exterior at great velocity and on to the drip line. The ball valve built into the bottom of the filter chamber allows you to flush out dirt by simply opening the ball letting the water run for a few minutes. The water passes through the interior of the screen at great velocity and flushes out the trapped silt and sand. Because a strong blast of water is best for cleaning the filter, the filter must be plumbed into the main assembly before the pressure regulator so it can get full, unrestricted water pressure. The second advantage of the Y-filter is its capacity to pass water. Y-filters have a much larger internal filter surface than tube-type filters, allowing for more water to pass per minute to supply a greater length of drip hose. The typical three-quarter-inch Y-filter with a 150 mesh screen is able to filter out particles down to 106 microns. [A micron equals one millionth of a meter. Looked at with a more practical description, a grain of salt is between 90 and 110 microns. Netafim's Techline CV® in-line tubing passes up to 130 microns. So clogging is not

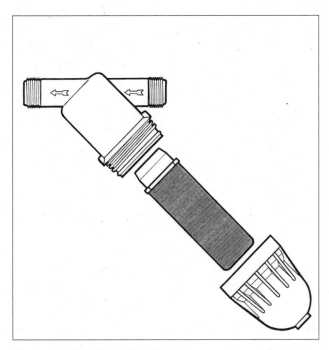

Figure 10 An Arkal™ filter looks strange, but really does a good job filtering small particles like rust in iron-laden well water with a series of plastic disks. It doesn't have a simple ball valve, but is a necessary effort well worth the benefits where water is plagued with iron, calcium, and other minerals.

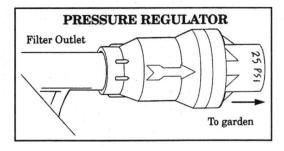

Figure 11 A pressure regulator is required to protect the easy-to-use drip irrigation fittings from blowing apart. The pressure should be between 10 and 25 psi [pounds per square inch] depending on the type of system. Regular water from the faucet is usually between 40 to 60 psi. Pictured is the best I've found, made by Senninger™.

have the 200 mesh screen as used in the filter described in Figure 10. The Arkal filter in Figure 10 does not have a flush valve. You must take the filter chamber off and scrub the disks aganst each under running water. If that doesn't work, try a high-pressure nozzle, or put it in a dishwasher. However, this is the best filter for use with well water that has iron. The filter in Figure 8 passes more than 800 gph, or over four times as much water as a tube-type filter. Thus, while Y-filters appear to be more expensive, they are far more efficient and cost-effective.

Be sure to purchase a Y-filter with a metal screen filter cylinder, not one made of plastic mesh. The metal screen can be scrubbed periodically, usually once a season, with a toothbrush and a solution of 10% bleach to remove any algae or scum buildup. Plastic mesh screens won't stand up to such scrubbing for very long.

The Pressure Regulator

Every drip irrigation system also needs a pressure regulator to prevent the simple non-threaded drip irrigation parts from blowing apart. A regulator which keeps the pressure below 25 pounds per square inch [psi] is often sufficient, but with some drip system parts, an even lower psi is required. Regulators are available with 10-, 15-, 20-, and 25-psi ratings. Porous hose [see page 24, 150, and 154] must be kept below 10 psi so the fittings don't leak. Laser™ drip tubing [1/4-inch tubing with small slits cut at regular 6- or 12-inch intervals by a laser] is especially useful in large pots or in small vegetable and flower beds, but it can work correctly only at 10 to 15 psi.

Good-quality pressure regulators, the ones I use, are made by Senninger™ [see Figure 11] and sold for a specific range of minimum and maximum flow. This is one of three pressure regulators recommended by the city of Santa Monica, CA in their handbook for profes-

much of a risk.] The larger the mesh number on a screen, the smaller the particle which is trapped. Some filters are rated at 200 mesh. City water needs only the 150 mesh. But well water should sional landscape contractors. The regulator I use most often is the Senninger 25-psi low-flow model marked 1/8 to 8 gallons per minute [gpm]. This means that the regulator only functions correctly when the flow rate is greater than 6 gallons per <u>hour</u> [1/10 gpm times 60 minutes per hour] and less than 480 gallons per hour [8 gpm times 60 minutes]. At higher or lower flow rates, the regulator will not control the pressure effectively.

Here's how to find the flow rate for each of your drip lines in order to purchase the correct regulator: determine the flow of your system by counting the number of emitters you have, or plan

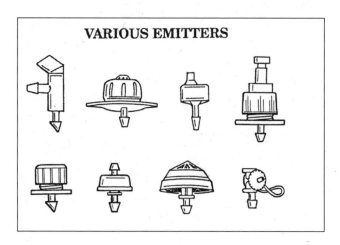

Figure 13 These are some of the emitters you can punch into 1/2-inch drip tubing or add to the end of 1/4 inch tubing. From left to right, the top row are: Hardie DBK™, Spot Scubbler™ adjust 0.0-10 gph, Rainbird Rainbug™ pressure compensating, and Hunter Dail-a-Flow™ 0.0-25 gph. From left to right, bottom row: Hunter Dial-a-Flow™ 0.0-10 gph, Netafim Woodpecker™, Netafim RAM™ pressure compensating, and Spot Vortex™.

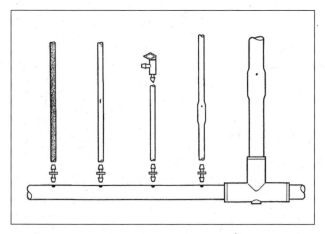

Figure 12 These are the five most common types of tubing that you can use to water your garden. From left to right: porous hose, laser tubing, tubing with emitters at the end of the tubing, 1/4-inch in-line tubing, and 1/2-inch in-line emitter tubing.

to have, on each line. Multiply by the flow rate of the emitters to get the total flow rate. [If you have emitters with various flow rates—something I do not recommend—total the flow rates for all the emitters.] Make sure this total falls within the range of the pressure regulator you've chosen.

For example, if you have a total of 37 emitters along a length of drip hose and each emitter passes 1/2 gph, the total flow is 18.5 gph or 0.3 gpm. This is within the flow rate of the Senninger low-flow model: 6 to 480 gph, or 0.1 to

8 gpm. As another example, using in-line emitter tubing [to be described soon] with 1/2-gph emitters every 12 inches, the Senninger low-flow pressure regulator passes enough water to use 12 to 960 feet of tubing. Or, the same regulator could supply between 3 and 240 emitters rated at 2 gph.

Different Ways to Drip Your Landscape

There are five major, generic types of tubing that can be used in the garden or landscape—porous hose, drip irrigation hose with punched-in emitters, laser tubing [referred to by its manufacturer–Agrifim–as "Laser Drilled Soaker Hose"], 1/4-inch in-line tubing, and 1/2-inch in-line emitter tubing. Each has various benefits and limitations.

Note: You may have heard of "spaghetti" tubing, thin 1/4- or 1/8-inch tubing which is used to run from a 1/2-inch solid drip hose to each plant. I

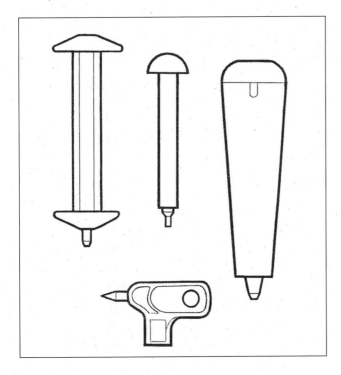

Figure 14 Some of the hand-held tools to punch a hole in solid tubing to insert a emitter or transfer barb. Pick one that's gentle on the palm of your hand. I find the larger tool's handle on the right [John Deere], offers the least discomfort on my hand and wrist.

think "spaghetti" is a good description—the stuff really gets tangled. Also, it is practically impossible to weed or mulch around and can easily snap off of the 1/2-inch drip hose. Personally, I never use "spaghetti" in the landscape, reserving it for limited use with container plants only [to be discussed later].

Porous Hose

Porous hose, also called soaker hose, oozes water through a labyrinth of minute channels in the hose and out of its entire surface. The soil is watered along the entire length of the hose and out from it to a width which depends upon both the type of soil being irrigated and how long the system is left on. Porous hose is made of either used tires or new tire trimmings combined with low-density polyethylene. The fittings sold to install porous hose are inserted inside the hose and will either leak or come apart if the pressure is too high, so be sure to use a pressure regulator that will keep the pressure below ten psi. Porous hose is often sold without a filter, but you should install one to prevent possible clogging. Even with city water, a 200-mesh filter [which traps all particles 74 microns or larger] will help protect your investment.

The benefits of porous hose include: it is sturdy, is readily available through mail order companies and garden centers, is very easy to hook up to your existing faucet, is simple to snake around your existing plantings, can be buried in the soil, drains itself for freeze protection, and works with pressures as low as ten psi. The cost is about $50 for the 1/2-inch roll 50 feet long.

Drawbacks include: the 5/8-nch version is rather bulky [the 1/2-inch hose has a much lower profile] and ugly if left uncovered, the metal hose clamps [often sold to guarantee that the insert fittings don't leak] are expensive, and will eventually rust. Unchlorinated well water can produce an algae slime or calcium build-up that eventually seals the pores on the interior of the tubing. Flow rates can vary considerably from the beginning to the end of a line and, to avoid differences in flow, it should be used only on flat ground.

Be wary, by the way, of manufacturers' guidelines on how far apart to space each length of porous hose. I know an employee of a prestigious mail order company which carried porous hose who followed the company's own guidelines for spacing the hose below the ground for a lawn. His lawn ended up striped a charming green-brown-green-brown. Before you bury any porous hose, do a test run to see how wide the wet spot will be in your soil for a given length of irrigation.

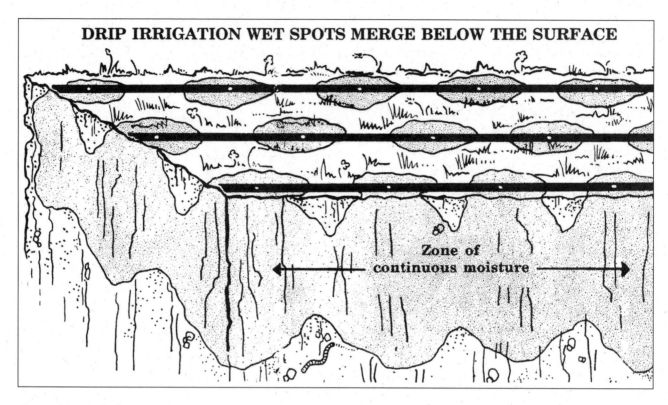

Figure 15 This illustration shows how the wet spots beneath each emitter merge to form one continous zone of moisture. The soil for the entire length of the in-line tubing is moist some four to six inches beneath the surface, depending on the soil type. Sandier soils require tubing with the emitters pre-installed 12 inches apart. While heavier, clayey soils only need emitters every 24 inches.

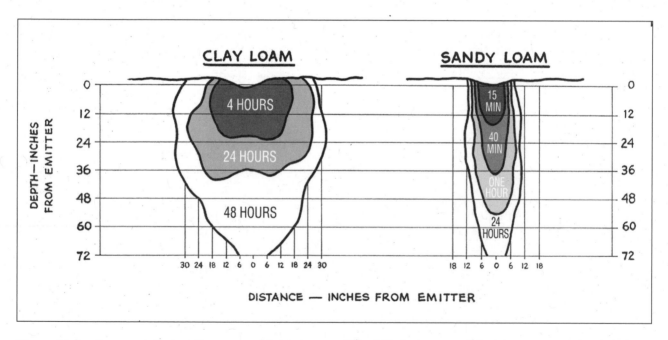

Figure 16 Another way to look at the pattern of the underground "bulb" of water spread. In this case, as per the time the system is on. Notice how wide the bulges are in just four hours in clay soil. Sandy soil could use emitters every six inches.

Emitters

Emitters come in dozens of configurations [see Figure 13], usually in flow rates of 1/2-, 1-, 2-, and even 4-gph, and are inserted into 1/2-inch polyethylene drip irrigation hose. [18mm] A hand-held tool is used to pinch a hole very much smaller than the barb's shaft. When the emitter's barb is inserted, the plastic hose naturally forms a tight compression around the shaft. [See Figure 12.]

Punched-in emitters do have the advantage over porous hose of being able to allow more than 200 linear feet of total drip hose per valve—up to 1000 feet, providing the total amount of water emitted is less than 110 gph. An example would be 220 emitters rated at 1/2 gph each or fifty-five 2gph emitters. The limit of a total flow of no more than 110 gph is to compensate for the reduction in flow caused by the friction of water moving through the extra length of hose. With more than 200 linear feet of tubing, you must use pressure-compensating emitters so that all emitters pass the same amount of water, regardless of the length of the hose. [See Figure 18 on the next page.]

Emitters are commonly used for what I call point-source drip irrigation, in which only one or two emitters are placed near the stem of each plant. There are both regular and pressure-compensating emitters. With regular emitters, the flow rate from one

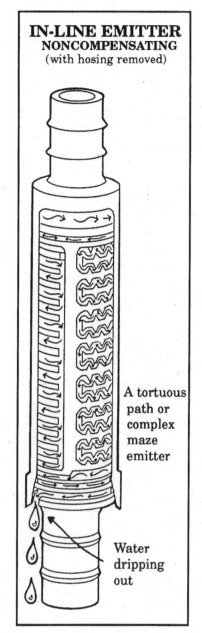

**IN-LINE EMITTER
NONCOMPENSATING**
(with hosing removed)

A tortuous path or complex maze emitter

Water dripping out

Figure 17 The inside of non-compensating, in-line emitter tubing. The emitter shown here is inserted at the factory into solid drip hose at the most common intervals of : 12-inches, 18-inches, and 24-inches. [You can order custom intervals like 6- or 48-inch spacings.] The water and any sediment left over from passing through the filter enters what is called the "tortuous path". This regulates the flow somewhat. More importantly, any debris is kept in a little tornado pattern due to all the right angles.

end to another [on lines totaling more than 200 feet or from one elevation to another] can vary considerably. If the total up-and-down change in your garden's topography is more than 20 feet, you must use pressure-compensating emitters, that are designed to put out almost the same amount of water regardless of topography and length. Even though pressure-compensating emitters can cost about 50% more, when I need punched-in emitters, I always use the pressure compensating type, to make sure the flow is consistent throughout the system.

The main limitations with the use of pressure-compensating emitters is that the stem of the emitter will get brittle with age and can easily snap off during weeding, hoeing, or mulching. In a large garden, installing hundreds of emitters can injure a "weekend warrior's" wrist or shoulder.

Laser Tubing

Laser tubing is not as easy to find as it used to be. It is still manufactured by NDS a wholesaler of Agrifim® [Fresno, CA. agrifimusa.com]. Check with your local retail irrigation supplier. Cost is about $25 to $35 for 100 feet of tubing.

It has largely been replaced by 1/4-inch in-line tubing in many

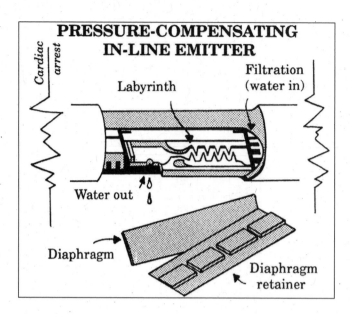

PRESSURE-COMPENSATING IN-LINE EMITTER

Cardiac arrest

Labyrinth

Filtration (water in)

Water out

Diaphragm

Diaphragm retainer

Figure 18 This cross-section drawing of a single pressure-compensating emitter shows a smaller tortuous path. The flexible diaphragm handles both the pressure regulation and helps prevent any particles from clogging the emitter. It also helps to prevent root intrusion. This example is from Netafim Techline®.

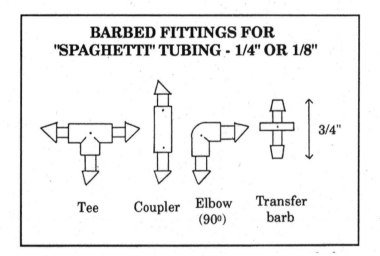

BARBED FITTINGS FOR "SPAGHETTI" TUBING - 1/4" OR 1/8"

3/4"

Tee   Coupler   Elbow (90⁰)   Transfer barb

Figure 19 One-quarter inch ["spaghetti"] tubing is joined together with these fittings. The transfer barb is used to make the transition from 1/2-inch drip hose to "spaghetti" tubing. No messy glue is required.

catalogs. It can still be found at irrigation supply stores.

Its main advantage is it is much cheaper than the comparable in-line tubing. As with 1/4-inch in-line tubing, it is fully adaptable to a range of barbed fittings and goof plugs used as end closures. It can be used to make tight circles for use in medium to large containers.

It's essential to make sure the tubing is installed with the arrows facing away from the water source, headed out toward the garden.

Laser tubing is another product for urban water supplies that don't have a lot of minerals in solution. The tiny slits can be easily clogged when calcium, iron, other minerals precipitate, and algae builds up at the slit.

I no longer use it in the landscape as 1/2-inch in-line tubing is self-cleaning, is just as easy to install, takes more abuse without getting sliced or cut, and can be used for much longer lengths of tubing [25 feet versus up to 326 feet, respectively].

In-Line Emitters

In-line emitters are the least well-known drip irrigation technology. In the 15 years since the first edition of this book and the writing of this

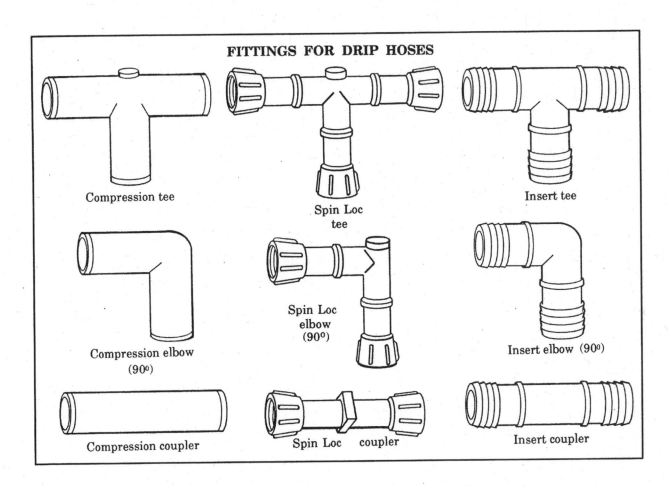

FITTINGS FOR DRIP HOSES

Compression tee

Spin Loc tee

Insert tee

Compression elbow (90º)

Spin Loc elbow (90º)

Insert elbow (90º)

Compression coupler

Spin Loc coupler

Insert coupler

Figure 20 Various compression and insert (barbed) fitings for 1/2-inch tubing. Easy to install. The 2006 guidelines for commercial landscapers from Santa Monica, CA specify only compression fittings. My favorite fittings.

revised edition, the in-line-emitter tubing is becoming more available—at least through certain retail and mail order outlets. It's usually found at stores that supply the landscape contractors with all types of irrigation products. [But not the "Big Box" stores. Yet.] In the 35 years since I've used this type of drip hardware, it is in my experience, the best mix of efficiency, ease of installation, and resistance to clogging and leaking. The tubing is nearly 1/2-inch in diameter [16 mm, as opposed to 18 mm for "regular" half-inch drip hose] and comes with an emitter pre-installed inside the tubing at regular intervals.

These internal emitters utilize what is known as a "tortuous path" [see Figure 17 and 21], the water must pass through a labyrinth of right-angled channels inside the emitter before exiting via a hole much larger than that of a typical punched-in emitter. The tortuous path causes the water to form a continuous vortex, a kind of horizontal tornado, which keeps any sediment, sand or silt in suspension so it won't settle out and clog the emitter. I used in-line emitters for Chester Aaron's 60 raised beds of garlic 15 years ago. I set up the system with a moveable filter and pressure regulator as depicted in Chapter 5. Even with well water full of iron oxide [notorious for clogging regular punched-in emitters], I've found only a few clogged emitters in a thousand feet of tubing.

Another person I know actually took off the filter and pressure regulator for four years and found no clogged emitters compared to the filter and pressure regulator assembly they originally installed. A true testimony to the cleaning action of these emitters.

In-line emitter tubing moistens the soil the entire length of the line but slightly below the surface, where the bulbous-shaped wet spots come together to form one nearly continuous moist zone. [See Figure 15.] The emitters come pre-installed in tubing with 12-, 18-, 24-, and 48-inch spacings [they can be custom ordered at just about any in-

terval—for an extra fee], but the type most commonly sold to gardeners is the 12-inch interval. The emitters inside the hose are rated to dispense either 1/2- or 1-gph [actually 0.6 and 0.92 gph]. The cost ranges from $22 to $30 for a 100-foot roll depending on the emitter [its flow rate and whether or not it's pressure compensating.]

Newer versions include tubing with pressure-compensating emitters at the same intervals

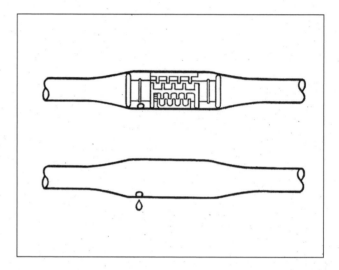

Figure 21 The 1/4-inch in-line pressure tubing is great for container plantings and short garden beds. This is a view of the turbulent, tortuous path that keeps the emitter clean.

as in the noncompensating in-line tubing and with 1/2- or 1-gph flow rates. [See Figure 18.] I always use the kind with 1/2-gph emitters on 12-inch centers because they will irrigate, depending upon how long the system is left on, both sandy and clayey soils.

The benefits of in-line pressure-compensating emitters are: they are very easy to install, simple to snake around your existing plantings, suffer less clogging than porous tubing and some punched-in emitters, provide consistent rates of irrigation without regard to slope or length, have no external parts to snap off, their connectors or fittings don't leak, and the connectors, either compression fittings or Spin-Loc™ fittings, seal better than metal hose clamps with porous hose.

The drawbacks are few: they are not recommended for plants placed far apart and at very odd intervals; they can't turn in as sharp a radius as porous tubing and they aren't carried by very many mail order or retail outlets. Much of this "newer" technology is available from suppliers to the commercial landscape trade. [See *Suppliers* in the back of the book and your local Yellow Pages.]

A very helpful product has been released since I wrote the first book in 1993. With 1/4-inch tubing with in-line, self-cleaning emitters placed every 6 to 12 inches we have a very important tubing to work with. There are two discharge holes opposite each other. Some people use this tubing for small vegetable gardens and in urban gardens because it costs much less than 1/2-inch in-line emitter tubing. The tubing is attached by simple, inexpensive "transfer barbs" and merely bent back at the end of the tubing or use a goof plug to seal the end of each line. This tubing has a small turning radius and is useful in medium- to large-sized round and rectangle container plantings. [One name brand is Agrifim's DURA-FLO™ JR Dripperline.]

The most exciting development in 1/2-inch drip irrigation technology is the pressure-compensat-

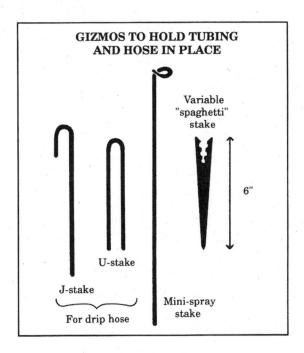

Figure 23 Various stakes and holders to keep drip irrigation hose and "spaghetti" tubing from walking around late at night and "breeding." Spaghetti tubing is the worst as it forms knotted messes that take the patience of a saint to untangle.

ing emitters that have a small flap that acts like a tiny check valve. This keeps all the water in the hose from draining to the lowest place in the system. An example is Netafim's Techline® CV Dripperline. The sneaky rascals have made the I.D. and the O.D. different than other tubings. So, you're forced to use their fittings.

The pressure compensation occurs when the psi is between 14.7 and 70 psi. But they prefer to limit the psi to 50 psi or less.

The cost is about $30 for a 100-foot roll with emitters every six inches. Or, $20 for 12-inch spacing.

Flow Rates Compared

The main assembly represents a major cost in any drip irrigation system. The total flow rate of each type of tubing or hose has a direct

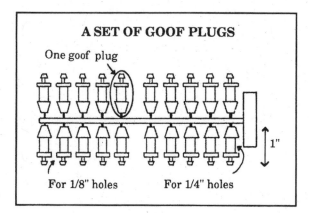

Figure 22 Most people make a few mistakes. These goof plugs are for repairing holes in 1/2-inch tubing after pulling out an emitter or a transfer barb. There are two sizes to plug most types of holes. They're also used to plug the ends of 1/4-inch in-line emitter tubing.

influence on the cost of main assemblies. The lower the flow rate of your water system, the more main assemblies you'll need. With porous hose, each valve can reliably serve up to a total of 200 feet of tubing without a substantial reduction in water flow [with a flow rate of 160 gph at 10 psi]. A main assembly or valve, servicing drip hose with punched-in emitters, can supply at least 200 feet of drip hose, for a maximum flow of 240 gph. With in-line pressure-compensating tubing, a single main assembly or valve can support up to 325 linear feet of tubing with 12-inch spacing and pressure-compensating emitters, or 458 feet with 24-inch spacing. [See Appendix #3 for the flow rates of various in-line emitter tubings.] This means that in-line tubing, at the lowest flow rates of 1/2-gph emitters on 12-inch centers, allows you to install about one-third more length of hose per main assembly than either drip hose with punched-in emitters or porous hose. Therefore, the use of in-line tubing means you spend one-third less on a main assembly than

you would for drip hose with punched-in emitters or porous hose. With more distant spacings between emitters, the savings are even greater.

Miscellaneous Stuff

Finally, there's a wide range of miscellaneous gizmos and widgets to personalize your system and make it more fun to work with. Figures 14, 19, 22, and 23 show various stakes, spaghetti-holders for container plantings, transfer barbs, "goof plugs," 1/4-inch right-angle barbs, emitters, and misters. I'll discuss each of these gizmos later in the sections that apply to their use.

All drip irrigation parts are either hand-threaded and hand-tightened or easily inserted into each other with compression fittings, Spin-Loc fittings, or insert fittings. [See Figure 20.]

With insert fittings, the drip hose fits over the barbed male portion of the fitting. And, depending upon the pressure rating on the regulator, hose clamps go around the outside of the drip hose to prevent leaks. Some people say the insert fittings don't need a hose clamp if the pressure is kept below ten psi. I would never trust an insert fitting without hose clamps. The greater the water pressure, the weaker an insert fitting becomes. Should an insert fitting fail, the water will flow out at the rate of three to five gallons per minute instead of one-half to two gallons per hour.

With compression fittings, the drip hose fits snugly inside the female orifice of the fitting. [You can easily figure out where the label of female and male parts comes from. If not, ask your doctor.] [See Figure 20.] Unlike insert fittings, compression fittings actually seal better as the pressure increases, up to a point. At pressures above 25 psi, most likely at or above 50 or 60 psi, the fittings may split apart. But no drip irrigation system should be operated above 25 psi.

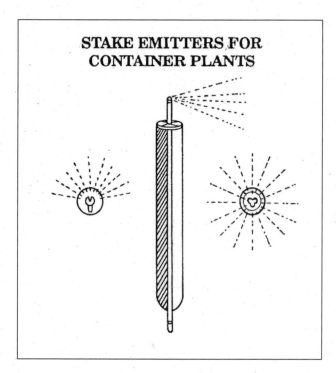

STAKE EMITTERS FOR CONTAINER PLANTS

Figure 24 There are many selections of stake emitters. These are Roberts stake (or spot) emitters–no relation to me, or else I wouldn't have to write this book. See the complete selection in the Appendix.

I've always preferred compression fittings because they are much less expensive than insert fittings with the appropriate hose clamps and they are quick and easy to install—for me. Other people I've worked with have a difficult time inserting the drip irrigation hose into compression fittings. This is especially true with the pressure compensating in-line emitter tubing which has an outside diameter [O.D.] of 0.708 inch, slightly larger than the inside diameter [I.D.] of the green-ringed compression fittings—0.63 inch]. I've always been able to grab the drip hose close to its end and wiggle it into the female-barbed opening. Sometimes, when other people are having problems putting the two together, I have them bring a thermos of hot water into the garden. If an inch or two of the end of the drip hose is stuck into the hot water, it softens up enough to wiggle into the fitting. Some folks, even with wiggling, hot water, well-placed curses, and repeated attempts, just can't get the hang of joining the two parts together. For these people the Spin-Loc fittings are the ticket.

Spin-Loc fittings have a smooth nipple which has a blue O-ring gasket around the outside and a female-threaded tightening ring which threads over the drip hose. You simply pull back the tightening ring, insert the nipple into the hose, pull the ring down over the end of the drip hose and thread the ring onto the drip hose. The threads of the tightening ring cut a shallow set of grooves into the soft hose and secure the inside of the drip hose against the blue O-ring. [Sexual plumbing at its best.] Unlike compression fittings, these fittings are easily reused. Spin-Loc fittings cost nearly twice as much as the equivalent compression fitting. Spin-Loc fittings offer one very nice advantage over compression fittings: the same Spin-Loc fitting works with standard 1/2-inch drip hose [O.D. 0.708-inch, blue ring] and with in-line emitter hose [O.D. 0.63-inch, green ring]. This means you won't have to stock two types of compression fittings.

A friend returned to compression fittings because he found the Spin-Loc fittings blew apart without a pressure regulator, while the compression fittings held their own. [Remember the Dripper's Mantra: "back-flow prevention, filter, then the pressure regulator".]

CHAPTER 3

Your First Drip Irrigation Project

If you live where there is a municipal water system, you probably won't have a supply problem, but you should know the water pressure at each existing garden faucet. [See Figure 25.] You can buy a simple pressure gauge to hook up to the faucets and test the existing pressure in, as mentioned before, pounds per square inch [psi]. See Figure 26 for an example of a pressure tester. Keep a written record of the psi for each faucet.

Checking Your Water Supply

People with wells should check the psi of the pressure tank at the well. The important figure for drip irrigation purposes is the sustained pumping rate, in gph or gpm. This is vital to know in order to ascertain the maximum flow

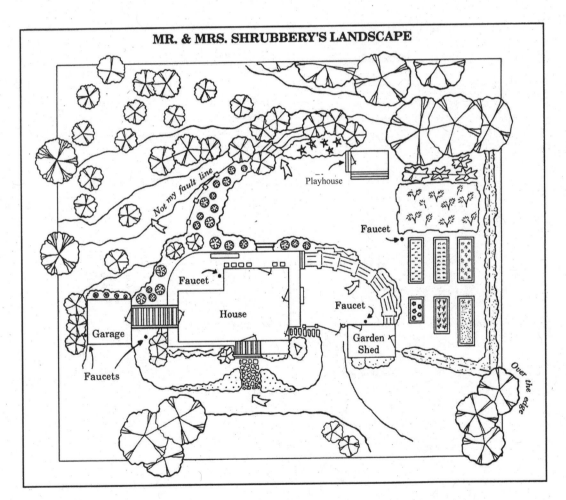

MR. & MRS. SHRUBBERY'S LANDSCAPE

Not my fault line

Playhouse

Faucet

Faucet

House

Faucet

Garage

Garden Shed

Faucets

Over the edge

Figure 25 Mr. and Mrs. Shrubbery live in a nice house with extensive landscaping. As luck would have it, they've installed every type of drip irrigation mentioned in this book. They've graciously allowed me to copy the plans of their yard as examples of a good drip irrigation design throughout the remainder of this book.

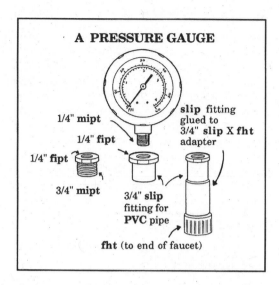

Figure 26 A pressure gauge will tell you the pressure in pounds per square inch [psi]. Some of these adapters may be needed to attach the gauge to your fixture. The gauge is not cheap, so you might want to hire a landscape contractor to do the survey.

rate for each drip irrigation system and what pressure regulator, if any, is required. If you have a storage tank, this information isn't very important, but knowing your well's performance record will help you maintain a conscientious program of water management. Also check your drilling records for any indication of dissolved iron and calcium; these minerals can clog certain emitters. If, for example, your well produces iron-rich water, that fact greatly affects your choice of emitters. Those who use water from wells should also test and make a written record of the psi for each existing faucet.

We find a main assembly in the Shrubberys' yard at an existing faucet near the perennial flower bed. [See Figure 27.]

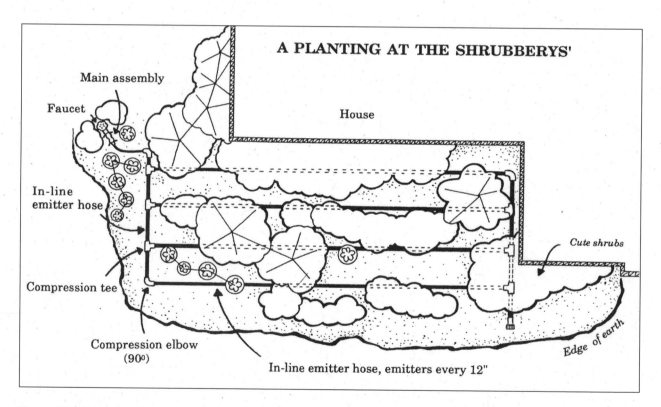

Figure 27 This view of the ornamental planting by the Shrubberys' house shows where the main assembly is located and the parallel line of in-line drip irrigation hose. The mulch was removed to show the tubing, Even though the foliage doesn't cover all the ground, the roots permeate the entire area and absorb moisture from all the emitters in the in-line drip hose.

Controlling Your Drip System

The most reliable way to control a drip system is to turn the faucet on and off manually. With a twist of the wrist, there's very little to go wrong. For your first drip irrigation system, stick with the existing faucet as the "controller." I picked this system as a way for you to easily use existing faucets and to keep everything visible for possible leaks. It is much easier to assemble than fitting all the parts in an underground irrigation box. And this assembly is easy to dismantle for winter storage in cold climates.

The Sexual Anatomy of Plumbing Parts [Rated NC-17]

At this point, it's time for a polite reminder that plumbing parts are much like human parts—the protruding round parts stick into the hollow,

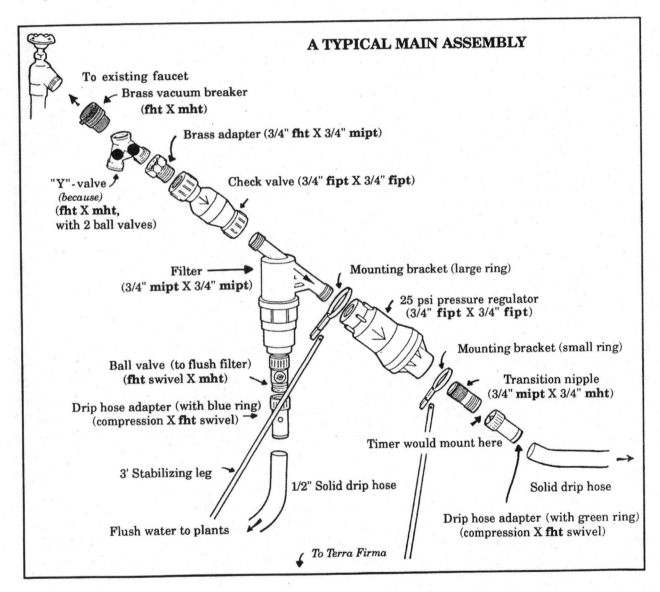

A TYPICAL MAIN ASSEMBLY

To existing faucet
Brass vacuum breaker (**fht X mht**)
Brass adapter (3/4" **fht** X 3/4" **mipt**)
Check valve (3/4" **fipt** X 3/4" **fipt**)
"Y"-valve *(because)* (**fht X mht**, with 2 ball valves)
Filter (3/4" **mipt** X 3/4" **mipt**)
Mounting bracket (large ring)
25 psi pressure regulator (3/4" **fipt** X 3/4" **fipt**)
Mounting bracket (small ring)
Ball valve (to flush filter) (**fht swivel X mht**)
Transition nipple (3/4" **mipt** X 3/4" **mht**)
Drip hose adapter (with blue ring) (compression X **fht** swivel)
3' Stabilizing leg
Timer would mount here
1/2" Solid drip hose
Solid drip hose
Flush water to plants
Drip hose adapter (with green ring) (compression X **fht** swivel)
To Terra Firma

Figure 28 All the parts of a typical system as I've developed over the years that allows all the parts to be visible to ward off most of PMLP axioms. The double approach to backflow protection is to keep the home's potable water clean. You can use a post instead of the harder-to-find mounting brackets.

tube-like parts. Therefore, the sticking-out parts with pipe threads on the outside are the male iron pipe parts, and the hollow tubes with threads on the inside are the female parts. The male parts are labeled "mipt;" that stands for male iron pipe threads. The female ones are labeled "fipt"— female iron pipe threads. Furthermore, some of these parts are made to be attached to a faucet and have unique threads called hose threads—[ht]. Thus, the end of a hose has a male hose thread [mht] fitting. The end that attaches to the faucet has a female hose thread [fht] fitting.

THE MAIN ASSEMBLY IN THE GARDEN

Figure 29 A main assembly in the garden. If you don't use the protective legs. Attach firmly to a post so that the weight of the assembly is taken off the faucet. Paint the entire assembly with exterior, latex paint to shield the PVC parts from harmful UV rays.

ply linens. Schedule 80 nipples and fittings are dark grey and best used as superior PVC fittings for main assemblies.

NOTE: I will be using the shorthand Sch 40 or Sch 80 for the rest of the book.

The PVC glue is toxic and requires special care in using. Used with care, there is little danger to the dripologist.

NOTE: I've used the lowercase letters to describe the fittings so as to not clog the text and illustrations with all capital letters. Most people use all capital letters, but they both stand for the same thing.

A length of pipe with mipt threads on both ends is called a nipple. Pipe nipples come in many lengths, from ones only 3/4-inches long [called close nipples] to 12 inches, 36 inches, and even 48 inches, and many sizes in-between.

Slip fittings [noted by slip x slip or slip x slip x slip] are PVC fittings that have smooth walls that require PVC glue to join the fittings with PVC pipe. [The "x" stands for "by." An example is: slip x slip 90-degree, elbow, PVC pipe comes in three grades: from the weakest—Schedule 125 PVC, to Schedule 40 PVC, to Schedule 80 PVC—the closest to metal. Schedule 125 is best used to hide wires from critters. Schedule 40 pipe is the most common for drip irrigation sup-

The collection of parts for a main assembly shown in Figures 28 and 29 are based upon years of trying many different manufacturers' products; these particular parts are the best I've worked with.

In the illustration, each fixture is referred to by its generic name, such as "check valve," and by its accurate plumbing moniker, such as "3/4-inch check valve, fipt x fipt." The "fipt x fipt" code isn't some kind of esoteric plumbing math, as mentioned earlier; it means "female iron pipe thread by female iron pipe thread," or, more simply, female iron pipe threads on both ends of the check valve.

Since some of the parts in the main assembly have hose threads and some have pipe threads, you'll need some adapters, or transition fittings, to join everything together. For example, in Figure 28, the transition nipple converts the female pipe threads of the pressure regulator into male hose threads to fit into the female hose threads on the swivel of the drip-hose adapter. Be sure to keep track of which parts have hose versus pipe threads. It's hard to spot the difference, but hose threads are more coarse and there are fewer per inch. You might want to mark the hose-threaded parts with a touch of paint or marker pen when you buy them. To try and join iron pipe threads with hose threads will ruin the threads of at least one part and produce a leaky union.

Putting the Assembly Together

Now, to assemble the assembly. You may want to loosely assemble all the parts first to become familiar with the fittings and their sequence, then take apart the assembly and lay out the parts in the same sequence. You may also want to have someone read the following instructions out loud as you put everything together. These instructions assume you already have an atmospheric vacuum breaker and a Y-valve attached to the garden faucet. The main assembly will attach to the faucet [mht] directly, but it's not recommended that you skip the atmospheric vacuum breaker.

1. To the mipt end of the brass adapter, add some Teflon™ pipe dope to make it easier to thread the parts together and to seal the threads against tiny leaks.

Now, keeping in mind PMLP #8, a little digression about covering iron pipe threads. Old-fashioned pipe dope is sticky grey stuff that tends to get all over your hands and sometimes dries out after it's applied—resulting in the inside-out *Titanic* effect. Many plumbers claim the solvents in traditional pipe dope are corrosive to modern plastic fittings. Teflon® pipe dope, on the other hand, duplicates the slickness of a Teflon frying pan to make it easy to thread two parts together, lubricates the parts for an easy fit, appears to stay somewhat flexible for a permanent seal, and is much easier to work with than the Teflon pipe tape discussed below. But, Teflon pipe dope still manages to adhere to hands, pants, shirts, and tools like balloons to a wool sweater. There is still much debate among plumbers as to the real or imagined damage from either pipe dope on plastic fittings.

Teflon pipe tape is a thin white material that is wrapped around male threads and doesn't have any corrosive compounds. Pipe threads seal up quite well with Teflon tape, in spite of the ease with which the parts go together. But, it is a real hassle to work with it out in the landscape. The gossamer-like tape blows around, knots up into useless balls, twists together just as you're about to apply it to the threads, and picks up gritty particles like a magnet—making it much harder to get a good seal. If I'm prefabricating a main assembly indoors at the workbench, I reach for the Teflon tape. Outdoors, I use the Teflon pipe dope instead of the bothersome tape. In the end, the choice is yours.

2. Next, apply the check valve until it is finger-tight. [In order to circumvent PMLP #6, be sure to note which direction the embossed arrow on the check valve is facing. The arrow should face away from the faucet and toward the drip hose.]

3. Use a pipe wrench to secure the brass adapter and another pipe wrench to twist the check valve a one-quarter turn—don't tighten any further as you may manifest PMLP #2 and crack the check valve.

4. Now apply Telfon pipe dope to the mipt inlet part of the Y-filter.

5. After finger-tightening the filter, hold the

check valve securely with a pipe wrench and rotate the filter by hand only one-quarter of a revolution [to avoid cracking the filter's housing].

6. Next, slip the larger of the two mounting brackets onto the fatter end [the intake] of the pressure regulator. [The two mounting brackets can be purchased at a hardware store; they're the same as the galvanized fittings used to attach chain-link fencing to its metal posts.]

7. Now more pipe dope goes onto the mipt outlet of the filter.

8. Add the pressure regulator and finger-tighten it, then rotate the pressure regulator another one-quarter revolution with a pipe wrench. Be sure to use the model of pressure regulator that is designed to handle the volume of water the system will pass. In most cases, I use a Senninger 25-psi low-flow regulator, rated at 1/10 to 8 gpm.

9. Now you can add the transition nipple. With this nipple, you need only apply pipe dope to the mipt side and hand-tighten it into the female end of the pressure regulator. The mht [male hose thread] end of the transition nipple allows you to add a swivel x compression fitting [again, x stands for "by"], also called a drip-hose adapter, to the end of the main assembly. One end of the drip hose adapter has female hose threads to attach to the end of the main assembly; the other has a special quick-couple orifice called a compression fitting. Compression fittings work by means of an internal ringed barb; the hose can be easily inserted into the fitting's hole, but the barb prevents its removal. [See Figure 30.] To insert the drip hose into the compression fitting, moisten the end of the cut hose and, holding the hose within two inches of its end, wiggle it into the hole until the barb pinches around the tubing.

10. Because the swivel end of the drip-hose adapter has a hose gasket, you can skip using pipe dope on the transition nipple and just hand-

twist the swivel onto the mht end.

11. Now attach the brass adapter, at the beginning of the main assembly, to the hose-threaded Y-valve that's already mounted on the faucet. The brass adapter's fht is designed to use a typical hose washer and therefore needs no pipe dope.

12. Tighten the main assembly finger-tight. Be sure to have the outlet of the filter pointing down. If the orientation is not correct, you can sometimes add another hose washer between the Y-valve and the brass adapter to change the amount of rotation the assembly will need to seat [tighten leak-free].

Finally, attach a length of drip hose to the flushing ball valve on the filter and turn on the faucet to check for leaks and flush the filter. If all goes well, and you haven't conjured up any of Pop Murphy's laws, you're done. The total length of the assembly in Figures 28 and 29 is about 18 inches. If left dangling from a faucet, the assembly's weight could stress the fittings near the faucet or the fittings could easily be accidentally hit and damaged. The assembly must be protected from damage and accidental "tweaking." In this example, two diagonal braces clamp onto the pressure regulator and stick into the soil. The braces triangulate the assembly, hold it firmly in place, and protect the Y-filter from bumps and collisions. Another option is to strap the end of the assembly to a firmly secured wooden post.

Mount the braces following these steps:

1. With the assembly mounted on the faucet, you can judge the angle at which the mounting bracket rods are to be pounded into the soil. The larger mounting bracket should be loosely attached to the pressure regulator. Drive one 4-foot length of 1/4-inch galvanized pipe [with one end flattened to make a point and a hole for the bolt drilled into the other end] into the ground so as to align

with the large mounting bracket, then attach the rod with a bolt, two washers, and a nut.

2. Next, disconnect the drip-hose adapter at the end of the main assembly and slip the smaller mounting bracket over the transition nipple and onto the outlet side of the pressure regulator.

3. Pound the second rod into the soil at the proper angle. Bolt this ring mount to the rod.

The main assembly should be painted with an exterior or anti-rust paint. Not only will this help disguise the hardware, but the plastic will also be protected from harmful ultraviolet rays, which can cause it to become brittle and crack. Dark forest green is a common choice, but an earthy brown seems more inconspicuous to me.

Laying Out the Drip Irrigation Hose

To get from the faucet main assembly to the flower bed, you'll need to add a length of solid drip hose. Make sure you have the correct size for in-line emitter tubing—16 mm or 600 series hose with an Outside Diameter [O.D.] of 0.67 inch.

If you have only the standard one-half-inch solid drip hose, 18 mm or 700 series with an O.D. of 0.708 inch, you can adapt it to in-line emitter tubing fairly easily. Purchase some compression adapters [also called ring adapters], a part that is just the barbed compression ring and made to glue into standard 1/2-inch PVC fittings. [See Figure 30.] To join the 16-mm and 18-mm tubings together: glue a 16-mm [green] compression

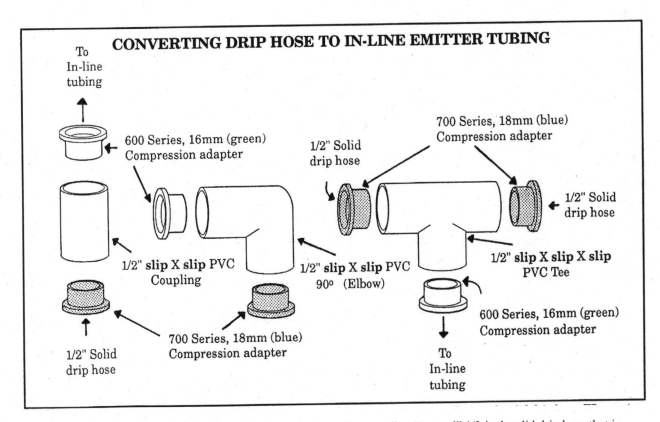

Figure 30 In-line emitter tubing isn't exactly the same size as "average" or "normal" 1/2-inch solid drip hose that is used as the supply line or header. When using compression fittings to join these two different hose diameters, you are stuck with gluing the compression adapters [also called ring adapters] to the slip part of the PVC fitting. Be sure to wear the rubber or latex gloves. Don't breathe the fumes. Since you're outdoors this is usually not a problem. The in-line tubing fits into the 16-mm green adapters, and the regular drip hose fits into the 18-mm blue fittings.

adapter into one end of a 1/2-inch slip x slip [s x s; slip means glued, not threaded] coupling and an 18-mm [blue] into the other end. You can use elbows [90°], tees and couplings with any combination of compression adapters to convert from one size of tubing to the other.

Where malicious gophers lurk just below the surface, you'll want to use solid 1/2-inch PVC pipe to get from the main assembly to the perennial bed. I use Schedule 40 pipe. Gophers can hear the tiny torrent of water in a pipe, and no solid drip hose is a match for their wicked, industrious teeth. [Many people report, however, that porous pipe can withstand the onslaught of a thirsty "soil rat."]

Solid drip irrigation hose is attached to the main assembly by a fitting called a "compression x female hose swivel." From the main assembly, the solid drip hose can curve gently down to the ground's surface and run to the flower border.

For superior growth, I prefer to design the layout of the in-line tubing, or any drip system, to water the entire soil volume of the planting. A water supply would have to be very limited to justify point-source watering; so, instead of being preoccupied about where the plants are located, I lay out parallel lines, or "laterals," of tubing throughout the entire bed. [See Figure 31.] I always stock the 1/2-gph, 12-inch-interval version because I install drip systems for different clients with different types of soil. The 1/2-gph tubing with the 12-inch spacing along the hose's length is the only one that will water sandy soil. [If you look hard enough, some stores carry 6-inch spacing in the hose. Yet, clay-loam soils can also be irrigated by turning on the system for a shorter period of time because the water easily spreads laterally. The parallel lines of tubing might be as close together as 6 or 12 inches in sandy soils and as far apart as 24 inches in heavy clay-loams. If you have a fairly heavy soil and want to save money, buy the tubing with 18-inch or 24-

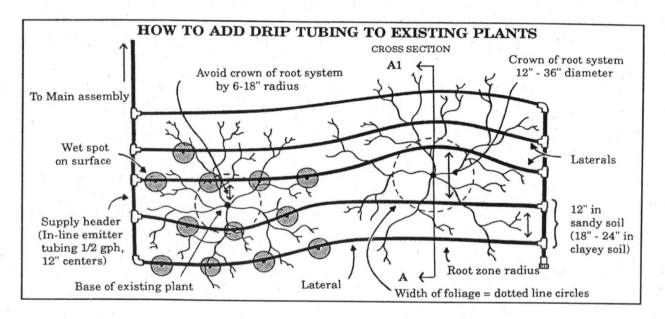

HOW TO ADD DRIP TUBING TO EXISTING PLANTS

Figure 31 Be sure to snake the in-line tubing around existing plantings while avoiding the base of the shrub or tree. This will reduce the chances of getting root rot. This is important with West Coast and arid climates that are irrigated during the warmth of spring, summer, and fall. The killing types of *Phytophthora* spp. are more prone to kill a plant if the normally dry soil is irrigated. Wet winters have lower soil temperatures that slow down the effects of root rots. Add warm soils and summer irrigation together, and you have the recipe for botanical homicide. See Figure 32 for a cross section, noted here as A and A1.

inch intervals between emitters, and you'll save 25% or 40% respectively. Also, a higher flow rate, such as 1 gph, will help the water to spread wider than with the slower 1/2-gph emitter tubing. At worst, you'll just have to run the system a little longer to get the wet spots to meet underground along the length of the tubing.

The logical time to install a drip system is during the warmer days of late spring or early summer. At these times of the year, the drip irrigation hose is soft and supple and easy to work with, but it can be deceiving. Gardeners often aren't aware that drip hose shrinks considerably as the weather cools off in the fall. Because of the type of plastic used with the most common types of 1/2-half-inch drip irrigation hose and in-line emitter tubing, each separate length of hose can shrink by as much as one to two feet for ev-

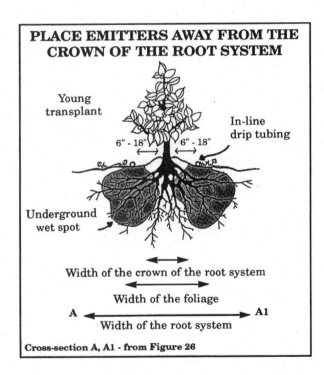

PLACE EMITTERS AWAY FROM THE CROWN OF THE ROOT SYSTEM

Young transplant

In-line drip tubing

6" - 18"   6" - 18"

Underground wet spot

Width of the crown of the root system

Width of the foliage

A ◄─────► A1

Width of the root system

Cross-section A, A1 - from Figure 26

Figure 32 Drought-resistant plants in the arid West should be planted on a mound for drainage away from the crown of the root system. Place the in-line tubing away from the trunk over the root system at or beyond the drip line of the plant. See Appendix for more details on root growth relative to the drip line of the plant.

ery 100 feet of hose. If you lay out the drip hose during a warm day and stretch it taut, there's a good chance, come cooler weather, that the tubing will shrink and pull out of some of the non-compression fittings. The tendency of drip hose to shrink will stress any coupling piece, even insert and Spin-Loc fittings; therefore, when laying solid drip irrigation hose, in a gopher-free zone in a trench [as the primary water supply from the main assembly] or on the surface with or without emitters, be sure to snake the hose loosely along the ground or in the trench. Also, don't stake the tubing in place too securely. When inserting the landscape stakes used to position the drip hose always leave a 1/8- to 1/4-inch gap above the hose to allow for shrinking and expanding. The stake will easily hold the drip hose in position without having to be hammered snugly onto the top of the tubing.

Many people, when they first start with drip irrigation, carefully place the emitters at the base of each plant. This is dangerous to many plants, as the upper portion of the root system near the trunk, the root's crown, is prone to crown rot, also called *Phytophthora* spp. Crown rot can quickly kill a plant that has been watered too much or planted in a soil with too much clay. Drip irrigation allows the gardener to avoid this problem easily by watering at least 6 to 12 inches away from the trunk. When laying out the tubing, make sure the emitters don't sit on top of an existing plant's root crown and cause rot. Also, because the roots grow well beyond the width of the plant, there is no reason to put the emitter near the trunk. Therefore, the tubing should snake slightly around the base of each plant and not be rigidly parallel—even in rainy places that have short droughts. [See Figure 31.]

All these not-quite-parallel lines join a main supply line, also called a "supply header," along the length of one side of the flower bed, usually the side closest to the faucet. For the header, I also use in-line emitter tubing so that another portion of the bed's soil gets watered.

The solid drip hose from the main assembly to the edge of the flower bed is connected to an in-line emitter header by joining the two pieces with a compression coupling or Spin-Loc coupler. Look at Figures 27 and 33 to see how the header and parallel lines were placed in the Shrubberys' yard.

Each parallel line, or lateral, attaches to the header with a "compression tee." To make the header, lay out a length of in-line tubing along one side of the flower bed, cut between two emitters in the tubing where each parallel line or lateral is to be attached, and wiggle the tubing into the compression holes of the cross-piece

of the tee. To attach the first lateral, cut halfway between two emitters on the roll of tubing and insert the tubing into the base of the first tee on the header. The second length of lateral tubing should be cut very close to an emitter and inserted into the next tee down the line in the header. [Remember to lay out the tubing loosely and leave some slack on the end of each lateral for contraction of the cold tubing.] Staggering the beginning of each subsequent lateral line like this helps to provide a more regular application of water. Instead of closing off the end of each lateral line, join the ends of each lateral with what's called a drain header, drain-down header, or exhaust header. The purpose of a "drain-down

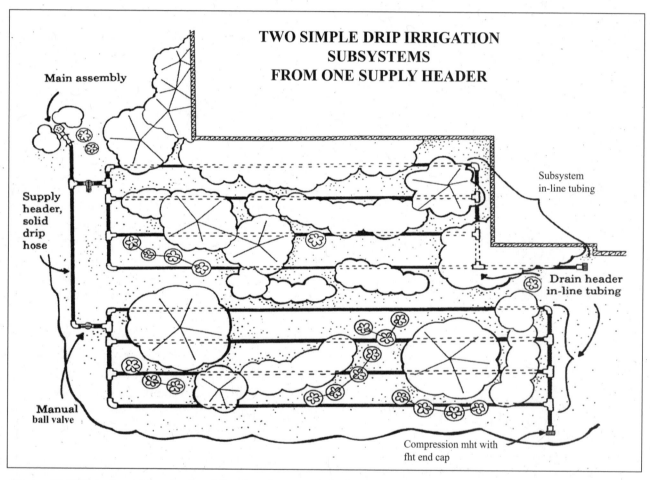

Figure 33 With in-line tubing that has 1/2-gph emitters on 12-inch centers, each subsystem, or two subsystems as in this illustration, can have no more than a total of 326 feet from each valve. Each subsystem has a drain header to allow for having to mark and find only one flushing point. Use compression by threaded drain-down caps. [See Figure 34.] Threaded end caps last much longer than the Figure-8 end closures seen in Figure 34A.

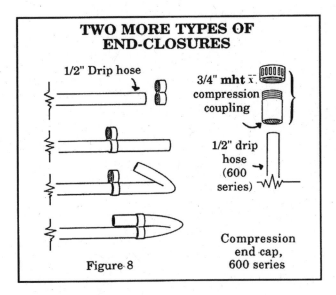

TWO MORE TYPES OF END-CLOSURES

1/2" Drip hose

3/4" mht x̄ compression coupling

1/2" drip hose (600 series)

Compression end cap, 600 series

Figure 8

Figure 34A Figure 8 end closures are inexpensive, easy-to-use, and can be reused, but can crack the drip hose over time. I use slip compression x mht with a fht cap. It costs more, but it will not cause your pipe to leak or burst open. Mr. and Mrs. Shrubbery chose to save money by using the Figure 8 end closures.

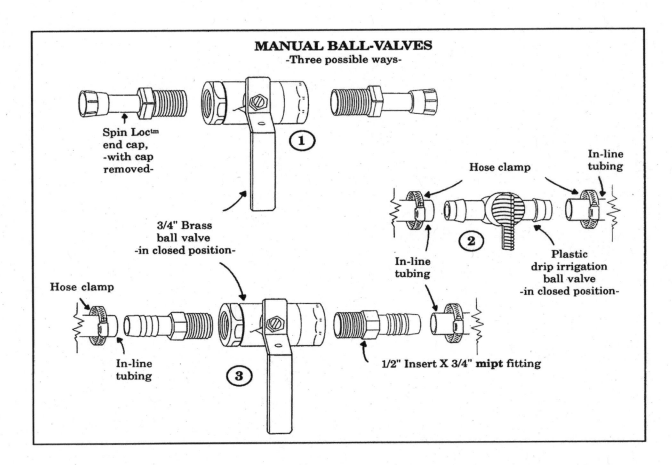

MANUAL BALL-VALVES
-Three possible ways-

Spin Loc™ end cap, -with cap removed-

3/4" Brass ball valve -in closed position-

①

Hose clamp

In-line tubing

In-line tubing

Plastic drip irrigation ball valve -in closed position-

②

Hose clamp

In-line tubing

③

1/2" Insert X 3/4" **mipt** fitting

Figure 34B Here are three ways to plumb a ball valve. The least expensive is number two. But this plastic fitting is the one most likely to break. Yet, a friend has used the these plastic valves for ten years.

header," as I'll refer to it, is to equalize the pressure throughout the system and to speed up the flushing or draining of the system. For example, in Figure 33, instead of opening and flushing eight separate lines in the two subsystems, only two end closures, one for each subsystem, need to be opened and closed.

To plan the layout of the tubing: first, on a scale drawing of the flower bed, sketch the pattern of all the parallel laterals [the lines attached to the supply header] needed to irrigate the bed's soil type. With in-line emitter tubing, I usually place the parallel laterals 12 inches apart in sandy soil and up to 24 inches apart in clayey soil. Next, sketch in the supply and drain headers that will supply and drain all the laterals, making sure the supply header is on the side of the bed closest to the main assembly. Remember, the recommended maximum length per valve or main assembly should be no longer than 326 feet for 1/2-gph, 12-inch-interval in-line emitter tubing.

If the total length of tubing in a planting area is more than 326 feet, then one or more manual valves must be added to break the entire system into 326-foot, or shorter, subsystems. To install a subsystem, add a tee, as seen on the right side of Figure 33, for each subsystem at the appropriate spot along the supply header. You can insert an inexpensive barbed ball valve made especially for drip irrigation systems to control each subsystem. Some people simply insert the in-line drip tubing over each barb on the ball valve. [Remember, if you have difficulty inserting the drip tubing, dip the end in hot water to soften the plastic.] According to the manufacturer, the barb will hold with pressures up to 60 psi. I prefer not to risk a failure while the system is on and unattended, in the tradition of Pop Murphy, and add two hose clamps to ensure a leakproof fitting.

Figure 34B shows three ways to install a ball-valve if you have difficulty inserting the tubing onto the barbs of the plastic ball valve. Each uses a quality ball valve instead of the more tradition-al gate valve. Ball valves seal more securely with repeated use over time than a gate valve. If your local supplier doesn't carry Spin-Loc products [or Perma Loc™ fittings], they most probably stock simple insert fittings. [See Figure 20.] After each shut-off ball valve, there should be no more than 326 linear feet of in-line tubing, but the laterals can have any configuration. A larger PVC pipe may be needed to supply more than one set of subsystems. See the chart in the Appendix for the maximum flow rate for different diameters of pipe.

One main assembly can service two or more laterals. While the filter in the main assembly in Figure 28 [page 37] can pass over 1980 gph, remember, the limiting factor is the pressure regulator, with a maximum flow rate of 480 gph. In my example, 326 feet of in-line tubing passes 163 gph of water, less than one-half and nearly one-third of the pressure regulator's limit of 480 gph assembly after it's attached to the faucet. Flush the open-ended hose of the main header line and then close the end. After all the lateral lines have been added to the header line, flush for several minutes and then close each lateral, starting with the line at the highest elevation or the line closest to the main assembly. Or, to simplify the whole process, plumb a drain-down header, with the single end closure at the lowest end of the header. [See Figures 27 and 33.]

When planting a new area that's to be drip-irrigated, I take the following steps:

1—Do all necessary soil preparation for the entire area.

2—Install the drip irrigation lines on top of the soil. Hold the hose in place with U-stakes [landscape staples], placed every four to six feet. Don't forget to leave the staples loose so the tubing can swell and contract throughout the year. Flush the hose for several minutes and close using a compression end cap. [See Figure 34A.]

3—Use an overhead sprinkler to irrigate the entire area to premoisten the soil for planting. Wait one or more days for the soil to dry enough to be planted. The soil should be moist and easily crumbled, not wet and sticky.

4—Plant according to the landscape plan. Make sure each plant is 6 to 12 inches away from all emitters so as to prevent crown rot.

5—Hand water each plant with a garden hose to settle the soil and eliminate any air pockets.

6—Cover the soil with newspapers and hide it and the hose with an attractive mulch.

Many people have a hard time with this concept when I first describe it. If they've heard or seen anything about drip irrigation, they are used to the usual system of each plant getting only one or two emitters—period. This is what I call the drought-stress approach to drip irrigation. While the plant may stay alive and even grow some, it will usually not flourish with such a small fraction of its natural root system being irrigated. The most difficult part of my approach to drip irrigation is getting people to experiment with what appears, at first, to be such a great distance between the emitters and the newly transplanted seedling, sapling, or shrub. This approach depends upon the premoistening of the soil and the hand watering of each plant before mulching. With the entire volume of the soil at an ideal moisture level, the new root hairs of the transplant could grow for days or even weeks without any additional water. By starting the drip system right away, and irrigating with tiny amounts of water on a daily basis, you will maintain an ideal moisture level, avoid transplant shock, and promote the best growth possible. The system's timer might be set to be on only one or two minutes per day which, with 1/2-gph emitters, is just tablespoons of water on a daily basis. Check the soil to be sure it's not drying out too fast after transplanting. After the plants are established, you can go to more traditional run times for the timer. The emitters, that appear to be a "waste" because they are so far from the transplants, will soon be irrigating the fast-growing roots. Remember, roots grow in an area up to three times wider than the foliage. [See Figures 31 and 32.]

No matter how you install a drip system, you should mulch. To use drip irrigation without using mulch would be like wearing pants without a belt—you get most of the effect, but without that last measure of protection. While drip irrigation doesn't waste any water through windblown spray or runoff, some moisture can be lost by evaporation from the soil surface. Two to four inches of mulch will virtually eliminate evaporation loss while at the same time hiding the tubing. Mulch also helps extend the life of the drip irrigation system by blocking harmful ultraviolet rays, that degrade the plastic hose.

Now you're ready to figure out how often, and for how long, to turn on your new drip irrigation system.

CHAPTER 4

When and How Long to Irrigate

Many gardeners think it's necessary to water deeply, which often leads to the habit of infrequent but lengthy irrigations. Of course, "deeply" is a very relative word. When teaching a drip irrigation seminar, I stress maintaining good soil moisture in the top two feet, and I tell people not to worry about soaking any deeper. At one workshop, a woman from a local nursery pointed out that for many of its customers, watering even six inches down was considered radically deep. On the other hand, I've run into well-intentioned gardeners who plunge root-watering rods 18 inches deep into the soil and then run the water for hours on end, which mostly floods soils below two feet. Watering should be a function of how roots really grow, not how we imagine their growth.

Deep Roots Doesn't Mean Deep Watering

In all the studies I've been able to find, the usual conclusion is that for the sake of quality growth, as opposed to sheer survival, the upper one to two feet of the soil accounts for over 50% of all the water a plant absorbs. [See Figures 2 and 3.]

While many plants, including herbaceous flowers, can have roots deeper than two feet, these deeper roots are more important for stabilizing the plant, absorbing some micronutrients, and surviving severe droughts than for supporting an abundance of growth.

Again, here's my theory of what lies behind this interesting phenomenon. The upper layers of the soil have the highest population of air-loving soil flora. [See Figure 4.] As mentioned earlier, the top three inches of the soil have nearly four-and-one-half times more bacteria, almost eight-and-one-half times more actinomycetes, more than twice as many fungi, and five times the algae as soil eight to ten inches deep. The soil's flora assist in the liberation of nutrients into a soluble form that the plant can absorb. This beneficial soil life needs plenty of oxygen to fuel its activity. In addition, each consuming and liberating critter of consumption also excretes either liquid or gaseous waste. These gaseous by-products, tiny subterranean soil farts and belches, can be toxic to young roots and some of the soil's bacteria and fauna. These noxious fumes must slowly migrate up through the minute labyrinth of the soil's pore space to dissipate into the atmosphere. The deeper the soil's flora and fauna, the longer it takes for the poisonous fumes to be "exhaled" and life-promoting gases such as oxygen and nitrogen to be "inhaled." The more aerobic layers of the upper soil horizons are quick breathers, with higher levels of oxygen and lower amounts of the noxious fumes of respiration. This allows for more rapid and extensive root growth. Deep soils aren't as aerobic; the inhalation of life-giving gases and the exhalation of toxic vapors are greatly slowed down and far less supportive of active root growth.

As mentioned earlier, plants can absorb nutrients only in a water solution. Dry soil inhibits nutrient uptake because the soil life can't thrive, and what little water is in the soil is held tightly to the soil particles. Drying out the soil between irrigations means that nutrients also "dry up." When water is supplied to the soil to the point of saturation, the roots hairs and air-loving soil life may be stressed or killed from waterlogging, and nutrient uptake is reduced due to the lack of air. As the wet soil dries, it takes some time for the aerobic flora to repopulate the soil. Either extreme, too wet or too dry, causes a biological lag before the root hairs get their best meals. Infrequent and deep irrigations produce two periods in the cycle in which the plant's growth is reduced or hindered—during the drought stage and when the soil is saturated.

Soils Aren't Always Deep

Remember, deep, glacially deposited topsoil is more the exception than the rule. Even if you have such a deep, loamy soil, remember that the majority of moisture and nutrient absorption for quality growth still happens in the top two feet of the soil. More typically, most suburban yards have a very shallow layer of topsoil. If, for example, there is a continuous deposit of rich orange clay just 12 inches under the ground, then for all practical purposes, the 12-inch layer of topsoil is the only place where your plant's roots will be absorbing water and nutrients.

Irrigate Frequently

As mentioned earlier, frequent waterings produce the best-looking foliage growth, the most abundant bloom, and the highest yields.

I prefer frequent or daily watering for the most beautiful and productive crops. This relies on knowing the local ET rate. The ET rate combines the amount of moisture lost from the soil's surface [evapo-] and the foliage [-transpiration]. It represents the amount of water a plant uses, regardless of the method of application, and is determined with a formula that factors the temperature, wind speed, humidity, and percentage of ground covered by foliage. The rate varies considerably, depending upon the season—the coolest days of early spring, windy days in

March, hot, muggy summer weather, or dry winds in August. Each spring or early summer, try to start watering only when the soil reaches an ideal moisture level: not too anaerobically wet and not too dry, barely as moist as a wrung-out sponge. The frequent irrigations are meant to maintain this ideal moisture level and eliminate the stress of soil that is too wet or too dry. In areas with summer rain, you should wait until the soil naturally drains to an ideal moisture content and then water frequently with small amounts of water until the next rain saturates the ground. [See Chapter 11 for more information.]

Frequent Irrigation Can Use Less Water

Daily irrigation doesn't mean using countless gallons of extra water. In fact, with infrequent irrigation, it takes a certain amount of water just to rehydrate the soil before the plant can even make use of the moisture. Oddly enough, infrequent waterings can use more water than the same planting would receive with frequent, even daily, irrigation.

Years ago, for example, I planted a drought-resistant landscape, with plants such as lavender, santolina, rockroses, and rosemary, for a neighbor. I followed the same steps for soil preparation and preirrigation outlined on pages 46 and 47. The day after planting, the timer was set to irrigate each zone for 15 minutes. After the risk of transplant shock was over, the irrigation lines were turned on each day for only eight minutes. The plants flourished, even though each 1/2-gph emitter was distributing the paltry amount of seven tablespoons of water for each emitter, every day. Contrast this with a nearby garden with a similar soil and lavender plants arbitrarily watered only twice a month for four hours. This amounts to two gallons per emitter for the two-week period, or just more than 18 tablespoons of water per day—more than twice the water used in the flourishing landscape.

No matter how you use drip irrigation, frequently or every once in a while, it will always be more efficient than any sprinkler you're currently using. All sprinklers, except the most modern of micro- or mini-sprinklers, can apply water faster than many silty and clayey soils can absorb it. This leads to anaerobic puddling and runoff, especially on steep slopes. Every sprinkler is vulnerable to wind- and sun-induced losses, with as much as 25% or more of the water wasted. In general, sprinklers are rated at an overall efficiency of 75% to 80%, compared with drip irrigation's 90%. [Furrow irrigation can have an efficiency rating as low as 50%.]

How Long to Water

There are two general approaches to watering, the empirical and the more analytical, which use the evapotranspiration rate as a guideline. Each works, but the ET-rate approach can be a far more accurate starting point for water conserving.

The most immediate, or empirical, way to understand your soil's response to drip irrigation, and to determine how long to leave the system on, involves digging. Even after doing your experiment with the milk jug, you should test for the drip system's underground pattern of moisture. Turn on the drip system for an hour, then turn off the hose and dig a number of small holes in the flower bed to see how deep and to what width the water has soaked in. Then turn the system on for another hour, to equal a test total of two hours, and check to see how much farther the water moves. Do this for several more intervals of time and observe vague changes in the wet spot. This test will reveal the shortest length of irrigation time to produce the widest wet spot, based on which test hole revealed the widest spread of the wet spot during the elapsed time. Without doing this test, you'll just be guessing in the dark.

ET-Based Irrigation

Another approach involves using the ET figures for your local climate. Your local Cooperative Extension office should be able to tell you either the current week's ET rate or the month's average rate; both are expressed in inches per day or month. If they don't know, fire them.

WARNING: Math Ahead

The chart in Figure 35 [next page] shows the daily water use for ten different ET rates. Remember, the amount of water needed to replace the ET losses depends upon the amount of soil covered [like a shadow] by the planting's foliage. If the plants are young, the ET rate is less, corresponding to the smaller area of coverage. With a mature flower border, the coverage is complete and all you need to determine is the total square footage of the border. For example, a 5- by 20-foot border [100 square feet] uses 18.7 gallons of water per day during a hot day when the ET rate is equivalent to nine inches of water per month. [Derived by cross-referencing the columns in Figure 35.] If you still prefer to water once a week, multiply the daily ET rate by seven to determine the total amount for the weekly watering.

To determine the length of each day's watering, take the total amount of water the flower border requires and divide by the total flow of the drip irrigation system. Consider again the illustration of Mr. and Mrs. Shrubbery's 5- by 20-foot border with a daily ET rate of 18.7 gallons. [See Figure 27.] Since the total length of in-line emitter tubing in the bed is 84 feet [this figure is reached by adding together one header four feet long and four 20-foot laterals], the sum flow of the system is 52 gph [eighty-four 1/2-gph emitters times their actual flow of 0.62 gph]. [See the Appendix, the "Maximum Length of Tubing" chart.] Thus, dividing the daily water need of

Daily Water Use (In Gallons per Day)

BASED ON VARIOUS EVAPOTRANSPIRATION RATES

Square Feet of Plant Cover	ET Rate (in inches/month)									
	1"	2"	3"	4"	5"	6"	7"	8"	9"	10"
1 sq. ft.	0.0187	0.0374	0.062	0.083	0.104	0.125	0.145	0.166	0.187	0.208
4 sq. ft.	0.075	0.15	0.248	0.332	0.416	0.5	0.58	0.664	0.75	0.832
10 sq. ft.	0.187	0.374	0.62	0.83	1.04	1.25	1.45	1.66	1.87	2.08
75 sq. ft.	1.403	2.805	4.65	6.225	7.8	9.4	10.875	12.45	14.0	15.6
100 sq. ft.	1.87	3.74	6.2	8.3	10.4	12.5	14.5	16.6	18.7	20.8
200 sq. ft.	3.74	7.480	12.4	16.6	20.8	25.0	29.0	33.2	37.4	41.6
300 sq.ft.	5.61	11.22	18.6	24.9	32.2	37.5	43.5	49.8	56.1	62.4
1 acre solid cover	815	1629	2701	3615	4530	5445	6316	7231	8146	9060

Figure 35 A number of daily ET rates. Ask your local Cooperative Extension agent or Master Gardener for the ET rate for your area. These rates are just a starting point; you can adjust the amount up or down depending on your water supply and how much growth or yields you desire. The square footage of the cover represents the surface of the soil covered by the shadow at noon or the "footprint" of the plant's foliage, regardless of the shape or type of foliage.

18.7 gallons by 52 gph yields 0.36 hour, or 22 minutes per day [0.36 of an hour times 60 minutes]. If you want to water once per week, then multiply 22 minutes per day times seven days to get a weekly watering time of 154 minutes, or nearly three hours.

The above calculation is fairly simple because I chose the example of emitters on 12-inch intervals and the rows of tubing 12 inches apart. What if your system has emitters or tubing at odd intervals? The calculation in Figure 36 may appear difficult at first, but it is rather easy. Another advantage of this calculation is that the rate of irrigation is converted to inches, which has been a more common way to gauge irrigation rates.

Rate of Application Formula

$$\text{RA (Rate of Application)} = \frac{231.1 \times \text{GPH}}{\text{sq. in. spacing}}$$

Figure 36 The rate of application [RA] formula is used to calculate the total flow, per square foot, of emitters spaced at odd intervals such as tubing 18 inches apart with emitters every 12 inches

The first part of this formula is another way to calculate the rate of application in inches per hour.

For example, if you have 1-gph emitters on 18-inch centers on the tubing and the lines of tubing

Rate of Application Math

$$RA = \frac{231.1 \times GPH}{\text{sq. in. spacing}} = \text{inches per hour (in/hr)}$$ *then,*

in/hr $\times$ 7.48 g/cu.ft. = gallons per hour per square foot (g/hr/sq.ft.)   *then,*

g/hr/sq.ft. $\times$ total sq.ft. = total flow rate (g/hr or gph)   *then,*

$$\frac{\text{total daily ET needs, in gallons (g)}}{\text{total flow rate (g/hr or gpr)}} = \text{total length of daily irrigations, in hours}$$ *then,*

total hours $\times$ 60 = **Total minutes of irrigation per day**   *[Finito!]*

Figure 37 This is a specific example of the math involved in computing the rate of application formula—the RA. It's not as scary as it looks.

Daily Irrigation Need Formula

$$DN \text{ (Daily Needs), gallons} = \frac{.623 \times \text{Area of the root zone} \times \text{Plant Factor} \times \text{ET rate}}{\text{Efficiency of drip irrigation by climate}}$$

Figure 38 The daily needs formula [DN] is a more efficient way of calculating the irrigation needs of your plants, and is more accurate than just using the table of ET rates on the facing page. You needn't use this formula if it scares you; just use the simpler ET table and adjust the length of irrigation based on your observations of the plant growth.

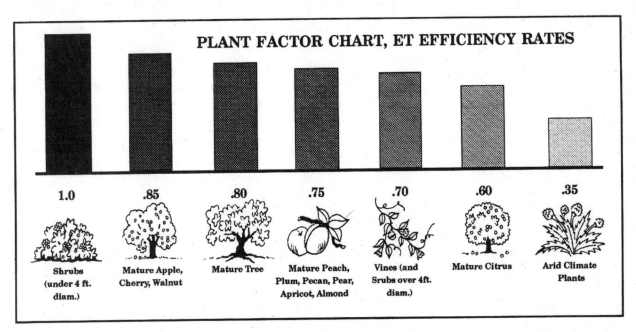

Figure 39 Not all plants have truly identical ET rates. Some plants are more moisture-conserving than others. This chart lists the ET-rate efficiency of a number of plants and trees. The rates of efficiency are still somewhat imprecise, but offers more accuracy than the rates listed in the ET chart on page 52.

are 24 inches apart, multiply 18 times 24 to get 432 square inches. Divide 432 into the product of 231.1 times 0.92 [the actual flow rate of the 1-gph emitters]. This gives a result of 0.49 inch per hour, the average irrigation rate in inches per hour for the entire system.

Many gardeners are used to irrigation guidelines given in inches per week. With the knowledge of your system's inch-per-hour rating, it's easy to figure how long to leave the system on to satisfy the plants. If, for example, the local farm adviser recommends two inches per week for peach trees, then the above system would have to run slightly more than four hours per week. [Two inches divided by 0.49 inches per hour equals 4.08 hours.] This four hours of irrigation could be all at once, or two irrigations per week of two hours each, or even, although I don't recommend it, 16 hours of irrigation once a month.

If you want to irrigate on a gallonage basis, the results of the RA formula must be converted to gallons per hour per square foot [g/hr/sq. ft.] To convert, divide the RA by 12 to get the cubic foot [cu. ft. amount of water per hour–cu. ft./hr]. In this case, 0.49 divided by 12 equals 0.04 cu. ft./hr. To convert to g/hr/sq. ft., multiply 0.04 cu. ft./hr times 7.48 [the number of gallons-per-cubic foot.] For this example, 0.04 times 7.48 equals 0.3 g/hr/sq. ft. [Take a deep breath.]

So, returning to the example of the 100-square-foot border that requires at least 18.7 gallons per day. If the tubing is configured with 1-gph emitters and 18 inches in the tubing by 24 inches between the lines, you could apply 30 gph [0.3 g/hr/sq. ft. times 100 sq. ft.] The length of irrigation equals 0.53 hour [18.7 total gallons divided by 0.53 gph—231.1 divided by 432 sq. inches] of irrigation per day, or 35 minutes. [See Figure 36.]

I hope this math doesn't make your head hurt as much as it did mine initially! The first time may

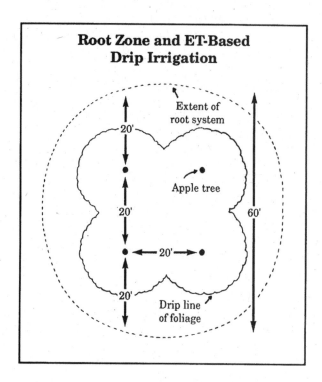

Figure 40 Use this sample planting plan as the basis for calculating daily needs [DN] in the example as given in Figure 38.

seem like a mind-bender, but if you work them through a few times, these calculations will soon become routine. Besides, once you've struggled through the initial math, you will have established a basic guideline for all of your subsequent irrigation. From that point on, the length of irrigation is adjusted up or down depending upon the quality of growth desired or on your water supply. If you want to fine-tune the system throughout the growing season, once you know the flow rate for each system, you can just do the math for the ET rate for different seasons.

Refining ET-Based Irrigation Rates

The above ballpark approaches to ET-based irrigation are the simplest, but the formulas ignore two important realities: all plants are not identical in their ET rate, and drip irrigation, in spite of its high efficiency, isn't perfect. There is yet another formula that makes ET-based irrigation even more accurate and less of an assumption. This formula for computing daily water needs is outlined in Figure 37.

The 0.623 figure in the formula is a constant that mathematically adjusts the varying square footage of root zones to the ET rate, and functions to convert the result to gallons. This number was derived by dividing 12 [inches] into the number of gallons in a cubic foot of water [7.48 gallons].

Since my approach to drip irrigation involves watering the entire root zone, the area of the root zone is equal to the area covered by the tubing plus the lateral movement of water away from the outermost emitters. In most cases, this is the area of the entire bed, container, or planting. Don't forget that the true width of the root zone is one to three times wider than that of the foliage. If you're watering an individual shade tree that is isolated from other plantings, then simply calculate the area of the root zone. For circles, the area equals the radius-squared times 3.14. For some, it's simpler to square the diameter and multiply by 0.7854.

Plants actually transpire at different rates; depending upon their size, type, and age, each plant can have a different factor of ET efficiency. For the sake of this calculation, shrubs smaller than four feet, unless an ET factor is known, are rated at 100%, or a 1.0 factor. Generally speaking, drought-resistant plants have a 0.35 plant factor. This means they use 65% less water than a normal water-loving plant. Refer to Figure 39 for more plant factors.

Finally, the ET rate is based on Figure 35. Instead of using the daily gallon rate from the one-square-foot column, use the daily ET rate in inches. This can be determined by dividing the ET [in inches per month] figure by 30 days. For example, in Figure 35; one, two, three, four, five, six, seven, eight, nine, and ten inches per month become 0.03, 0.07, 0.10, 0.13, 0.17, 0.20, 0.23, 0.27, 0.30, and 0.33 inch per day, respectively. Choose an ET rate on the high end of your monthly ET.

All of this is to be divided by the efficiency of the drip irrigation system. While I mentioned earlier in the book that drip systems are 90% efficient, this is really just an averaged figure. The efficiency of any irrigation system is affected by the climate. Figure 41 shows the efficiency rates for three simplified climate zones. When in doubt, select an efficiency rate from a harsher climate than yours.

Let's consider the irrigation of four apple trees planted in a moderate climate in a square pattern on 20-foot centers. [See Figure 40.] The root zone and the drip system cover a total of 3600 square feet [60' X 60']. From Figure 39, the plant factor is 0.85; the ET rate is 0.2 [6 inches

Efficiency of Drip Irrigation Systems

Climate	Factor
Dry-Warm/Hot	.85
Moderate	.90
Humid	.95

Figure 41 While drip irrigation is the most efficient way to irrigate, its efficiency is still influenced by climate. A factor of one would indicate an absolutely efficient system.

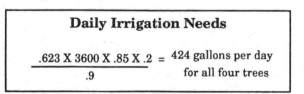

Daily Irrigation Needs

$$\frac{.623 \times 3600 \times .85 \times .2}{.9} = \begin{array}{l}\text{424 gallons per day}\\ \text{for all four trees}\end{array}$$

Figure 42 This illustrates the math for calculating the daily needs [DN] outlined in the text.

per month] and the efficiency of the drip system is 0.9. See Figure 38 for the calculation.

Now you've got the actual water needs of the trees. Next, total the number of emitters in the system and calculate the flow-rate per hour, then divide into 424 gallons per day to get the total number of hours the system must run each day.

ET Facts for Trivia Buffs

Even this last formula for using ET rates to calculate irrigation rates relies upon generalized assumptions about plants. Yet plants, like people, are unique; each has a different physiology and distinctive needs.

David Johnson, while working as a technician at the Laboratory of Climatology at Arizona State University, developed, after considerable library research, some very interesting figures about maximum ET rates for various crops and plants. Who would suspect that the more petite pomegranate [*Punica granatum*], with a mature height of less than 12 feet, would transpire more water [35 inches per year] than a lofty Aleppo pine tree [*Pinus halepensis*], with a mature height of 30 to 60 feet and a maximum transpiration rate of 25 inches per year?

I was surprised to find from Johnson's data that an olive tree's annual transpiration of 25 inches is higher than that of a pineapple [20 inches]. Perhaps this difference is due to the thick, waxy covering on the pineapple's leaves or the humidity of a tropical climate. Or it may simply be due to the large difference in total surface area of the leaves of olive trees and pineapple plants. While the exact mechanism is uncertain, the discrepancy is striking.

More remarkably, a number of Sonoran desert scrub trees, including several species of *Acacia* spp., growing in one of the drier climates in the country, have a maximum transpiration of 35 inches, more than the average of 33 inches for deciduous fruit trees. This may be due to the capacity of many desert plants to grow very extensive and lengthy root systems. While some desert plants use more moisture than some humid-climate plants, they compensate by having root systems that are better able to explore for and secure elusive soil moisture.

In other cases, desert plants behave the way we would expect. Desert cacti transpire no more than 15 inches of moisture per year and need less than one inch of water to survive, compared with an orange tree's maximum use of 35 inches and survival need of 11 inches of water.

CHAPTER 5

Hiding and Expanding Your Drip System

The main assembly for the flower border or any other section of the landscape can be discreetly hidden at or below the soil's surface.

[See Figure 43.] This makes for a less cluttered-looking garden, but beware. You may easily forget to flush the filter or bring the assembly indoors for the winter [if necessary in your area]. Also, please note, when considering a "buried" assembly: if the main assembly is below ground level, all plants to be irrigated must be at least 12 inches downhill from the level of the assembly in order for the atmospheric vacuum breaker and check valve to be effective. If this is not possible in your yard, you can add a brass vacuum breaker [see page 63] near the house where the main irrigation line joins the house's water pipes. Instead of a faucet, a ball valve is plumbed into this assembly to turn the system on and off.

Due to the space limitations of this assembly

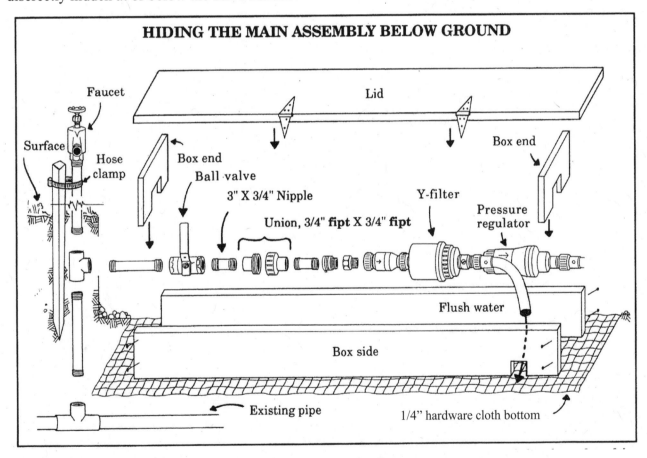

HIDING THE MAIN ASSEMBLY BELOW GROUND

Faucet

Lid

Surface

Hose clamp

Box end

Box end

Ball valve

3" X 3/4" Nipple

Y-filter

Union, 3/4" **fipt** X 3/4" **fipt**

Pressure regulator

Flush water

Box side

Existing pipe

1/4" hardware cloth bottom

Figure 43 Some gardeners prefer to have their drip irrigation main assembly hidden in a box just below the surface of the soil. Remember the "out-of-sight, out-of-mind" syndrome, which may cause you to forget to flush the filter or bring main assembly indoors during cold winters. If you skip the protective wire hardware cloth bottom, gophers may fill the box in less than one night with their "throws".

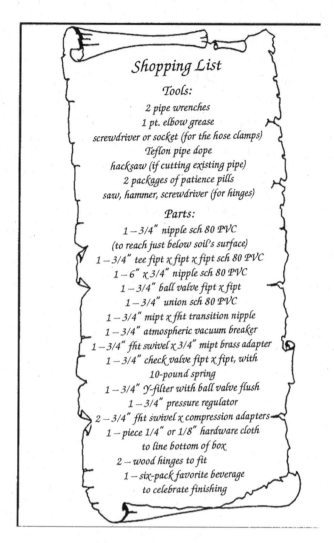

along with some plumbing tools and all the parts you'll need. In Figure 44, I've provided a shopping list for both the tools and the plumbing parts you'll need. Be sure to check your purchases twice so that universal law of plumbing, PMLP Numero Uno, doesn't rear its ugly head.

Now You Can Begin

1—Pull the soil away from the base of your existing faucet riser. Carefully dig down to where you find the riser [actually a very long nipple] attached to a threaded fitting. This might be a threaded "tee" if the riser is in the middle of a long irrigation line. Or there might be a threaded elbow [a 90° fitting or "ell"] if it's the end of an irrigation line. Be sure to dig below the level of the fitting to prevent soil from spilling into the open pipe when the riser is removed.

2—All risers should be attached to a post to keep them from "tweaking" the underground fitting. Loosen the fastening so you can unthread the riser. [If there is no post, you'll need

Figure 44 Here's your shopping list for the project to construct a main assembly that is cleverly hidden below the surface of the garden. NOTE: Remember this assembly must be at least 12 inches above the highest point of the drip system. Or, a separate agricultural water supply.

housing, you won't be able to rotate the filter easily to thread it onto the assembly. A union [see Figure 45] allows you to add the main assembly just after the ball valve without having to rotate any part. The union has three parts: one end with fipt threads and nonpipe male threads with a flat seat; another end with fipt threads, and a flat seat with an O-ring gasket; and a large ring with female threads that joins the flat faces of the two other parts together into one leak-free fitting.

Before you begin, gather your wits about you,

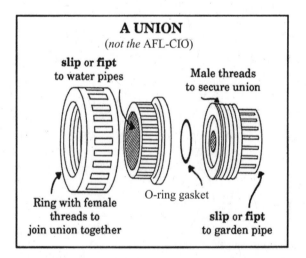

A UNION
(*not the AFL-CIO*)

slip or fipt
to water pipes

Male threads
to secure union

Ring with female
threads to
join union together

O-ring gasket

slip or fipt
to garden pipe

Figure 45 The union allows you to take a main assembly off the water main supply line without having to take the entire assembly apart. The larger outer ring joins the two sections together, and the gasket seals against any leaks.

to add one after you've finished re-plumbing the riser.]

3—With a pipe wrench, grasp the riser above the soil level and turn it counterclockwise to remove it from its fitting on the underground pipe. When backing the riser out, use another wrench [watch out for PMLP #3] to hold the fitting, to make sure it's not tweaked. If the fitting appears rusty, treat the base of the riser with some Liquid Wrench™ or WD-40™ to loosen the threads.

If the riser is just a white plastic pipe that is glued, not screwed, into a white fitting, you should cut the irrigation pipe and glue a new schedule 80 threaded fitting [a grey-colored fitting] into the existing irrigation pipe. Schedule 80 PVC pipe fittings, while not as sturdy as metal pipe fittings, are many times stronger than the white schedule 40 fittings. Be sure to use the special glue made to bond the grey schedule 80 fittings to white PVC pipe; check the description on the label or ask the store clerk for assistance. Try to avoid manifesting PMLP #7. Make sure the fitting you glue has fipt threads on the outlet portion.

4—Now, using either threaded schedule 80 parts or galvanized metal fittings, add a new, shorter riser nipple to reach three inches below the natural level of the soil. [Be sure to use Teflon pipe dope, in spite of PMLP #8, to seal all the threads mentioned in these instructions.] The length of this nipple will vary according to how deep the original irrigation pipe was laid. Install the nipple with two pipe wrenches, one grasping the nipple between the threads, the other firmly holding the fitting below ground to prevent it from getting tweaked. [If any dirt fell into the old irrigation pipe before the new, short riser was added, turn on the water briefly before rethreading the old riser to help flush the dirt out.]

5—Install a threaded 3/4-inch tee [fipt X fipt X fipt] to the bottom of the old riser with the faucet. Install the tee so that the pass-through openings

will be straight up and down and the "leg" will be parallel to the ground. As the tee gets snug, make sure the "leg," when you're looking down on the faucet, is perpendicular to the direction of the faucet.

6—Thread the old riser on top of the new fipt tee. [Don't drop it or PMLP #5 will come into play.]

7—Next, add a six-inch nipple to the "leg" of the fipt tee. Be sure to hold the riser securely while threading on the nipple.

8—Attach one of the fipt openings of the ball valve to the end of the nipple. You will have to dig a hole deep enough and wide enough to rotate the ball valve in its open position onto the nipple.

9—Add a three-inch nipple to the end of the union with the fipt threads and the seat with the O-ring gasket. Be sure to slip the union's female-threaded ring over the end of the union before adding the nipple. Keep an eye on the O-ring, as it can easily fall out during the precarious act of plumbing.

10—Because the simplest brass atmospheric vacuum breaker has hose threads, you'll have to thread an adapter into the outlet side of the union and onto the inlet side of the check valve. The adapter looks much like a short nipple but has, on one end, male pipe threads to screw into the union and, on the other side, male hose threads. Use some Teflon pipe dope only on the mipt portion. Hand-tighten the atmospheric vacuum breaker onto the adapter's mht end. Add the next adapter, a 3/4-inch brass fht X mipt fitting, to the vacuum breaker. Hand-tighten.

11—Apply some pipe dope to the brass adapter's mipt end and carefully twirl on a complete main assembly as described in the chapter titled *Your First Drip Irrigation Project*. Be sure not to misalign the assembly and ruin the threads by "cross-threading" the plastic threads on the check valve.

12—Tie or fasten the riser back to the support post. If there was no supporting post, carefully hammer in a wooden stake 2" by 2" [with a pointed end for easier insertion], a length of 3/4-inch rebar, or a length of 1/2-inch galvanized pipe with one end pounded flat to make it easier to drive into the ground. Using large hose clamps, strap the riser to the post in two places—one near the faucet and the other on the lower half of the riser.

13—Join the finished main assembly to the portion of the union that's attached to the ball valve. Double-check to make sure the O-ring didn't fall out. Also make sure both flat surfaces of the union are clean and free of any dirt or mulch. As you tighten the union's female-threaded ring, make sure the filter's discharge valve is parallel to the ground.

14—Add a swivel X compression fitting to the mht fitting of the ball valve at the end of the filter. Insert a length of solid drip hose into the compression fitting. This allows you to flush the filter without filling up the box with water. Place the end of the flush hose near a plant to utilize the water. Stop, relax, and reward yourself.

Now construct a box to surround the main assembly. Be sure to cut a slot over the filter's discharge hose. All worries of PMLP #11 aside, if you have moles or gophers, before you place the box around the assembly, lay a doubled-over piece of 1/4-inch metal hardware cloth on the ground. The hardware cloth helps keep the box from filling up with soil from these tunneling pests. Or, pour a thin slurry of concrete into the bottom of the box.

The union allows you to remove the main assembly for repairs or winter storage without digging up the box. To remove the main assembly, close the ball valve, unscrew the swivel that attaches the drip irrigation hose to the pressure regulator, unscrew the swivel fitting from the filter's flush discharge, and unthread the large outer ring of the union. You can then lift the main assembly out of the top of the box.

With the assembly hidden, you will probably need some kind of reminder system to help you remember to flush the filter periodically and bring the main assembly indoors in cold-winter climates.

Plumbing the Main Assembly at Ground Level

To give your main assembly a low profile while avoiding the "out-of-sight, out-of-mind" drawback of the hidden main assembly, you can use the same configuration of parts mentioned above but plumb them to lie nearly on the soil's surface, at the base of the faucet. A little ruffle of evergreen herbs or shrubbery will veil the assembly from view in the garden but still leave it visible enough to be a reminder for seasonal maintenance. If you're the kind of person who requires visual reminders to get things done, this is a still-visible but more elegant solution than constructing the main assembly off the faucet well above ground.

Figure 46 shows that this approach is very similar to plumbing the main assembly below ground. Follow steps #1 through #14 as mentioned above. The exception, in step #4, is to add a longer nipple to bring the tee, and subsequently the main assembly, two to three inches above the ground. The nipple in step #7 can also be reduced to just three inches, since you're not building a box around the assembly. You can skip the addition of a union [steps #8, 9, and 10] if you want, but you'll have to dig a shallow hole to allow for the rotation of the Y-filter while threading it onto the check valve. The union, however, makes it much simpler to remove the

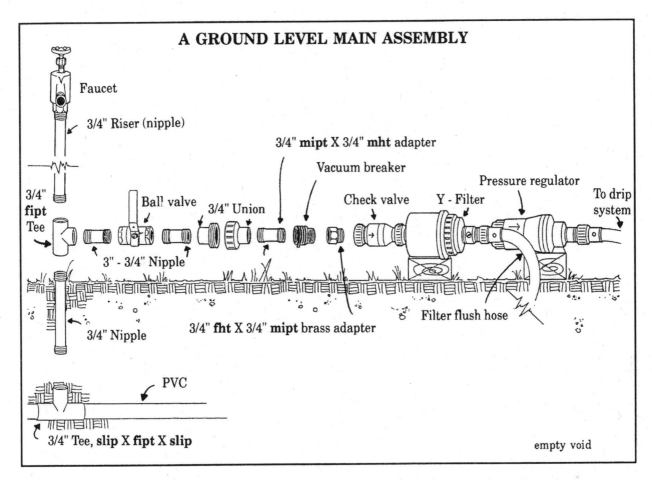

A GROUND LEVEL MAIN ASSEMBLY

Faucet

3/4" Riser (nipple)

3/4" **mipt** X 3/4" **mht** adapter

Vacuum breaker

Pressure regulator

Check valve   Y - Filter

To drip system

3/4" **fipt** Tee

Ball valve

3/4" Union

3" - 3/4" Nipple

3/4" Nipple

3/4" **fht** X 3/4" **mipt** brass adapter

Filter flush hose

PVC

3/4" Tee, **slip** X **fipt** X **slip**

empty void

Figure 46 These parts allow you to have a main assembly near the ground, where it won't show from a distance but will be more accessible for cleaning the filter. Be sure to place blocks of wood under the filter and pressure to reduce stress on the fittings. NOTE: As mentioned, this assembly must be 12 inches or higher than any part of the drip system.

main assembly in cold-winter climates. Be sure to add, as illustrated, some blocks of wood beneath the assembly to keep it from tweaking any of the parts leading back to the faucet's riser. You must paint the entire assembly with exterior latex paint to help delay the brittling of the plastic by the sun's ultraviolet rays. Beneath the entire assembly, put down a weed barrier—a piece of carpet with the less noticeable brown backing facing up, or a piece of woven landscape fabric, which allows water and air but not weeds to pass through.

Attaching the Main Assembly to the Hose

Perhaps the easiest approach to the main assembly is to attach the main assembly permanently to the end of a length of garden hose. The other end of the hose can be attached to one side of a Y-valve at a faucet and the main assembly can then be taken to whichever section of the landscape needs watering. In this case, the main assembly is constructed exactly as it would be for mounting on a faucet, except the fht fitting at the beginning of the assembly is threaded onto a metal in-line ball valve with hose threads and then onto the mht end of the hose. [See Figure 47.] The ball valve permits you to turn on the

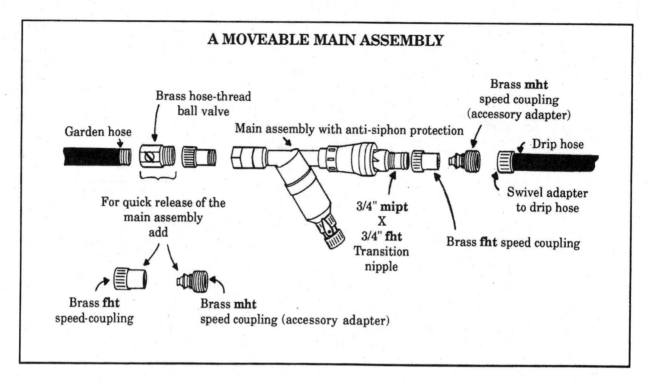

A MOVEABLE MAIN ASSEMBLY

Garden hose

Brass hose-thread ball valve

Main assembly with anti-siphon protection

Brass **mht** speed coupling (accessory adapter)

Drip hose

For quick release of the main assembly add

3/4" **mipt** X 3/4" **fht** Transition nipple

Swivel adapter to drip hose

Brass **fht** speed coupling

Brass **fht** speed-coupling

Brass **mht** speed coupling (accessory adapter)

Figure 47 A moveable main assembly allows the gardener to use one assembly for numerous irrigation systems and subsystems. Because the parts for a main assembly are rather expensive, the moveable assembly can save you plenty of money.

water at the main faucet but not waste any water before you've joined the assembly to one of the drip systems in the landscape. It's imperative that you do not pick up the assembly by grabbing the end of the hose. The weight of the assembly may crack the assembly. Lift the assembly up by the filter, which is the easiest part to hold and is more or less in the middle. Again, be sure to apply a protective layer of exterior latex paint to the assembly.

Out in the landscape, each separate drip system begins with a fht swivel X compression fitting. These fittings are commonly sold with a combination gasket and cone-shaped screen in the swivel. The screen must be left in the swivel to keep bugs, worms, various disgusting creatures, and dirt from entering the drip hosing when the main assembly is not attached. These work very well with assemblies that don't use a speed coupling.

An even better way, compared to a Figure 8 end closure, is to is to use an end cap, made from a compression by mipt fitting. Or, close the fht end of your system with a simple 3/4-inch mipt hose plug.

You can streamline your watering by adding brass speed couplings to both the end of the main assembly and all fht swivels in the landscape. Speed couplings work much the same way the gizmo you use to inflate your car's tires attaches to the end of the air compressor's line. I always recommend solid brass speed couplings over the plastic versions, even the European versions, because they can take much more cold and abuse without breaking. To add a speed coupling to the end of the main assembly, add a mipt X mht transition fitting [see Figure 47], then thread the female threads of the brass speed coupling's connector onto the male hose threads of the transi-

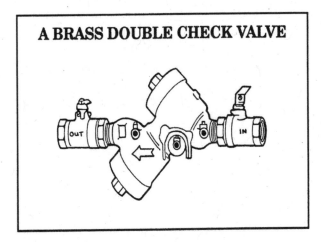

A BRASS DOUBLE CHECK VALVE

Figure 48 The highest quality and most expensive backflow preventer—a double check valve. This can be placed level or lower than the irrigation lines.

tion fitting. At the beginning of each drip system, add a permanent male hose-threaded speed coupling, sometimes called an accessory adapter, into the fht swivel. In order to attach the male hose-threaded piece, you will have to reverse the typical position of the cone-shaped screen. Face the convex side of the screen into the throat of the fht swivel; otherwise, the cone will block the tightening of the male speed coupling. Then, you can attach or unfasten the main assembly with a quick snap or release of the speed coupling. The small cost of the speed couplings will be repaid many times over by their convenience.

Using One Main Assembly for Several Sections of Your Landscape

The best way to save money is to design your drip system [and, if possible, your landscape plantings] to allow for one main assembly to service several or all drip irrigation systems. This is usually most easily done at a faucet or water pipe next to the house. The idea is to have one main assembly serving several rigid plastic PVC pipes, which are buried in trenches leading out to each separate drip system.

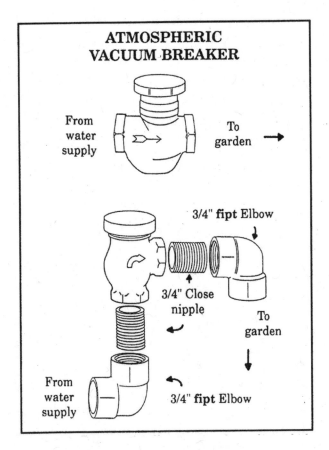

ATMOSPHERIC VACUUM BREAKER

From water supply

To garden

3/4" **fipt** Elbow

3/4" **Close nipple**

To garden

From water supply

3/4" **fipt** Elbow

Figure 49 Two ways to plumb an atmospheric vacuum breaker into the main assembly. Note: These parts must also be 12 inches or more above the highest point of the drip system.

If this centralized main assembly is 12 or more inches lower than any portion of all the separate drip systems, you can't use a single check valve. Even a brass atmospheric vacuum breaker [see Figure 6] has to be 12 inches higher than any portion of the drip system. The only safe anti-siphon device plumbed lower than the drip system is a brass backflow preventer [see Figure 48] with a double check valve. These are expensive [$125 or more for the 3/4-inch model and $140 or more for the 1-inch size] but worth the price compared with the alternative of contaminating your family's drinking supply. These seemingly expensive anti-siphon devices can be cheaper than installing a lot of brass atmospheric vacuum breakers with manual valves at various points in the landscape.

For example, if your landscape needs six or more vacuum breakers, at nearly $21 each, brass atmospheric vacuum breakers with manual valves are more costly than a single $125 backflow preventer.

This device should only be installed by an

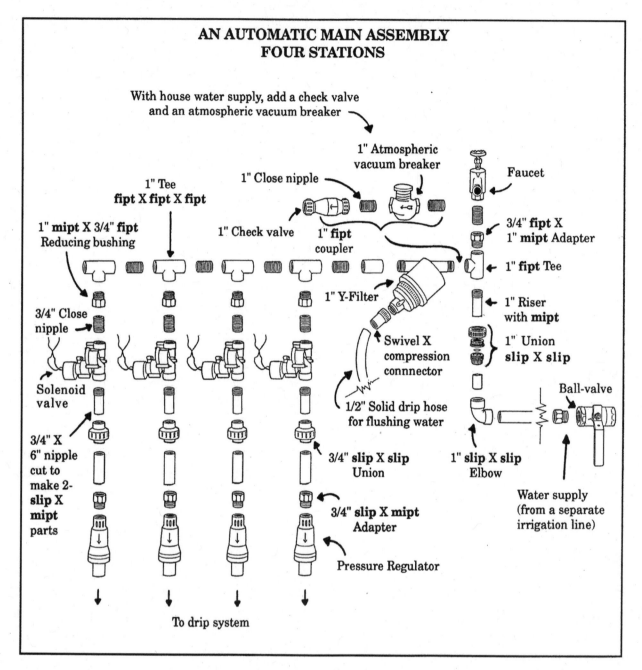

AN AUTOMATIC MAIN ASSEMBLY FOUR STATIONS

With house water supply, add a check valve and an atmospheric vacuum breaker

1" Atmospheric vacuum breaker

Faucet

1" Close nipple

1" Tee
fipt X fipt X fipt

1" Check valve

1" **fipt** coupler

3/4" **fipt X** 1" **mipt** Adapter

1" **mipt X 3/4" fipt** Reducing bushing

1" **fipt** Tee

1" Riser with **mipt**

1" Y-Filter

3/4" Close nipple

1" Union **slip X slip**

Solenoid valve

Swivel X compression connnector

Ball-valve

3/4" X 6" nipple cut to make 2- **slip X mipt** parts

1/2" Solid drip hose for flushing water

1" **slip X slip** Elbow

3/4" **slip X slip** Union

Water supply (from a separate irrigation line)

3/4" **slip X mipt** Adapter

Pressure Regulator

To drip system

Figure 50 All parts that make up a centralized assembly for four separate zones. Each irrigation line has a solenoid 24 VAC [Volts Alternating Current] controller. The solenoid valves are automatically activated by an electronic controller. If this assembly is outdoors, be sure to paint all the PVC parts with outdoor latex paint or something like Rust-Oleam®. This is a big project. But for a first multiple zone system you can see how all is working. Be sure the filter comes before the solenoids as they can easily clog.

irrigation contractor trained to install and check that it is functioning properly. You should have the contractor come once a year to inspect the double check valve to make sure it's protecting the home's water by eliminating a back flow siphoning.

For this centralized main assembly, you'll need to know if you plan to irrigate any two sections at once. If so, you'll have to install the larger 1-inch versions of the anti-siphon device, filter and all connecting parts to maintain sufficient flow. Remember, a 3/4-inch filter can pass only 660 gallons per hour, compared with 1200 gph for a 1-inch filter.

NOTE: In some yards, the pressure regulator is best installed at the end of the PVC pipe and the beginning of the drip hose to reduce friction loss problems.

Figure 50 shows what a centralized main assembly might look like. This one, for the west and south sides of the Shrubbery's house, supplies four lines, each leading to a separate drip irrigation zones. All parts plumbed in after the water supply line have 1-inch threads because they will be used to irrigate several drip systems at once. The assembly begins with a ball valve so the water supply can be shut off to work on any part of the assembly. Next comes a 1-inch union for easy removal of the entire assembly. The top "arm" of the 1-inch schedule 80 tee, just before the faucet, is stepped down to 3/4 of an inch with what's known in plumbing parlance as a reducer bushing [a 1-inch mipt X 3/4-inch fipt version] so that you can use a less expensive 3/4-inch brass faucet.

Off the "leg" of the first tee is where you add the atmospheric vacuum breaker and check valve combo if you're connected to the house's water pipes. In this example, the Shrubberys left out the anti-siphon devices because the assembly is connected to a water line from the well that services only the landscape, not the house.

A 1-inch Y-filter follows to allow for the simultaneous use of two or more irrigation valves. Everything up to this point is in the more expensive 1-inch fittings to allow for the possibility of running several drip irrigation lines at the same time. The "leg" of each one-inch tee for each separate irrigation line is reduced to 3/4-inch threads with what's known as a threaded adapter bushing. This allows for less expensive valves and pressure regulators. And because each individual drip irrigation line usually doesn't require the flow of a 1-inch valve, you can revert to less expensive 3/4-inch plumbing parts.

You can substitute any type of manual ball valve for the automatic solenoid if you don't want the complexity or cost of an automatic system. [The threads are the same for both—fipt.] To join the solenoid [or any valve] to the union, cut a 3/4-inch, 6-inch schedule 80 nipple in half. Now you have two pieces, each slip X mipt. Use one to thread into the valve, with pipe dope, and glue into the slip X slip union. Be sure to use the special PVC glue for cementing schedule 80 plastic parts. The 3/4-inch unions with female slip fittings are added after each valve to simplify the removal of the entire assembly for any repairs.

If the flower bed or trees you'll be irrigating are nearby [less than 50 feet away], you can install the pressure regulators after the valves, at the main assembly. As always, paint the entire assembly.

But if there is any distance at all to the beginning of your irrigation lines, it is better to run schedule 40 PVC pipe from the main assembly to the beginning of the line and then add the pressure regulator. [Don't forget PMLP #6.] If the pressure regulator were at the beginning of the system, the pressure drop from the friction of the water moving through the pipe out into the garden could severely reduce the flow. No matter where the pressure regulators are, be sure they have the right flow and psi ratings for each particular line or system.

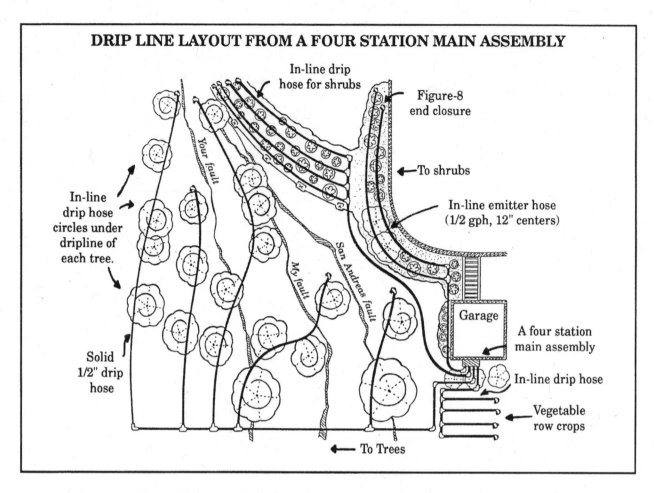

DRIP LINE LAYOUT FROM A FOUR STATION MAIN ASSEMBLY

In-line drip hose for shrubs

Figure-8 end closure

To shrubs

In-line emitter hose (1/2 gph, 12" centers)

In-line drip hose circles under dripline of each tree.

Your fault

My fault

San Andreas fault

Garage

A four station main assembly

In-line drip hose

Solid 1/2" drip hose

Vegetable row crops

To Trees

Figure 51 A view of the trees and shrubs at the Shrubberys' house. They are irrigated by the four valves of in-line drip irrigation tubing. The large well-spaced trees are serviced by a lateral of solid 1/2-inch tubing with a length of in-line drip line. They have a compression tee at each tree. A 1/2-inch 700 series, 18mm, blue compression fitting X 600 series 16-mm, green compression fitting X 1/2-inch 700 series, 18-mm, blue compression fitting. See Figure 20 for a refresher illustration. The Shrubbery's have Figure 8 end closures on all lines of tubing. They missed out on the part of my book that recommends drain-down headers where appropriate. The four lines in the vegetable garden and all the ends of the in-line tubing for the shrubs could easily be fixed by the addition of elbows and tees. As we'll see later in the book, dripper lines are most effective for the trees at or beyond the drip line.

When the regulator is at the end of the solid PVC supply pipe, it is connected with a male adapter, a mipt X slip 3/4-inch PVC fitting. Using pipe dope, thread the male adapter into each regulator. Then glue the male adapter to each solid schedule 40 PVC supply line. Finally, a 3/4-inch union with female slip fittings is glued [be sure to use the special glue for bonding white and gray PVC parts] into each line for simple removal of the assembly. As always, paint the entire main assembly.

Disregard PMLP #11 and bury the schedule 40 PVC lines at least 18 inches deep to protect them from future digging and cultivation. Leave the trenches open until all the below-ground parts have been glued together. Never bury the pipe until the glue has set for 12 to 24 hours and you've turned on the water to test for leaks. [A layer of sand placed around the pipe before backfilling with soil may help remind whomever is digging that they are about to hit a water line.] Use a 3/4-inch slip X slip elbow

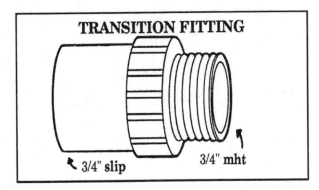

Figure 52 A transition fitting that glues onto the end of a schedule 40 PVC pipe and converts it to a male-hose thread. Found in irrigation contractor's supply houses or via the mail from some of the resources listed in the back of the book.

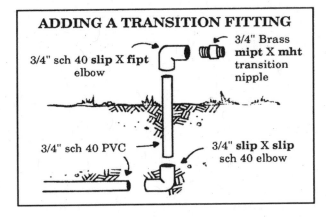

Figure 53 Brass transition fittings that convert pipe threads to hose threads are easier to find in hardware stores than a schedule 40 PVC pipe slip X mipt fitting. Be sure to use Teflon pipe dope or tape to seal only the fipt end. Any drip irrigation fitting with a swivel X fht or garden hose can be added to the transition fitting.

at the end of each PVC line to glue a piece of schedule 40 PVC pipe so that it reaches up a few inches above the soil's surface. Add another 3/4-inch slip X slip elbow above ground, facing toward your plantings. This is where you'll probably be adding the pressure regulator. Add a three- to four-inch length of PVC pipe parallel to the ground. Thread the male adapter [3/4-inch slip X mipt] into each regulator and glue the male adapters to each solid PVC supply line. Then the outlet side of the regulator is threaded with a mipt X mht transition nipple.

If your supply line doesn't have a regulator out in the garden, you can use slip X slip elbows to come up out of the ground and then connect directly to the drip hose. To easily adapt to drip irrigation fittings, glue a special male adapter, a 3/4-inch slip X 3/4-inch mht transition fitting [see Figure 52], to the horizontal PVC pipe coming out of the last elbow. Now simply thread the drip irrigation fht swivel X compression adapter onto the hose threads of the transition fitting, insert the in-line drip hose and you're all set—if Pop Murphy hasn't meddled with your plumbing—to irrigate the modern, efficient way.

The slip X mht fitting is not an easy part to find in an ordinary hardware store, and certainly not any big box store. Another method is to glue onto the vertical riser pipe an elbow that has female threads on one side—a 3/4-inch 90° slip X fipt. [See Figure 53.] Into the fipt threads add a mipt X mht transition nipple. For both of these parts, see the mail-order suppliers in the Appendices.

CHAPTER 6

Drip Irrigation for Containers

Container plants—whether grown in expensive Italian terra-cotta pottery, plastic tubs, old olive oil cans, wooden planters, or hanging baskets—add delightful accents to patios, porches, decks, windowsills, and rooftops. For many urban gardeners, container plants are the only option for a soothing touch of foliage, color, and fragrance, or even a modest harvest of fresh herbs, vegetables, and some tree-ripened fruit. In all gardens, bedding plants in glorious full bloom, displayed in attractive pots, are a wonderfully easy way to provide colorful seasonal highlights throughout the garden.

Compared with their down-to-earth cousins, however, container plants are unforgiving of neglect, especially when it comes to watering. Pots dry out fast. Periodic and/or infrequent drenching harms the plant by allowing intermittent periods of drought stress and by leaching valuable and limited nutrients from the soil. Daily watering with tiny amounts of water is often essential to maintaining consistent moisture and therefore consistent nutrient availability in the soil.

Enter drip irrigation, which fits container gardening like jelly on a peanut-butter sandwich. With a well-planned drip system you can add a very small, measured amount of water to each plant every day. Consistent watering of container plants will reward the gardener with better growth and a longer period of bloom [and fruit if you're lucky enough to have a large deck with your apartment]. Furthermore, drip irrigation can eliminate the mildew and fungus problems encouraged by overhead watering.

Drip irrigation of pots calls for a variety of hardware that I seldom use in landscapes. This is virtually the only situation where I mess with the dreaded "spaghetti" tubing. Its small diameter, either 1/8- or 1/4-inch, provides a low visual profile and makes it easy to hide among foliage. When carefully installed in small- to medium-sized containers, spaghetti in-line tubing is manageable and doesn't end up the tangled mess so accurately suggested by its name.

Trickle Your Pot's Fancy

Start with the same main assembly that I've described for flower borders. Remember, if you use a combination check-valve and atmospheric vacuum breaker or just an atmospheric vacuum breaker, all the containers must be at least 12 inches below the level of the anti-siphon device. Only a more expensive brass-bodied reduced pressure backflow preventor with a double check valve can service container plants or hanging baskets below the level of the main assembly.

Use the same quality of Y-filter but make sure the stainless-steel screen is at least 150 mesh or up to 200 mesh. This smaller-sized screen will help prevent clogging of the smaller orifices of some of the emitters and emitter-like tubing used with pots.

Remember, quality pressure regulators are rated for a specific range of flow. You may not have many pots on any one container drip system and thus will be using only a very low volume of water. The Senninger low-flow pressure regulator, which comes in 10- and 15-psi models, is rated at a 0.1 to 8 gpm (6 to 480 gph) capacity. This is usually the best pressure regulator for containers, providing all the emitters or 1/4-inch in-line hose in the system pass at least 6 gallons per hour.

Let's take a look at all the components for various sizes of pots, starting with a guide to matching the emitters to the container's size. Then I'll show you how, with a little sleight of hand, to make all the emitters and tubing virtually disappear.

Before adding the spaghetti tubing and planting your pots, be sure to seal the inside. Terra-cotta pots are especially prone to wicking lots of moisture through their walls. I brush an inexpensive, nontoxic cement sealer on all the inside surfaces of clay pots. Sometimes the clay soaks up so much sealer that two coats are required.

Small Pots

For small pots, up to 12 inches in diameter, it's best to use a single emitter, no matter how many plants are squeezed in. To avoid overwatering small pots, I find it best to use 1/2-gph

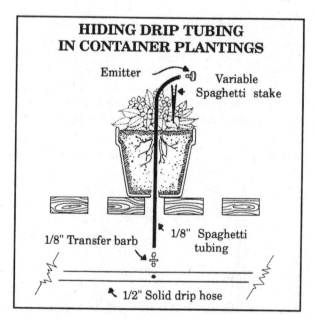

HIDING DRIP TUBING IN CONTAINER PLANTINGS

Emitter

Variable Spaghetti stake

1/8" Transfer barb

1/8" Spaghetti tubing

1/2" Solid drip hose

Figure 54 If you pot your plants with drip in mind, it's easy to hide the drip paraphernalia. Feed a length of 1/8-inch tubing through the pot before planting. Attach the tubing to a solid 1/2-inch drip irrigation supply hose. Plant. Flush the system. Cut the 1/8-inch tubing to fit onto the stake.

emitters. If more water is needed, I can always set the timer to stay on a little longer. As with landscaping, I always use pressure-compensating emitters for all my containers. While they might cost as much as 30% to 100% more than the noncompensating ones, I figure it's a small price to pay for the assurance that all emitters are dripping the same amount of water. The emitters will be attached to a main supply line [1/2-inch solid drip hose], using a length of spaghetti tubing. The barbed post on most emitters attaches to 1/4-inch spaghetti tubing, but a few emitters require the smaller 1/8-inch tubing. The emitter should be placed at the end of the tubing. DO NOT punch the emitter into the 1/2-inch tubing and then add a length of solid 1/4-inch tubing. Be sure to buy the right spaghetti tubing for your emitter's barbed post.

Medium Pots

For medium-sized pots [12 to 18 inches in diameter], the rule is to use one emitter for every one to two plants. In a multiplant container you might get away with a single emitter with a higher flow rate, but if the water spreads unevenly through the potting soil, some roots may go unwatered and the soil may dry out and pull away from the sides of the container. Water could then drain out the sides without moistening the plant's roots.

If you don't want to load up the pot with emitters, there's another solution: a spot spitter. It's not as rude and crude as it sounds. The brand I use is the Roberts Spot Spitter™ because it is the most readily available and comes in the widest selection of flow rates and spray patterns. These spitters consist of a four-fluted plastic stake with a V-slotted post on the top and a solid, round post at the bottom. [See Figure 24 in Chapter 2.] Spaghetti tubing is inserted over the V-slotted post and water shoots out over the soil in a horizontal fan spray, which extends 12 to 18 inches, depending upon water pressure. The solid post on the bottom can be used to close the spaghetti tubing if the pot is empty. Simply lift the stake out of the soil, pull it off the spaghetti tubing, reverse the stake and insert the solid barb into the spaghetti tubing to plug it shut.

Spitters are not even closely related to emitters, as they distribute far more water. The width and depth of the V-slot in the top post determine, respectively, the pattern of the spray and its volume. At 10 psi, the amount of water distributed ranges from 5.5 gph for the 90° spray pattern to 9.3 gph for the 160° spray to 19.20 gph for the high-volume 360° spitter. Therefore, spitters cover a much larger area of the pot's soil surface than true emitters and add humidity to the atmosphere around a plant's foliage. One spitter can provide enough water for all the plants in a

pot up to 18 inches in diameter. Make sure there is no foliage in the way of the spray pattern or you'll have dry spots in the potting soil. Spitters are best suited to containers which are deeper than they are wide; this allows the soil to absorb the higher volume of water more readily and prevent it from running out the bottom.

It's best to use spitters with plants that prefer, or at least tolerate, high humidity and wet feet. Azaleas (*Rhododendron* spp.), Rhododendrons (*Rhododendron* spp.), daphnes (*Daphne* spp.), ferns and sweet woodruff (*Galium odoratum*) are much more suited to spitters than are drought-resistant plants like rockrose (*Cistus* spp.), rosemary (*Rosmarinus* spp.), santolina (*Santolina* spp.), and California fuschia (*Zauschneria californica*–also classified as *Epilobium* spp.). Better solution—1/4-inch in-line emitter tubing.

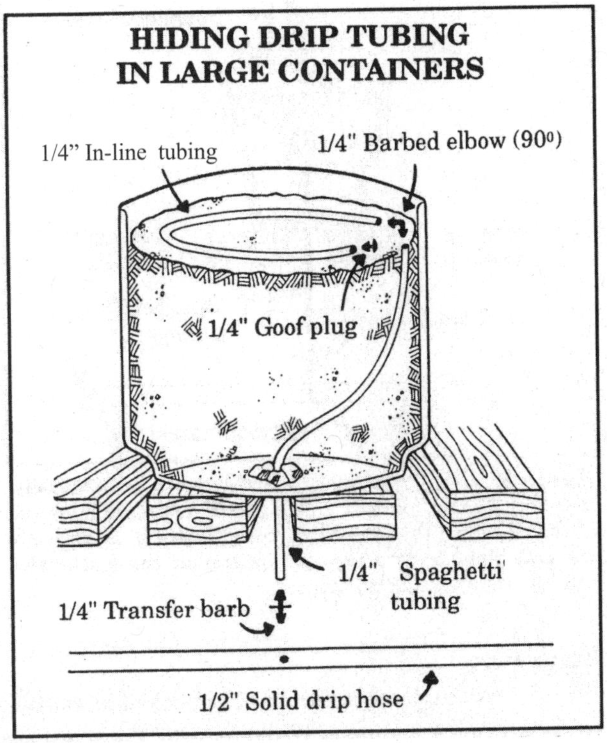

HIDING DRIP TUBING IN LARGE CONTAINERS

1/4" In-line tubing

1/4" Barbed elbow (90°)

1/4" Goof plug

1/4" Transfer barb

1/4" Spaghetti tubing

1/2" Solid drip hose

Figure 55 Much like the smaller-potted plants, bigger pots can be planted with the supply tubing hidden in the soil. The difference is a circle of 1/4-inch in-line tubing in the soil's surface with emitters every six inches. This is easy to install and provides more evenly-spread moisture.

Installing Drip In Small and Medium Pots

Before adding the spaghetti tubing and planting your pot, be sure to seal the inside. Terra-cotta pots are especially prone to wicking lots of moisture through their walls. I brush an inexpensive, nontoxic cement sealer on all the inside surfaces of clay pots. Sometimes the clay soaks up so much sealer that two coats are required.

The most invisible drip system for pots is installed as the containers are planted. To begin, lay a length of 1/2-inch solid drip hose from the main assembly near to the base of all the pots. You must bring the 1/2-inch tubing close to the respectivly, the pattern of the spray, and its volume. Medium pots are hard to do without relying on spaghetti tubing to travel a long distance. As listed in the "Maximum Length of Tubing" chart in the Appendix, the longest possible length for consistent and adequate flow with 1/8-inch spaghetti is five feet, and 15 feet for 1/4-inch spaghetti. The solid drip hose can be, in spite of PMLP #11, in a trench alongside a patio, under the wooden flooring of a deck, or hidden beneath the handrail of a porch. After the drip hose is in place, turn on the main assembly and allow the hose to flush any dirt out the open end. Turn off the water and close the end of the drip hose with a compression end closure with a fht threaded cap.

Next, use a single piece of broken pottery or a flat pebble to close off any space around the spaghetti where it comes through the drainage hole; this will keep any potting soil from falling out.

At each pot, punch a hole in the solid drip hose and insert a transfer barb—which has two barbed posts, one to go into the drip hose and the other to insert into the spaghetti. Be sure to use a transfer barb that is the same size as the spaghetti tubing. Use spaghetti tubing to go from the drip hose to beneath the pot. [See Figure 54.] Cut a piece of spaghetti four to six inches longer than the soil depth will be in the pot, attach one end to the spaghetti elbow beneath the pot, and thread the tubing through the hole in the bottom of the pot before you add any potting soil. If your pots are on a patio or rooftop, you'll need to block each one up off the surface a bit to allow the spaghetti to come up through the bottom of the pot without getting flattened. With wooden decks,

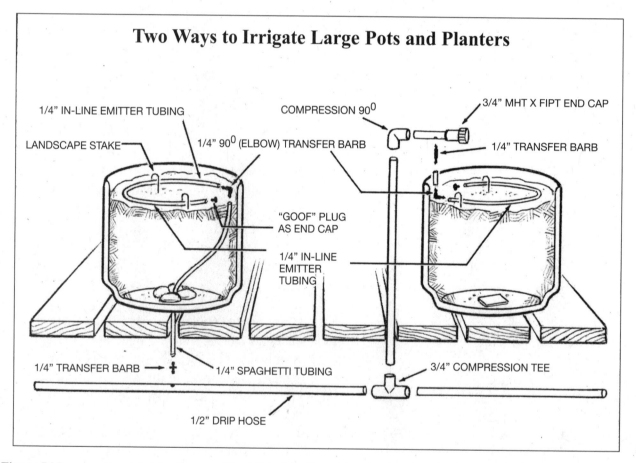

Figure 56 Large pots are ripe for the use of the 1/4-inch in-line tubing. The pot on the left is irrigated after the plant[s] have been planted. To replant or exchange potting soil, simply disconnect the 1/4"-90⁰ [elbow] transfer barb from the in-line tubing and the solid 1/4-inch spaghetti tubing. Dump out the old soil and repeat the installation steps as found in the text. Pull the tubing through the bottom hole. The pot on the right shows how to irrigate a planting already installed.

simply set the drainage hole of each pot over the space between two boards but set the pot on blocks to help prevent the decking from rotting. Now plant. Fill the container with a rich, well-drained potting soil. Leave the spaghetti tubing above the soil open and flush it for several minutes to clear any soil out.

Now trim the tubing to fit and add the appropriate emitter or spitter to each length of spaghetti. You can use a spaghetti stake to hold the emitter in place. Be sure to keep the emitter away from the base of the stem or trunk to prevent crown

rot. If you need more than one emitter in the pot, use a spaghetti barbed tee to branch out for two emitters. Or have more than one length of spaghetti coming up through the bottom of the pot, each attached to its own transfer barb. A little bit of mulch will further disguise the tubing and emitter. Even the day you plant, your container drip system should be practically invisible.

If any one pot in a system should become empty, you can save water by pulling the emitter or spitter off the spaghetti tubing and inserting the right-sized barbed goof plug.

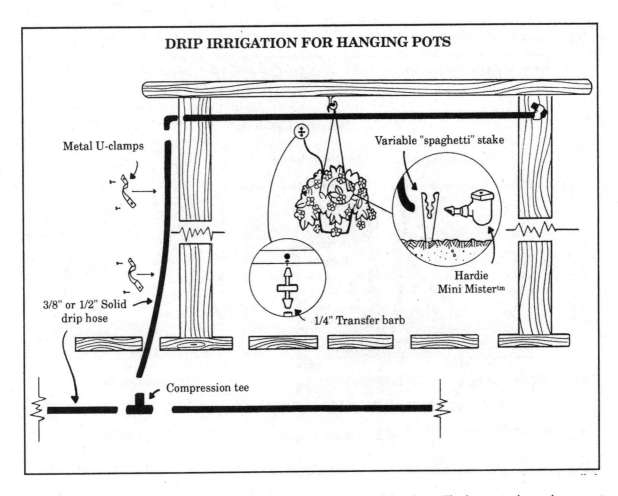

DRIP IRRIGATION FOR HANGING POTS

Metal U-clamps

Variable "spaghetti" stake

Hardie Mini Mister™

3/8" or 1/2" Solid drip hose

1/4" Transfer barb

Compression tee

Figure 57 Hanging plants are vulnerable to drying out and the death of the plants. The lowest emitter releases water at 1/2- gph. Using emitters may require frequent start times per day. Be sure to buy a timer with multiple start times and low run rates. This will prevent the soil from pulling away from the container. After there is a gap between the pot and the soil, much of the subsequent watering finds its way down the gap to be wasted. Thus frequent irrigations for very short times on a daily basis. A mister may cover more of the planting and has a lower gph rate. Hide the tubing on the backside of the posts. The elegant approach is to use a router to cut a channel in the wooden post deep enough hide the tubing.

Large Pots

You could use a number of punched-in emitters in pots over 18 inches in diameter. Or use the spot spitters mentioned earlier.

Remember, spitters are not even closely related to emitters, as they distribute far more water. The width and depth of the V-slot in the top post determine, respectively, the pattern of the spray and its volume. As mentioned, at 10 psi, the amount of water distributed ranges from 5.5 gph for the 90° spray pattern to 9.3 gph for the 160° spray to 19.20 gph for the high-volume 360° spitter. Therefore, spitters cover a much larger area of the pot's soil surface than true emitters and add humidity to the atmosphere around a plant's foliage.

More preferable is the use of the 1/4-inch in-line tubing with emitters every six inches. Use the tubing that passes 1/2 gph. Plant and install your pots as described above, leaving only a few inches of solid 1/4-inch spaghetti tubing above the potting soil. [See Figure 56.] After potting the plant and tubing, flush the system. Next, clip the spaghetti off just above the soil and attach a 1/4-inch barbed spaghetti elbow (90°). Add a length of 1/4-inch in-line tubing to the elbow and circle the pot just a few inches in from the perimeter. With large pots you can coil the tubing in a spiral pattern, but make sure you don't water directly on top of the crown of the root system. Flush again and close the tubing with a goof plug. You can hold the tubing in place with metal J-stakes every foot or so.

As noted earlier and in the "Maximum Length of Tubing" chart in the Appendix #3, 1/4-inch in-line tubing should never be used in lengths of more than 15 feet per lateral or, in this case, per pot. If your pot or container is so large that more than 15 feet of tubing would be required, you can switch to 1/2-inch in-line emitter tubing.

Hanging Up Drip Emitters

You can use regular emitters in hanging pots, but the pots usually need more water than the same-sized pot on the ground. So if you're using, for example, a single 1/2-gph emitter in a 10-inch pot on your patio, try at least two emitters or one 1-gph emitter in the same-sized hanging pot.

Spot spitters put out a good amount of water over a large area, but the flow rate is so great that the water may run off the surface or down the sides of the pot faster than it can percolate into the potting mix. I don't recommend them in most hanging plantings.

Many hanging plants are water and humidity lovers. While a spitter does produce some humidity, it's nothing compared with the fog-like vapors of a micro-mister. While they pass more water than some of the lowest-flow emitters, misters use only three gallons per hour to generate a delightfully cool cloud. With the mister placed beneath the plant's foliage, the moist fog condenses on the plant's leaves and drip-irrigates much of the pot's surface, although some water will dribble off the foliage outside the pot. Two name brands for 3-gph misters are Hit ProMist™ and the Hardie Mini-Mister™. Each comes with a special stake to hold the mister upright so the spray billows up into the leaves. The Hardie Mini-Mister costs less and its stake and mister are considerably less bulky and therefore not as noticeable as those of the Hit ProMist. The use of these misters requires a 200-mesh filter screen to prevent the tiny misting hole from clogging.

Hanging plants are often high enough off the ground that 1/4-inch spaghetti, with its 15-foot limit, won't reach. In this case, 3/8-inch solid drip hose can be laid out for up to 100 feet and is much less visually bulky than 1/2-inch solid hose. Use 3/8-inch tubing [with an outside diameter of .455 inch] and the appropriate number of compression elbows and tees [called series 400 fittings] to get as close to each hanging plant as possible. The tubing is cut and wiggled into the compression fittings in the same way you put together in-line emitter hose. Try to hide the 3/8-inch tubing beneath the batten of a board-and-batten wall, in a routed notch up the backside of a post, or beneath a railing or eaves. Use the newer plastic clamps with a nail to secure the tubing flat to the post or wall. It's important neither to fasten the tubing securely to the post nor to stretch the hose taut, because winter's cold will significantly shrink the tubing and may damage fittings. [See Figure 57.] Paint the tubing to protect it from ultraviolet rays and to help it blend in with the surroundings. At each hanging pot, use a 1/4-inch transfer barb to attach a length of spaghetti tubing. Run the spaghetti down one of the wires which holds the pot, tying the tubing at intervals to keep a low visual profile. Flush the system and add the appropriate emitter, spitter, or mister.

Segregating Your Drip System

A drip system for hanging plants with 1/2- to 1-gph emitters cannot easily include high-flow devices such as spitters and porous pipe, that have gph ratings ranging from several gph to nearly 20. Irrigating long enough for the emitter-watered plants would waste a lot of water on the spitter or porous pipe irrigated ones and could even drown them.

Hanging plants should also always be on their own valve with a timer because their water needs are so special. If you live in an especially hot or windy area, get a timer which allows you to turn on the system automatically several times during the same day to keep hanging plants well moistened and healthy.

Hanging container plantings usually demand daily irrigation so that the soil doesn't dry out and pull away from the walls of the vessel. If this happens, subsequent irrigations can simply run

off the soil surface and down the cavity between the soil and the planter to drain away unused.

Slight amounts of daily water keep the soil mixture moist, plump, and in full contact with the walls of the container. The daily amount of water added should equal what is lost by evaporation from the soil and container and by transpiration from the plant's leaves. By adding just enough water to equal these losses, you will also prevent leaching of the limited and valuable nutrients in the potting mixture.

Only experience and experimentation can provide the specific answer to "How long do I leave the drip system on?" Start with very short times of only a minute or two. If you're going to automate your container irrigation, beware—not all irrigation timers or controllers can be set for times as short as one or two minutes. Check with your supplier to make sure you purchase a timer with short "run" times.

CHAPTER 7

Drip Irrigation for Trees and Shrubs

On a sloped, east-facing hillside in Sebastopol, CA, was a remarkable orchard that produced a cornucopia of fruit while serving as a testing ground in the mid-1990s for many types of drip irrigation hardware. Sponsored by the University of California Cooperative Extension, Roy Germone—who provided the land, and the Master Gardener Program [which is sponsored by the Cooperative Extension] and several local businesses that provided raw materials and services, this unique demonstration plot featured 200 fruit trees and dozens of cane and bush fruits. Each row utilized a different type of drip irrigation emitter or micro-sprayer [tiny sprinklers similar to large rotating lawn sprinklers, such as the Rainbird™ impact sprinklers]. This allowed Paul Vossen, local UC Cooperative Extension tree crops farm adviser, to test many possible kinds of drip systems for fruit trees simultaneously, evaluate their performances for both home and commercial plantings, and demonstrate to both home gardeners and farmers how this hardware might work for them.

The trees at the Germone Demonstration Orchard showed some impressive results. Paul's records during the six years the project was monitored showed that "with some of our peach trees, we're getting 14 tons per acre in the third year while local growers are only getting seven tons, and on three-year-old apple trees we're getting 20 tons per acre, while established, unirrigated, and mature apple orchards are only getting 13 tons per acre." [These impressive increases in yields correspond to an increase in abundant foliage and plentiful bloom produced on ornamental trees when appropriate irrigation is used.]

Drip Irrigation for Good and Healthy Root Growth

To get such superior yields, one needs to know how roots grow. Paul begins with his knowledge that contrary to popular belief, "the top two feet of soil represent 50 to 80 percent of the tree's root mass. Therefore, most of the water and nutrients absorbed by the trees come from this zone in part because that's where the oxygen is to fuel the soil biota that provide the nutrients." Paul maintains that "the roots will develop where there is water, but they can't grow any distance at all from a dry spot toward moisture. The tree's roots don't explore for water; they exploit available water."

The Germone Demonstration Orchard trees were planted on top of 18-inch-tall, 4-foot-wide berms that run the entire length of each row of trees. So as not to counteract the effect of a dry, well-drained berm, Paul reasoned that the irrigation system should keep the tree's root crown and trunk dry at all times. Conventional sprinklers, especially large Rainbird-type high-impact sprinklers, wet the entire surface of the orchard, the root crown, the trunk, and even the tree's foliage—thus encouraging diseases of the roots, trunk, and leaves.

This study has shown that drip irrigation not only avoids all the potential drawbacks of conventional sprinklers but also keeps the top two feet of soil at optimal moisture levels and reduces weeds. Furthermore, drip irrigation puts less demand on the orchard's well pump and makes better use of the water supply.

Each row of trees had one type of drip irrigation emitter or micro-sprinkler installed along its entire length. In all, there were working demonstrations of seven types of emitters, one version of drip tape, and five kinds of micro-sprinklers. Each row of fruits had a single line of 1/2-inch solid drip hose running down the length of the row near the base of each tree, on top of a raised planting berm. The emitters were punched into the drip hose at 18- to 24-inch intervals on either side of each tree's trunk to keep the drip irrigation applied water away from the root's vulnerable crown. The raised soil berm allowed for plenty of drainage to protect the upper portion of the root system from crown rot [*Phytophthora* spp.]. There were no hoses in the flat area between berms; this allowed for periodic mowing of the permanent ground cover of either Dutch white clover or subterranean clover and Zorro fescue.

For extra protection, every set of three drip irrigation lines (three rows of trees) had a 200-mesh metal screen filter in addition to the filter at the well. Most homeowners, with smaller plantings than the Germone Demonstration Orchard and with cleaner water or city water, will need only a 150-mesh filter.

Every set of three rows is controlled by a 24VAC electric solenoid valve. Each solenoid valve was, in turn, automatically controlled by a circuit, usually called a "station," on an electronic microchip irrigation controller. The orchard required a seven-station electronic irrigation controller, which controls the irrigation start and stop times to all 20 rows—this includes tree crops and bush and cane fruits. [This summons up PMLP #12, but that is discussed in Chapter 11 "Controlling Your Drip Irrigation."]

Evaluating Drip-Irrigation Emitters

Conventional thinking has held that emitters with lower flow rates, such as 1/2-gph and 1-gph emitters, are more likely to clog and that the larger 2- to 4-gph emitters are less likely to become clogged with silt. Paul used all sizes in the Germone Demonstration Orchard, and, with the exception of the 4-gph emitter, emitters for each given flow rate came from several different manufacturers.

According to Paul, "The 1/2-gph emitters didn't plug up on us very much. They did plug up more than the 2- and 4-gph emitters, but not very much at all." Some of the 1/2-gph emitters had approximately 20% clogging due to the high level of iron in the well water. The 1- and 2-gph emitters, with the name brands Spot Vortex™, DBK™, and Netafim RAM™ worked well.

Drip Irrigation for Landscape Trees

The Germone Demonstration Orchard was a model for conventional row-based orchards.

Now, returning to our ideal drip-irrigated garden, Mr. and Mrs. Shrubbery have chosen, as seen in Figure 25, to arrange their fruit trees in the more informal style of an edible landscape. The trees are grouped together because they have similar water and fertilization needs. The layout, however, is more like a forest, with random spacings and clusters of certain trees, which puts the pollinators next to each other. The entire area is mulched with a substantial layer of shredded trimmings from the local tree service. This thick layer of chipped bark and shredded leaves serves a number of purposes: it hides the in-line emitter drip hose, conserves moisture, keeps the sun from overheating the soil, prevents wind-blown soil erosion, provides safe and easy footing for pruning and harvesting the trees, and makes fallen fruit easily visible for a thorough cleanup to prevent the wintering over of pests and disease.

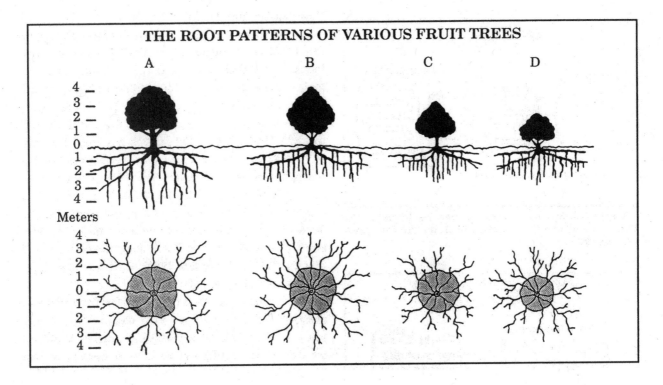

THE ROOT PATTERNS OF VARIOUS FRUIT TREES

Figure 59 Contrary to popular belief, a tree's or shrub's roots grow well beyond the drip line [foliage]. This illustration is based on the work of the Timiryazev Agricultural Academy, USSR; A=apple, B=pear, C=plum, D=sour cherry. All the trees were 13 years old.

Irrigating All of the Tree's Feeder Roots

This design allows for a layout even more efficient than that of the Germone Demonstration Orchard. The limitation of conventional drip irrigation in a typical orchard is that it consists of only a single row of hose with emitters, running straight down a row of trunks. This layout limits the water to a relatively small proportion of the tree's root system. Generally speaking, the roots of a tree actually extend one-and-a-half to three times farther than the width of the foliage. In heavy clay soil the roots are limited to an area one-half again as wide as the foliage.

The roots responsible for absorbing water and nutrients are the very young and tiny root hairs found near the tips of new roots. Older roots, much like older branches, have a bark-like covering that protects the root but doesn't produce root hairs. In one study done with radioactive isotopes in England, the roots 4.5 feet away from the trunk of a 10-year-old apple tree absorbed less than 10% of the water and nutrients absorbed by the entire root system. The study showed that proportionately, many more feeding roots are found at, or beyond, the drip line of a tree's foliage. Because of this, I prefer to place a ring of in-line emitter tubing at or beyond the tree's drip line. This produces a "doughnut" of moisture, and far more of the root zone is adequately irrigated than with a single line of hose down a row of trees. [See Figure 31, page 42.] As the tree grows, extra lengths are added to this circle of moisture to correspond with the new growth in the canopy. By setting the circle of emitters farther out every few years, you're encouraging the tree's roots to explore more soil volume and gather more nutrients for superior growth. Other than placing parallel rows of in-line emitter tubing, like that in a flower border,

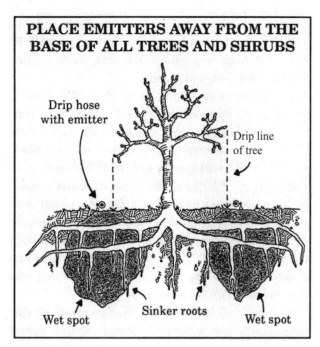

PLACE EMITTERS AWAY FROM THE BASE OF ALL TREES AND SHRUBS

Drip hose with emitter

Drip line of tree

Wet spot   Sinker roots   Wet spot

Figure 60 To protect the root's crown and supply moisture to the largest number of root hairs, place the emitters at or beyond the drip line of each tree and shrub. The underground moist spot will provide moisture to a bigger area than what the wet spots on the surface show.

this is the most efficient way to irrigate a large volume of the tree's roots.

To get from tree to tree, use solid 1/2-inch drip hose with an outside diameter of 16 mm, or 0.620 inch. Placing the emitters as far away as the drip line of the newly planted or established shrub or tree is necessary to protect the upper portion of the root system from moisture-induced rot. The wide wet spot spread below the soil surface by the emitters guarantees that the young feeder roots will receive moisture. At the drip line of each tree, use a Spin-Loc [or equivalent] tee to add the correct length of in-line pressure-compensating emitter hose. After all the trees have been encircled, turn on the main assembly for five minutes or more to flush the hosing. Use a threaded end cap at the end of each in-line hose. [See Figure 34A .] Start with the tree closest to the main assembly. Close each tree's in-line hose in sequence until you've worked your way to the end of the assembly. You can keep the hose in place with a U-stake

every four to six feet. When it comes time to add another length of in-line hose, add a compression or Spin-Loc coupling, attach the new length of hose, flush, and close the new end. Remember, the total length of in-line emitter hose per valve or main assembly has to be 326 feet or less. If your trees are very far apart, the solid drip hose which runs from tree to tree should total less than 240 feet.

This same process of encircling a tree with a doughnut of moistened soil works fine with ornamental trees. Shade trees in particular respond with excellent growth and a fast-growing, shady canopy. Ornamental flowering trees will have superior growth, enhanced blossoming, and an extended length of bloom.

How Much Water?

It was from Paul Vossen's remarkable flyer titled "Water Management for Fruit Trees and Other Plants" [published in 1985] that I first learned about evapotranspiration-based irrigation rates [ET rate]. The publication begins with a provocative question: "Did you know that a large apple tree, on a hot summer day, will use about 50 gallons of water?" That's right, 350 gallons per week for each individual, mature ornamental or fruiting tree with a canopy that covers 300 square feet of the ground.

This small blue leaflet of Paul's caused quite a skeptical stir among gardeners, landscapers, and farmers back in '85. But after a thorough review and several years of applying Paul's suggestions, I realized that the "Daily Water Use (ET)" chart was one of my most valuable irrigation "tools."

Remember, the ET rate varies from place to place, season to season, and even day to day, but once you know the ET rate [expressed in number of gallons per day or per month], you know, more accurately than by any other method,

Daily Water Use (In Gallons per Day)

BASED ON VARIOUS EVAPOTRANSPIRATION RATES

Square Feet of Plant Cover	ET Rate (in inches/month)									
	1"	2"	3"	4"	5"	6"	7"	8"	9"	10"
1 sq. ft.	0.0187	0.0374	0.062	0.083	0.104	0.125	0.145	0.166	0.187	0.208
4 sq. ft.	0.075	0.15	0.248	0.332	0.416	0.5	0.58	0.664	0.75	0.832
10 sq. ft.	0.187	0.374	0.62	0.83	1.04	1.25	1.45	1.66	1.87	2.08
75 sq. ft.	1.403	2.805	4.65	6.225	7.8	9.4	10.875	12.45	14.0	15.6
100 sq. ft.	1.87	3.74	6.2	8.3	10.4	12.5	14.5	16.6	18.7	20.8
200 sq. ft.	3.74	7.480	12.4	16.6	20.8	25.0	29.0	33.2	37.4	41.6
300 sq.ft.	5.61	11.22	18.6	24.9	32.2	37.5	43.5	49.8	56.1	62.4
1 acre solid cover	815	1629	2701	3615	4530	5445	6316	7231	8146	9060

Figure 61 I've replicated this chart, so you won't have be flipping the pages. This chart is a good place to start to help you manage how much to water your plants. The evapotranspiration [ET] chart is based on continuous cover of a lawn grass. Plants vary considerably compared to this idealized chart. For example, lavender sub-shrubs can do well with only 25% of the water recommended by the chart. Thus, keen observation, poking in the soil to check on moisture levels, and experience are important factors in settling on a final amount of water per plant or planting zone.

how much water to apply. To find out the ET rate for your area, by month or season, call the local Cooperative Extension, the local library's reference desk, or a local university, college, or junior college horticulture department. Get the monthly ET rate, since it can vary considerably from the cool days of April to the dog days of August.

Paul's guide, "Daily Water Use (ET)," which is the basis for Figure 61, gives you the irrigation rate for replacing what is lost each day or month, but you can also increase the irrigation rate from this basic figure if you want to increase growth and yields. Because the ET rate is the only "uni-

versal" guideline, no longer should a gardener in Texas have plants die after reading an article by a New England garden writer who casually and misleadingly says to "water every 10 to 14 days until the ground is wet." Nor will a New England reader drown plants by using the rule-of-thumb watering rates proposed by a California garden writer.

Once you have the ET rates for various months, or an average one for the entire growing season, refer to Figure 61. Notice how the ET rate is listed in inches per month across the top—one through ten inches. Match the number you got for your local ET and read down the column. Within the body of the chart, the numbers represent gallons [or a fraction thereof] of water per day. The left-hand column represents the square footage of the canopy or foliage cover. It is important to focus on the square footage, since a plant's size at any given age can vary. Paul cautions the reader to always consider the amount of ground covered by all the foliage. "Percent of cover," he cautions, "pertains to everything that's growing on the area that's to be irrigated. If you have young fruit trees far apart, but there's a perennial ground cover over the whole area—then, you'll have to water based upon solid cover rate to keep both the tree and the perennial ground cover happy." For such a planting, divide the one acre solid cover rate by the number of square feet in your planting or landscape to get the daily water use for a given ET rate. [Or multiply the area of your planting by the 1-square-foot figure at the top of the chart.] Since this is such an important concept and is so often ignored or misunderstood, Paul always adds another reminder—"Water is water, and roots is roots. If it's green, it's using water. Base your irrigation upon the ET rate and the area of total foliage cover."

The number you get from the chart is really just a starting point. The amount can be increased quite a bit to make growth and yields go up correspondingly. For example, with an ET rate of six inches per month, my newly planted Asian-pear orchard, with each tree's foliage covering four square feet, needed only 0.5 gallon per day or 3.5 gallons per week per tree. I decided to water a larger area around each young tree and let the natural grass ground cover grow. For the first year, I applied 35 gallons per week per tree, and I was amazed. The trees put 3.5 to 4.5 feet of new growth on four or more primary branches per tree, yet the trees didn't appear overly watered or too weak or spindly. This increase in watering follows in the footsteps of Paul's recommendation to create "water junkies." "Don't hold back on the water when your trees are young," he advises. "You've got to build a well-branched and extensive branching to the trees before they come into fruiting." This also applies to ornamental trees for shade and blossom.

As with herbaceous flowers, you can water daily [for the best growth] or weekly, or even monthly, providing the amount is based on the ET rate. To determine the length of each irrigation, start by totaling the number of emitters built into the in-line hose in a system and multiply by the flow rate of the emitter to determine the system's total capacity in gallons per hour. To determine how many hours to leave the system on, divide the number of gallons recommended in the ET chart by the total gallonage the system can distribute.

For example, a tree covering 300 square feet of ground might have 11 lines (1.5 feet apart) of in-line pressure-compensating hosing, each 18 feet long, for 198 total feet of in-line hose. Since the emitters are every 12 inches, the total number of emitters is also 198. With a rating of 1/2 gph, the entire system has the capacity to distribute 99 gallons per hour. Where the ET rate is 3 inches per month, 300 square feet of canopy requires at least 18.6 gallons per day. Dividing 18.6 gallons, the plant's water needs, by 99 gallons per hour, the system's total capacity, we get 0.19 hour. Leave the system on for a little more than 11 minutes (0.19 times 60 minutes) each day to equal the ET rate for 300 square feet of foliage. This can be adjusted up or down, based upon your observations and needs.

Drip Irrigation of Shrubs

On the south side of Mr. and Mrs. Shrubbery's house, they have an area of . . . well, how else can I say it . . . shrubbery. Most shrubs are planted close enough together that their roots, if given adequate irrigation, are all intertwined. Instead of the complications of circling in-line hose around each shrub, they simply irrigate the entire area as described for the flower border. Parallel lines of in-line hose are placed every 12 inches apart in well-drained soils and up to 24 inches apart in heavy soils—as per your initial test with the emitter punched in a plastic milk jug or your personal experience with the flower border. Be sure to jog the in-line hose around the base of each shrub to protect the root's crown from rot. [See Figure 31 in Chapter 3.]

Again, start your irrigation program by basing your irrigation schedule on the appropriate ET rate. Adjust as you watch the plants grow [or not grow!].

CHAPTER 8

Drip Irrigation for Vegetable Beds

The trick to drip-irrigating vegetable beds is to make the system as simple as possible and easily adaptable to routine tasks such as weeding, hoeing, digging, and fertilizing. For many years I never recommended drip irrigation for vegetables to my clients because I couldn't figure out how to make the system efficient, convenient, and safe from damage.

Early "experiments" in vegetable drip irrigation by my gardening friends started with the use of Mono-tubing™ or Bi-wall™. Mono-tubing is a single thin-walled plastic tube with minute holes every 12 inches, much like the old-fashioned soaker hoses my grandfather used, which were flat and green with white stripes. Mono-tubing is so thin-walled it collapses flat like a long balloon after each irrigation. While not exactly balloon-thin, Mono-tubing is extremely easy to pierce or tear; it practically splits open if it sees a hand trowel coming. Furthermore, the minute holes are prone to clogging, even when proper filtration is used. The next generation of low-cost tubing was Bi-wall. It is made with a bit heavier-gauge polyethylene tubing and with a second, smaller chamber or tube, which has tiny holes spaced every 12 inches, piggybacked on top of the larger supply tube. The second chamber helps to moderate the pressure along the length of the line, but it, too, is very prone to clogging, even with a 200-mesh screen in the filter.

T-Tape™ is a more recent product and is similar to Bi-wall. T-Tape is the least expensive product

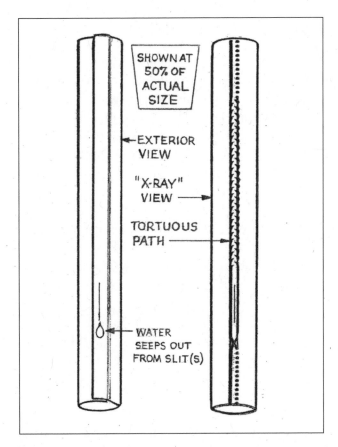

Figure 62 T-tape, shown here, has more integrity than Mono-tubing and Bi-wall and has some pressure compensation. It is stonger than flimsy "tubing" such as Mono-tubing and Bi-wall. All three can't hold a candle to the strength and practicality of 1/2-inch or 1/4-inch in-line tubing. Mono-tubing, Bi-wall, and T-tape are much less expensive than other options but are more easily damaged or severed than "true" emitter tubing. They shouldn't be used in most landscapes as they can't be installed in curved patterns. Best used by farmers or gardeners growing food or flowers in straight rows.

for straight rows and raised beds; it cannot be used in curved rows. It requires a low pressure of no more than 15 psi maximum for the 15-millimeter tape. The tapes with 6-, 8-, and 10-millimeter thick walls must have a 12-psi regulator. It does have turbulent flow track emitters. Every emitter acts as a true drip emitter, providing reliable drip flow without squirting. The slit outlet impedes root intrusion and virtually eliminates plugging from external contaminants, but not internal sediment, algae, or iron water. Thus, a 200-mesh filter is absolutely required. The tubing flattens out after each irrigation. It uses 5/8-inch fittings. The manufacturer rates it to last up to seven years when covered or two to five years when left exposed to sunlight. While T-tape is sturdier than Mono-tubing or Bi-wall, it is so much more likely to be damaged than either 1/2-inch or 1/4-inch in-line tubing. It is cheap in both senses of the word. It's more appropriate for agriculture as opposed to horticulture.

I think the original fascination with these three products was the low cost of the materials and the ease of use in linear rows of crops because there are some serious drawbacks. All three tubings must be carefully stretched in straight lines, evenly secured at the far end with a stake, to prevent twisting and kinking, which can cut off the water's flow. They cannot be easily plumbed to make 90° turns except with a fairly expensive fitting.

While some of the material is rated for more than five years of careful use, most grades are damaged within three years. None can compare with the factory-rated guarantee of ten years for both solid and in-line drip hosing. [The 1/2- tubing I used in landscape I designed for Lou and Susan Preston's Vineyards and Winery has lasted 30 years.]

The Spaghetti Nightmare

I have, in the past, also seen a number of ambitious gardeners use 1/2-inch solid drip hose to supply a Medusa's thicket of spaghetti tubing with spot spitters or emitters attached at the ends of the tubing. And I've also watched these same gardeners curse in frustration: at the tangled mess of tubing, at how easily the spaghetti tubing pops off the drip hose, at how readily the emitters separate from the spaghetti, and at how often the tubing is damaged while weeding. Some ended up, like Hercules burdened down by the manure of the Aegean stables, dragging large heaps of snarled spaghetti tubing to the local

dump. As far as I'm concerned, spaghetti tubing with emitters is out of the question with annual plants because of its need for periodic care and seasonal cultivation. In fact, the guidelines for profession landscapers in Santa Monica forbids the use of spaghetti tubing for any commercial installations. As mentioned earlier, this does not apply to the 1/4-inch in-line tubing. It's more forgiving as it can curl around without pinching off the flow of water.

Drip hose with punched-in emitters would have been the next logical choice for annuals, but I found out that the heat of summer and the sun's ultraviolet light soon cause the rigid plastic of the emitter to become brittle. Then, during routine tasks such as weeding, tilling, or hoeing, the brittle barb snaps off at the base of the emitter. When this happens not only must the gardener find the hole, plug it with a goof plug and punch in a new emitter, but the end of the drip line must also be opened to flush out the broken tip of the barb. Snapped-off emitters under mulch can go undetected, and not only are large amounts of water wasted but the soil in that area also gets puddled and anaerobic. While certainly superior to the three versions of thin-walled soaker hoses and to spaghetti with emitters on the ends, this still didn't seem to be the ultimate solution.

The best material didn't present itself to me until 1980, when I was tending a booth at an agricultural trade show. The booth next to mine featured something I'd never seen before—drip hose with the emitters pre-installed *inside* the polyethylene hose. I immediately tried some out on rows of fruit trees and was pleased, but it was another four years, after lots of testing in various landscape settings, before I attempted using in-line tubing in a vegetable bed.

In-Line Emitter Tubing with Raised Vegetable Beds

I almost always design vegetable beds for my

clients' edible landscapes as raised beds with 2- by 12-inch rot-resistant wooden sides or plastic boards such as Trex™. By a remarkable coincidence, this is exactly what Mr. and Mrs. Shrubbery have in the section of their landscape just beyond the lawn. [See Figure 63.]

The wooden boxes solve a number of problems: there is a clear demarcation between the edge of the path and the beginning of the bed; the wood helps keep the gravel or wood-chip mulch of the path from mixing with the soil in the bed; the raised soil allows for good drainage during our wet, rainy Northern California winters; and a layer of 1/4-inch hardware cloth can be added between the box and the ground to exclude

destructive gophers and moles. In spite of the four-foot width I still recommend boxes typically three feet wide and eight to ten feet long. The three-foot width makes it easier for aging "boomers" to reach the middle without straining the lower back. Making the boxes 24 inches high gives the roots more soil to explore as the gophers graze on the roots that venture below the wire barrier. And the 24-inch height makes it even easier on the back.

The first time I tried in-line emitter tubing as a vegetable drip system was for a very small raised-bed design at Preston Vineyards and Winery near Healdsburg, CA. My goal was to design a harness or assembly of in-line tubing

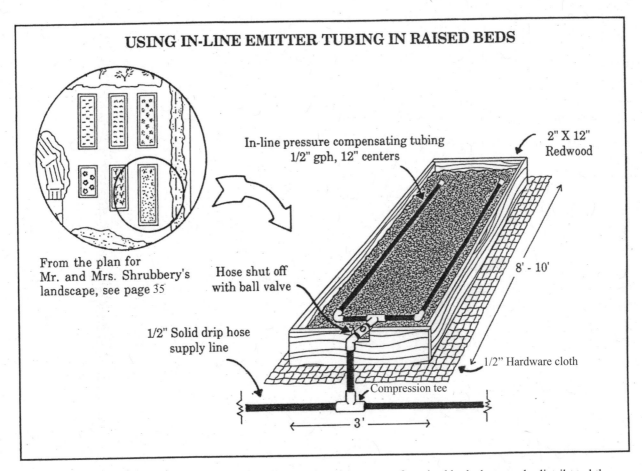

USING IN-LINE EMITTER TUBING IN RAISED BEDS

In-line pressure compensating tubing 1/2" gph, 12" centers

2" X 12" Redwood

From the plan for Mr. and Mrs. Shrubbery's landscape, see page 35

Hose shut off with ball valve

8' - 10'

1/2" Solid drip hose supply line

1/2" Hardware cloth

Compression tee

3'

Figure 63 For me, the toughest nut to crack was how to do a drip system for raised beds that evenly distributed the water, had a low profile, and more importantly, how to make it easy to remove for cultivation. After some failed experiments, this is what I came up with. The manifold has a fht fitting that allows the gardener to separate the assembly from the supply line. Then the manifold of two to three lines can be easily moved out of the way. A system like this has been working for my friend Chester Aaron's 60 boxes of garlic for over 20 years. We used four lines per box as they are four feet wide.

inside the vegetable boxes that could easily be removed from the boxes by one person in order to cultivate the soil. Due to Sue Preston's design criteria [she needed only enough vegetables for daytime salads and snacks for the winery staff], the beds for this design were a petite three by

six feet. The short length of the raised beds was to allow the gardener to throw amendments and mulch from a pathway along the backside of the boxes. At the Preston's, the other side is a long swath of lavender that hides the risers coming up and over the lip of the box. The harnesses,

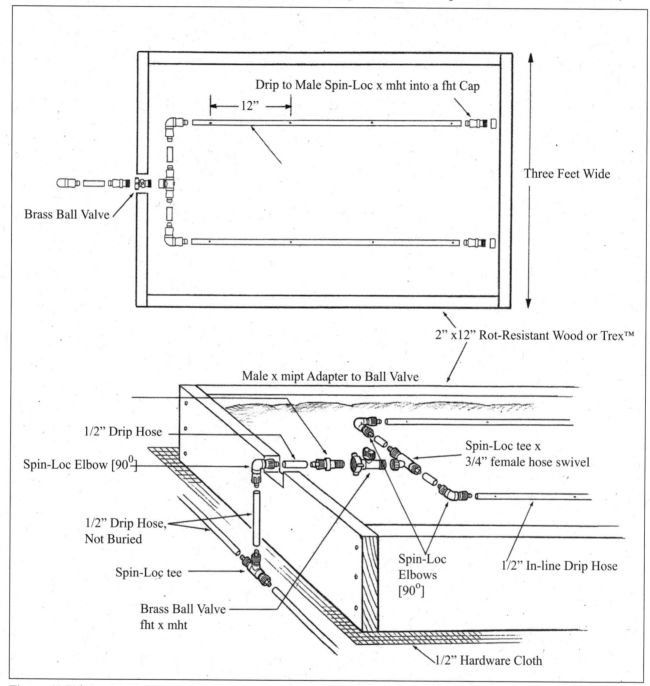

Figure 64 These are two views of the raised vegetable beds as installed for Lou and Susan Preston at the outside picnic area of their winery. This turns out to be a very convenient, elegant [if I do say myself] to use drip irrigation for annul crops. The same would apply to annual flower beds. No complaints from the Prestons for 30 years. You can substitute compression fittings instead of Spin-Loc fittings, but some people find compression fittings too hard to work with.

composed of two lines of in-line emitter tubing, for each box are easily removed and reinstalled by the quick unthreading of a single hose swivel fitting in each bed.

This system has been working for 30 years.

The one drawback with drip irrigation for vegetables is that small-seeded varieties that are grown rather close together, such as carrots, arugula, beets, and turnips, must be hand-watered until they show their first or second set of true leaves. The wet spot formed by drip irrigation on the soil's surface isn't usually wide enough to germinate small seeds broadcast over the entire area. Shortly after sprouting, however, these plants' taproots grow deep enough to tap into the continuous wall-to-wall drip zone of moisture, four to six inches beneath the soil's surface. Larger, big-seeded plants can be sown near each emitter and germinated solely with drip. Presoaking the larger seeds overnight in a dilution of water and seaweed powder will help ensure healthy germination. With transplants, it's a no brainer—simply plant near an emitter.

Since I conceived the design for Preston Vineyards, I have modified some of the parts. Figure 64 shows my current configuration. A main line of 1/2-inch solid 600 or 700 series drip hose is laid on the ground along one end of all the boxes. At the center point of each box, the solid hose in the trench is cut with hand pruners and a Spin-Loc tee is inserted with its "leg" facing up. Enough solid hose is added to come out of the ground and reach the top edge of the box, then the main line is flushed. In the center of the box, a 1-1/2-inch-square notch is cut into the upper lip of the 2- by 12-inch board. This permits the drip hardware to pass into the box without visually breaking the line of the end board. The following series of parts is assembled to allow for speedy and convenient removal of the drip irrigation harness from the box:

[NOTE: You can easily substitute compression fittings for all the Spin-Loc parts.]

1—Add a Spin-Loc elbow to the top of the solid drip-hose riser coming out of the main line. Trim the riser so that the elbow will pass its drip hose through the notched area.

2—Insert a three-inch length of solid drip hose into the end of the elbow that is parallel to the ground.

3—To the end of the short piece of solid drip hose, add a Spin-Loc x mht fitting. These are sometimes sold in a set with a fht cap as endclosures for drip lines. Just save the cap for that wonderful collection of parts kept in a large coffee can and labeled "Plumbing stuff I have no idea if I'll ever use but I'm too cheap to throw away."

4—To the mht, add the female end of a metal ball valve hose shutoff. This will allow you to turn off certain beds if nothing is planted in them or remove the harness from one bed while other beds are being irrigated.

5—Some hose shut-off ball valves have little holes built into each side of the valve. Use these holes to tap some small nails into the base of the wooden notch to secure the plumbing assembly, or use two screws with washers to hold the ball valve in place. Be sure the male hose threads of the hose shutoff extend beyond the wood, toward the inside of the box.

6—Next, add a Spin-Loc swivel x compression tee to the mht of the shutoff-valve. The "leg" of the tee has a swivel hose fitting, and the "top" of the tee has two Spin-Loc fittings for in-line pressure-compensating emitter tubing.

Now you can use in-line pressure-compensating emitter tubing to finish the harness, which rests on top of the soil in the bed. I usually recommend the in-line tubing with 1/2-gph emitters on 12-inch intervals because it works on both sandy-loam and clay soils, depending upon how long you run the system. One- and two-gph emitters, with their higher flow rates, work better in very sandy soils because the greater volume causes the water to spread more horizontally underground. This makes for a fatter carrot-like shape to the wet spot beneath the surface of the "bed" and distributes water more evenly to the roots. For a three-foot-wide bed with a fairly loamy clay soil, you'll probably need only two lines of tubing running the length of the box. A four-foot-wide bed may need just three lines of tubing. If you're growing a crop that is planted close together, such as garlic, beets, turnips, or small European butter lettuces, you may want to have four lines per box to ensure adequate irrigation. It's best to put together a trial system first to see how the harness configuration works with your soil. In any case, to get the spacing [in inches] between each line across the width, divide the bed's width [in inches] by a number that is one larger than the number of lines you'll be using.

From the swivel tee, next to the shutoff-valve, add the appropriate lengths of in-line tubing to reach the next fittings on the main header that runs the width of the bed. For the outer two lines, add Spin-Loc elbows. For any lines other than the outside ones, add tees at the appropriate intervals. Always remember to leave the length of these lines loose and not firmly staked, to protect the fittings as the tubing shrinks in the fall.

Flush the system. Close the ends of each line in all the vegetable beds with an end cap. Mulch to disguise and protect the tubing, and you're ready to grow some food.

Remember, your solid main line along one end of the boxes can supply no more than 240 gph. Determining the number of lateral lines running off one supply line can be done in two ways. First, simply use the "Maximum Length of Tubing" chart in the Appendix to determine the maximum number of feet for the type of emitter tubing you are using and make sure each lateral is equal to or less than the recommended length. If, for example, you're using in-line pressure-compensating tubing with 1/2-gph emitters on 12-inch spacings, make sure the total length of all the in-line tubing coming from one solid drip hose supply line to your vegetable boxes is less than 326 feet.

Sometimes the flow-rate capacity of the emitter tubing [from the Appendix] exceeds what the solid drip hose can supply. For example, the chart indicates that in-line pressure compensating tubing with 1/2-gph emitters on 24-inch centers can have a maximum length of 584 feet. But remember, the solid drip hose can supply only 240 gph. Technically, therefore, you must have three separate supply lines to service 584 feet of this tubing—two solid drip hose lines supplying 240 gph and another line to supply the remaining 52 gallons. In reality, there is enough of a fudge factor in these charts that you could divide up the 52 gallons among the other two lines and probably not notice a significant drop in the flow.

The other approach is to total the flow rates of all the emitters and make sure that number is less than 240 gph. If, for example, you had chosen to use 2-gph emitters on 12-inch centers, the maximum length would be 120 feet—240 gph divided by 2 gph = 120, times 1 [the interval of the emitters, in feet]. If, in another example, you were using 2-gph emitters that you've punched in [which I don't recommend, but it's hard to find a supplier that stocks 2-gph in-line emitters, although it can be special ordered if you buy a large quantity] on 18-inch centers, the maximum footage would be 160 feet—240 gph divided by 2 gph = 120, times 1.5 [the emitter interval in feet] = 180 feet. In this example, had you planned to use 1/2-gph emitters on 18-inch centers, the maximum length of tubing would be 720 feet—240 gph divided by 0.5 gph times 1.5 feet. [You would need one-inch Schedule 40 PVC to service the three subassemblies.]

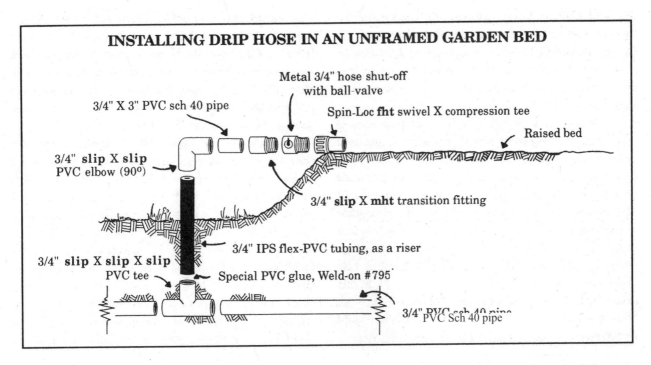

INSTALLING DRIP HOSE IN AN UNFRAMED GARDEN BED

Metal 3/4" hose shut-off with ball-valve

3/4" X 3" PVC sch 40 pipe

Spin-Loc **fht** swivel X compression tee

Raised bed

3/4" **slip X slip** PVC elbow (90º)

3/4" **slip X mht** transition fitting

3/4" IPS flex-PVC tubing, as a riser

3/4" **slip X slip X slip** PVC tee

Special PVC glue, Weld-on #795

3/4" PVC Sch 40 pipe

Figure 65 This system is virtually like the configuration of the way I install drip in raised boxes. The main difference is the use of the flexible hose called "IPS Flex-PVC." This helps prevent cracking of the buried tee fitting connected to the water supply line.

Drip for Vegetable Beds Without Wooden Boxes

Not everyone wants to go to the expense of wooden vegetable beds. The simplest and cheapest beds are merely dug in place, and often the only way to tell a pathway from a bed is by the vegetables growing in one of them. One considerable advantage to unboxed beds is that their shape can form any part of a curve or circle—an aesthetically pleasing alternative to boxes.

There is a simple way to connect the same type of harness in a ground-level bed with a buried main supply line. Without the gopher-retarding wire bottom of a box to deal with, you may be digging much deeper into the native soil as you cultivate. To protect the main water supply line that goes from bed to bed, use schedule 40 PVC pipe instead of solid drip hose and place it in a trench 18 inches deep, well out of reach of seasonal cultivation. A 3/4-inch main supply line

less than 200 feet long, will supply 480 gph. A one-inch main line can deliver up to 780 gph.

I don't recommend rigid PVC pipe for the risers from the buried main line to the beginning of a bed harness. A wheelbarrow or even a clumsy foot bumping into a rigid PVC riser, even if it's clamped to a post, can transmit enough of a shock to break the Sch 40 tee fitting on the main supply line. There is a flexible PVC hose called IPS Flex-PVC, which can be glued into regular Sch 40 PVC fittings. If you bump into the IPS Flex-PVC hose, it's limber enough to bend without snapping or cracking the Sch 40 tee below ground. With IPS Flex-PVC hose, the 3/4-inch hose can pass 480 gph and the one-inch hose, 780 gph. Be sure the total footage of each harness falls within this range.

Now, refer to Figure 65. Wherever you want a riser along the main supply line, cut the pipe with a hacksaw and use regular PVC glue [keeping in mind the likelihood of PMLP #7 occurring] to affix the correct-sized slip x slip X slip [all are glued] tee to the main line with its open "leg" facing straight up. [If you're using a 1-inch main supply line because it must serve a lot of beds, use a one-inch slip x 3/4-inch slip x 1-inch slip tee.] Use a special clear PVC glue such as WELD-ON #795, which is made to cement 3/4-inch IPS Flex-PVC hose to schedule 40 fittings, to attach enough hose to reach just above the soil's surface. Glue a 3/4-inch slip x slip Sch 40 elbow to the top of the IPS Flex-PVC hose with the open end facing the beginning of the bed. [Make sure to use the correct glue.] To the one open end of the elbow, cement a short, three- to four-inch length of regular 3/4-inch Sch 40 PVC pipe, using ordinary PVC glue, and then glue a 3/4-inch slip x mht transition fitting to the end of the PVC pipe. To this male hose thread you can add the ball valve hose shutoff and the rest of the bed's harness, as described above.

Small-Gauge Drip Tubing

With the introduction of 1/4-inch polyethylene tubing with in-line emitters, more and more gardeners are turning to this less expensive material. At current prices [as I write this book, circa 2008] the 1/4-inch tubing costs $28 for a 100-foot roll with emitters every six inches. This compares to $34 for 1/2-inch tubing with emitters every nine inches. With small beds of vegetables or flowers this makes a lot of cents.

The supply header remains a 1/2-inch solid polyethylene drip hose. Transfer barbs are used to make the transition from 1/2-inch tubing to the 1/4-tubing. Attach the transfer barb to the 1/4-inch tubing, punch a hole in the 1/2-inch solid hose, and then insert the other end of the transfer barb. Most gardeners don't build a drain-down header, but it would be the same as the supply header, but in reverse.

This tubing is easier to hide due to its diminutive size. This tubing tends to wander around more than the 1/2-inch in-line hose. For a proper spacing, use the smaller 1/4-inch by three-inch-long hold-down stakes and more of them compared to 1/2-inch tubing. For a bed four feet wide, I would use four lengths of tubing compared to three lines with the 1/2-inch "relative". Usually the ends are closed with a goof plug.

The beauty to these materials is that it's rather easy to remove the rows of tubing for soil preparation. Where winters are severe, it's easy to coil up and bring indoors for the winter.

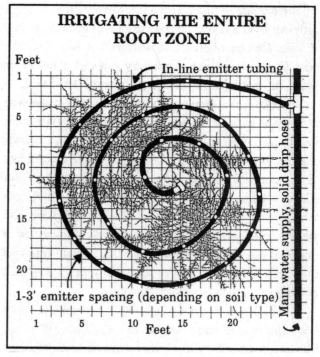

IRRIGATING THE ENTIRE ROOT ZONE

In-line emitter tubing

1-3' emitter spacing (depending on soil type)

Main water supply, solid drip hose

Figure 66 A friend plants his corn, squash, and pumpkins on a raised bed and irrigates it with a spiral instead of parallel rows to save money due to the reduced the number of fittings.

Row Crops and Drip Irrigation

If you prefer to garden in the time-honored fashion called row cropping, with wide paths between rows of vegetables, you can still use drip irrigation. Row cropping is well-suited to big patches of corn, long rows of tomatoes for canning, trellises of cukes for pickling, and lengthy rows of dry-shell beans. In some ways, row cropping is the easiest way to use in-line drip tubing because no harnesses are required.

You can use a main line of either solid drip hose or schedule 40 PVC pipe and plumb off of the main line as described above. The only difference is that you'll want to have each row's drip hose attached separately to the main line by its own riser with a fht swivel fitting. This makes it easier to disconnect the long lines of drip tubing and drag each one off to the side before rototilling the entire plot. When hoeing young seedlings, simply flop the tubing over to an already cultivated portion of the row, hoe where the tubing was, and flop it back. Once the crop is maturing you can still gently hoe as it's hard to slice the 1/2-inch tubing. At the end of the season, cut the plants back to just a few inches above the tubing and then remove the tubing before any more cultivation.

Vining winter squash and pumpkins have such an extensive root system, as shown in Figure 66, that it's better to drip irrigate more as you would with trees than with row crops. Use a large spiral of in-line tubing to water as much of the root zone as possible.

How Often and How Long to Water Your Vegetable Beds

Even more than with flowers, trees, and shrubs, I suggest experimenting with daily applications of tiny amounts of water on vegetables. As mentioned in the Introduction, unless your water supply is extremely limited, judicious daily waterings will produce the greatest yields, although with some crops, like tomatoes, to produce a more richly flavored fruit you may want to reduce or eliminate the amount of water as the vegetables begin ripening. Too much irrigation will plump up the 'maters with water; this dilutes the flavor and also makes it more difficult to cook them down into a sauce or paste.

Happy harvesting!

CHAPTER 9

Grey Water & Drip (?)

Sometimes yes. Sometimes no. Let's take a peek into a world even Pop Murphy has never ventured. The details are in the filth—the grit, sand, particulates, oils, soap, and many more potentially emitter-clogging detritus. The successful use of drip irrigation with grey water is the Holy Grail of drip irrigation.

Alas, an obligatory side step to the potential health risks. Then a review of the main components of a grey water system before we get to the nuts and bolts of drip irrigation. Because the proper selection or DIY construction of a grey water system is basically more important than the actual emitters.

Is Grey Water a Health Risk?

The potential for grey water (GW) to transmit pathogens has long been the concern of most Public Health Departments. Due to assumed health risks, the use of GW has been illegal, and no structure was permitted to have a code for a grey water system (GWS)—until the droughts in the west and southwest beginning around 1990 and continuing into the 21st century. GW was always classified before then as "sewage waste," making it potentially as dangerous, from a Health Department perspective, as black water [bet you know why it's called black]—the dirtiest water such as that from the toilet and kitchen sink. GW can contain the same types of pollutants and pathogens as black water—but, usually in very tiny amounts, if at all. However,

to date, and in spite of various theoretical scenarios, there has not been a single illness documented to be caused by GW. Those diseases that are potentially transmitted via GW include:

Common Name Disease	Latin Name Disease
parasite roundworm	*Ascaris lumbricoides*
food poisoning	*Salmonella* spp.
amoebas, amoebic dysentery	*Entamoeba histolytica*
typhoid, typhoid fever	*Salmonella typhi*
diarrhea, bacillary dysentery	*Shigella* spp.
fevers, strep throat scarlet fever, St. Anthony's fire	*Streptococci* spp.

Enteric viruses (also called enteroviruses)—a large group of human viral pathogens that can cause a number of diseases, including:

Diarrhea (loose bowels)
Encephalitis (inflammation of the brain)
Gastroenteritis (inflammation of the stomach and intestines)
Hepatitis A (inflammation of the liver)
Meningitis (inflammation of the brain and spinal cord membranes)
Myocarditis (inflammation of the heart muscle)
Nephritis (chronic disease of the kidneys)
Pericarditis (inflammation of the membrane around the heart)
Pleurodynia (disease of the lung membranes)

Most pathogens can reside out of the body of a host, in the soil, for some period of time. But, each disease has a different life span in the soil. Some of the survival times for various pathogens are:

Organism	Survival Time (in days)
Ascaris spp. ova [roundworm]	up to 7 years
Entamoeba histolytica	6–8

Enteroviruses	8–175
Hookworm larvae	42
Salmonella spp. [typhoid fever]	1–120
Streptococci spp.	26–77

Most of the above illnesses are transmitted exclusively via the "fecal-to-oral" path. The important caveat to the above list is that in order for you to get sick from a GWS: someone else in the household must have a disease; fecal matter contaminated with the disease organism or parasite ova must get in the GW, you must come in contact with the GW [or soil that has been watered with GW]; and your hand must come in contact with your mouth. If nobody's ill [including visitors], then there's nothing to transmit via a home's GWS. Also, all systems must have a manual or automatic valve that can divert the GW to the septic tank or sewer whenever someone is ill. All these scenarios and facts are irrelevant when the GW is distributed both automatically and out-of-reach—below the surface of the mulch or soil.

Even though you won't have any of these organisms in the garden if you're healthy, the prudent person will avoid using GW with annual ornamental bedding plants or vegetables that touch, or grow in, the soil—to avoid working the soil several times per season. The safest use of GW is in a well-designed landscape planted with perennial shrubs and trees which will not be moved or replanted. Or, fruit trees; being sure that you don't eat any fallen fruit. Caution dictates washing your hands—just like Mom always said—after gardening where GW is distributed.

Remember, with a GWS, you and your family are now acting partially as your own wastewater treatment "plant." and its judicious maintenance and management are your responsibilities.

The Reality of Exposure to Cooties

All this sounds pretty scary, no? But the reality is much more mundane. In 1992, the City of Los Angeles Office of Water Reclamation did a one-year study about the concerns of the public's exposure to pathogens. The report entitled *Gray Water Pilot Project* states: "if [the] data can be generalized, the implication is that gray water irrigation—below the surface of the soil—does not by itself elevate the health risk from handling the garden soil, as long as sanitary practices are followed." Furthermore: "Disease organisms, normally capable of surviving in the soil for a few days, were not present in gray-water-irrigated areas." As to the risks in cleaning the filter bags: "Individuals assigned the task of cleaning gray water filters—some doing so without protective gloves, in spite of instruction to the contrary—did not report any adverse effects."

Safe Cleaners and Soaps for a GWS

Since I don't recommend using laundry water, the list of products to clean the shower and bathroom sink is rather short. [Some say the shower, bathroom tub, and bathroom sink account for 40–60% of all GW generated.] Stop using boron-based products. Boron doesn't easily leach away once it has been added to the soil, and plants react negatively to it at very low levels—irrigation water with only 2 to 3 parts per million [ppm] boron will harm many agricultural crops. While boron seldom actually kills plants, it does cause a very noticeable blackening or browning of the leaf margin [its outer edge].

Reduce or eliminate chlorine bleach and any cleaner with chlorine bleach additives. Chlorine bleach is quite caustic to all life—that's why it's used as cleanser or purifier. Non-chlorine cleaning agents such as baking soda and Bon Ami™ are simple cleaners that don't harm plants.

Virtually all hand soaps are safe to use with a GWS. Avoid cleaners that are designed to remove greasy dirt. Just use the kitchen sink or switch the main GW valve to the sewer or septic tank.

Grey Water and Drip Irrigation

With all that said, can grey water be practically used with drip irrigation? The answer is maybe yes, maybe no. It greatly depends on where the GW comes from, how diligent you are in maintaining a GWS, and the proper selection of each component of the system. Yet, it is still an experiment in progress. [A system that did the best cleansing with a computerized dispersal system of GW in the Los Angeles 1992 study cost $5,000, but the developer simply stopped making any more systems—and disappeared.]

Tough times with water supplies will only continue as potable water becomes increasingly difficult to find and distribute. Drip irrigation is the most efficient way to distribute this valuable resource.

NOTE: Using GW with drip irrigation is far from easy. Most of the systems tested in 1992 in Los Angeles are not working today. Probably for two reasons: the most important reason was the owners stopped religiously cleaning the filter bag. And, probably, the sump pumps were too small for the load of GW. Also, all systems tried to clean and distribute laundry water along with the shower, bathtub, and bathroom sink GW.

The Basics of Grey Water Use in the Landscape

Because GW has the possibility, however remote, to transfer pathogens, it is never applied by sprinkler or hand-held hose. The goal is to make sure the GW never surfaces to see the light of day—referred to as preventing "daylighting." Therefore, the GW must be applied below the surface of the landscape. The "surface," in reality, can refer to the top of a thick, permanent mulch covering the soil or the top of an unmulched soil. The upper layers of the soil are the most aerobic and quickest to neutralize any pathogens due to its diversity of beneficial soil life. Also, the closer to the surface of the soil the GW is applied, the more efficient a plant's roots are in absorbing the water and its nutrients.

Thus, the most effective way to apply GW for the plant's growth and both the homeowner's and the soil's health is via drip irrigation tubing beneath a very thick protective layer of mulch. The mulch also ensures the tubing is hidden from view, the plastic is protected from damaging UV light, and the GW remains safely out of touch. [Theoretically, subsurface distribution would be ideal. But it is much easier to mange and fix any malfunctioning system if it's not buried. Gophers make it impossible to bury the tubing.]

The Basic Components of a GWS

All GWSs have a certain number of components in common. These include: collecting pipes, a surge tank, a main three-way switching valve, distribution valves, and in this case—drip irrigation tubing. Below is a brief listing of each major part or component. [See Figures 67 and 68.]

NOTE: The drawings here show only using grey water from the shower(s) and bathroom sink(s). Only the most meticulous person should try using washing machine water. It has so much lent and dirt that the filter bag needs to be cleaned often—sometimes after each load. Much like the lint filter in a laundry dryer.

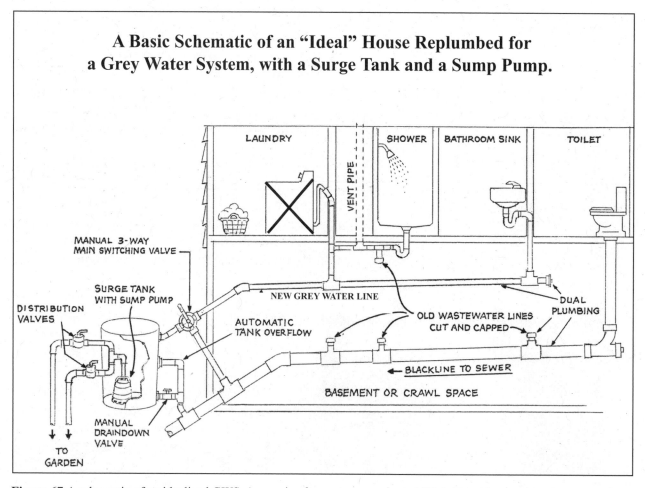

A Basic Schematic of an "Ideal" House Replumbed for a Grey Water System, with a Surge Tank and a Sump Pump.

LAUNDRY SHOWER BATHROOM SINK TOILET

VENT PIPE

MANUAL 3-WAY
MAIN SWITCHING VALVE

SURGE TANK
WITH SUMP PUMP

DISTRIBUTION
VALVES

NEW GREY WATER LINE

AUTOMATIC
TANK OVERFLOW

OLD WASTEWATER LINES
CUT AND CAPPED

DUAL
PLUMBING

BLACKLINE TO SEWER

BASEMENT OR CRAWL SPACE

MANUAL
DRAINDOWN
VALVE

TO
GARDEN

Figure 67 A schematic of an idealized GWS. Access is often not as easy in real life [at least in many western or modern suburbs]. Houses built on slabs have all the plumbing buried in the concrete pad. The only pipe out is GW mixed with black water. The X on the washing machine is to remind the reader that I don't recommend the use of laundry water due to all the fibers that quickly fill up the filter bag. [Fanatics or compulsive people who are able to do frequent cleaning of a filter bag can use laundry water with <u>due diligence</u>. [See Figure 71.]

Grey Water Collection Pipes

Many existing houses can be replumbed if there are any accessible pipe(s). [Many modern homes have all the plumbing connected and encased with a concrete. In such cases, the grey- and black-water pipes are connected in the concrete pad, making it impossible to have a GWS.] A simple three-way valve is installed to allow for quick switching, as needed, between the sewer and a GW landscape distribution system. Thus, if the use of GW is not desired by any current or future occupant, it can be diverted to the sewer or septic tank with a twist of a valve. [See Figure 69.] In gardens that go mostly dormant each fall and winter, the GW needs to be switched back to the sewer or leach field. Also, where it rains or freezes in the winter, it's easy for the GW to "daylight". Thus is dispelled the myth that GW reduces the size of a failing or new septic tank system.

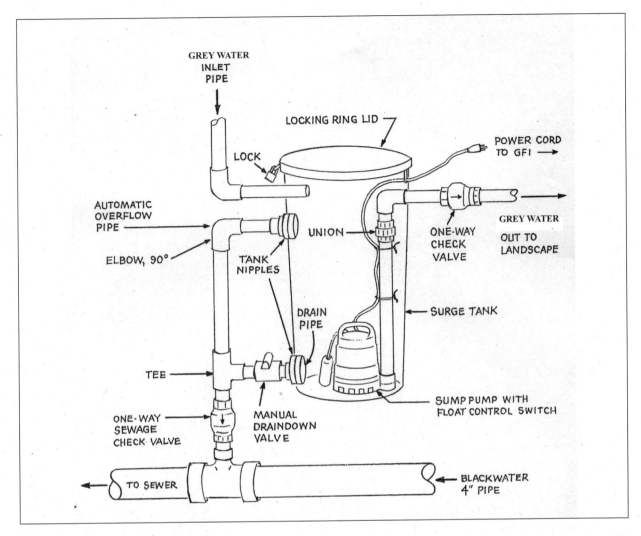

Figure 68 This is one possible configuration for a GWS. This is a gravity-fed inlet with a sump pump outlet. This GWS requires a considerable crawl space or basement to work. There are many possibilities. A plumber may help in states or counties that have approved GWSs. Check with your local building department. A surge tank with straight sides, no bulges, makes it much easier for attaching the fittings. An overflow port is important if the pump should fail. You could plumb both the overflow and draindown pipes to a gravel [river rock for air pockets to hold the draining GW.] sump covered with a deep mulch outside the tank in the landscape. This would eliminate the chances of a sewage check valve failure. A more expensive sump pump would be required if the level of the landscape is above the tank's sump pump.

The Surge Tank

All GW pipes drain by gravity to a tank, usually a 55–gallon, high-quality plastic drum. While this looks like a small storage tank, it usually only holds water for a short period of time–minutes, or an hour. If the GW is being generated faster than the distribution system can disperse it, the tank allows for the temporary backup of water—thus, the name "surge" [or buffer] tank.

A surge tank may simply drain out the bottom to the landscape—which is called a gravity system. However, a gravity GWS only works when all the plants are below the level of the bottom of the surge tank. Or, a pump—often a sump pump—can be installed to lift the water to any landscaping above the surge tank. [See Figure 72.] All surge tanks must have an automatic overflow pipe near the top of the tank in case something clogs after the tank or the sump pump fails. [See Figure 68.] The overflow port must be connected by gravity flow to the existing septic or sewer line with a one-way sewage check valve to prevent the septic tank or sewer from backing up into the surge tank.

Each surge tank also has a manual draindown valve that is plumbed to the sewer or septic line, with a protective one-way check valve, to allow for draining and cleaning the tank. [See Figure 68.]

If that fails to work, plumb the overflow and draindown pipes to a large gravel sump below the surface of the ground.

You can let the GW enter the tank through a hole cut in the tank. The drawbacks are: insects

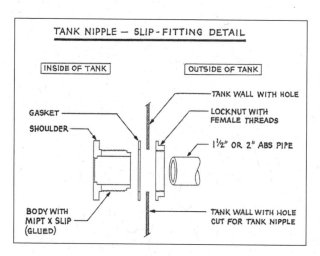

Figure 70 A tank adaptor fitting [sometimes called a bung fitting] is an easy way to pass a pipe thorough the tank's wall without leaking. Use plastic parts if possible, to avoid corrosion and make a tighter seal to elimante variations in the plastic surge tank.

[such as mosquitoes] can enter the tank and if the overflow pipe should fail, the GW will spill out. It's safer to use a tank adapter with a gasket to prevent leaks. [See Figure 70.] Tank adapters can be used for all inlets and outlets for a good seal. In Figure 68, the inlet of GW and the pumping of the GW from the sump pump are set higher than the overflow port. Thus, the tank adapter isn't required. However, seal any holes around the pipes with steel wool. Replace the steel wool after it rusts. Or, use a silicon caulk for tiny gaps.

For extra protection, add a filter bag that captures lint, hair, and all manner of detritus. The GW should enter the tank via a tank adapter. [See Figure 71.] Add a flange to the bottom of the pipe. Tie the filter bag around the flange. You can find these bags at beer- and wine-making supply stores. A better source for a finer mesh may be found at aquarium suppliers. When changing or cleaning the bag, be sure to use protective rubber gloves.

Switching Valve

A main valve is required to allow the homeowner

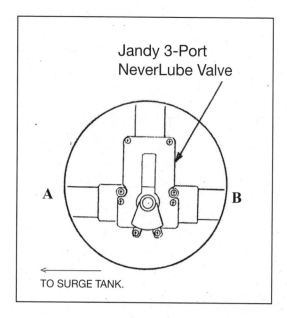

Figure 69 The Jandy® 3-port NeverLube® valve is the best way to direct GW to the garden or to the sewer or septic tank. The arrow points to the main body of a manual model. You can use an electric model if you want to control the switching from a distant location—like the garage or bathroom. Here the GW enters from the top. As an example, the handle can be turned clockwise to shut the "B" pipe sending GW to the sewer. A counterclockwise turn would send the GW to "A", the surge tank. Swimming pool stores are the best place to find a Jandy valve. To alternate between two landscape areas, add another three-way valve after the surge tank "A".

A FILTER BAG IS <u>REQUIRED</u> TO USE GREY WATER THROUGH A DRIP SYSTEM

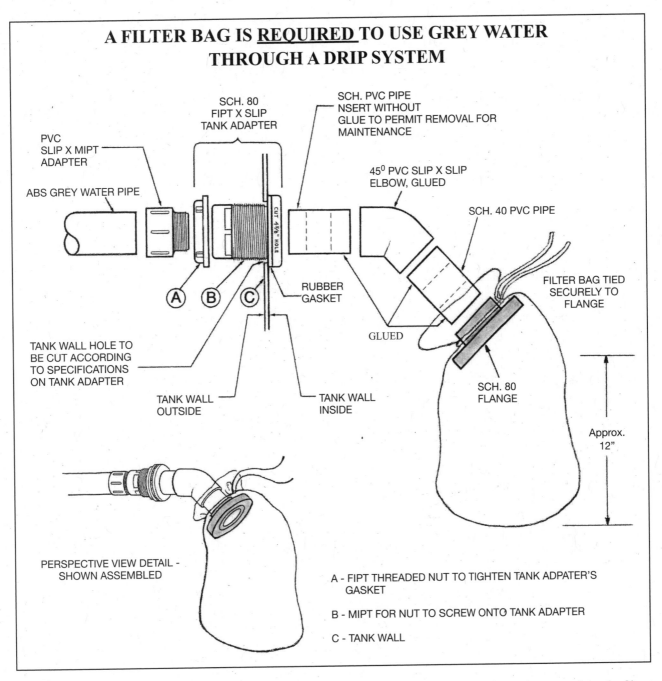

Figure71 A way to add a filter bag to screen out particles down to 100 or higher mesh bag. If you change or clean the filter bag often, you can avoid a Y-filter. [This is only true if you're not using the laundry GW.] Get the bags at a local beer-making supply house. Or, look for finer mesh bags at aquarium suppliers. Try to get bags with a mesh size rated more than 100 mesh [150 microns]. [See the "Mesh to Micron" chart in Chapter10, "Drip Irrigation with Cisterns & Tanks?" chapter.] This drawing shows a 3-inch set of fittings to connect with the 3-inch GW inlet pipe. This takes nearly $250 of parts. You can use the same configuration in smaller sizes: 2-, 1-, and even 3/4-inch pipes [with appropriate adapters to save money. But depending on your pipe configuration, smaller-sized pipes can cause the GW to backup and cause messy indoor spills. Be sure to place the inlet port with its flange so nothing, including the filter bag, blocks the switch for the sump pump. Use a surge tank with straight sides to make sure the tank adapter's gasket seals properly. [See Figure 70.] Some sump pumps have a float switch that slides vertically instead of a tethered float switch. Use a vertical float switch for a measure of protection from a wayward filter bag. Leave the pipe on the inside tank nipple unglued so the unit can be removed for important periodic maintenance [i.e., cleaning the tank, or the sump pump].

to alternate between the GWS and the septic tank or sewer as desired. [See Figure 69.] The main valve is used when the ground is saturated with rainwater, when someone is ill with a dangerous infectious disease, when flushing high concentrations of cleaner from the shower and/ or bathtub, or the occupants don't want to use the GWS irrigation system. The main valve(s), whether manual or electro-mechanical, is best plumbed near the anticipated location of the future surge tank.

The Distribution Valves

After the surge tank, a series of two or more manual or electromechanical valves will control the application of the GW to various portions of the landscape. For the sake of the plant's health, the GW should be alternated between two separate watering areas (zones) or rotated through a number of zones. This rotation allows a resting time so the soil's pores can drain and breathe in fresh air. The soil's beneficial bacteria and microorganisms use the oxygen to thrive as they consume the GW's residual "bad" bacteria, nutrients, and particulates (organic matter).

If all the GW is distributed to the same zone every day, the soil can become anaerobic and its loose, well-drained structure can be destroyed. Also, daylighting may occur due to saturation and the plant's root hairs may be crippled or killed.

The manual valve I use for switching back and forth drip lines is a Jandy 3-port NeverLube. [See Figure 69.]

Sump Pumps

When the plants to be irrigated are at the same level as the surge tank, but far away or above the surge tank, a pump is required. The usual solution for a disposal system is a sump pump. Sump pumps are designed to be submerged in

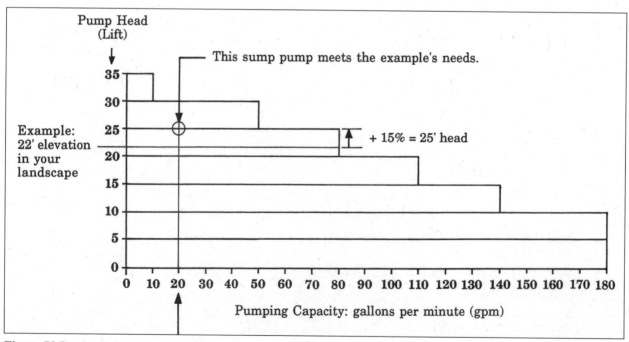

Figure 72 Don't go cheap on purchasing a sump pump. Make sure you get one with all metal parts. [Or, mostly metal, not plastic.] Make sure you have one that has the intake ports as close to the bottom of the surge tank as possible, after determining the head of the pump for your situation, and an extra 15% or more to deal with friction losses.

water, to automatically turn on when the water reaches a predetermined level and to pump the water a certain maximum height and distance—at a specific rate, in gallons per minute (gpm) or gallons per hour (gph). Sump pumps are installed in the surge tank. [See Figures 67 and 68.]

Sump Pump Specifications

1—Sump pumps are usually more convenient for homeowners to install because the pump and automatic on/off switch (called a level control) comes pre installed together and the pump is waterproof and designed to prevent electrical shock.

2—Sump pumps are basically designed to evacuate a large amount of water as quickly as possible, with little regard as to pressure or high lifts. While sump pumps can move plenty of water in a short period of time, they often can't lift the water very high (called "head"), nor develop much pressure—which is a function of the head.

3—The sump pump must be wired with grounded direct-burial wire to a GFI outlet located inside the nearest building, not the dry well. All electrical work must be done by an electrical contractor and meet UBC guidelines.

4—All sump pumps must be constructed primarily of metal parts and have a metal housing. (Plastic-bodied pumps usually must have four or more inches of standing water at all times to keep the pump's body from overheating, but the standing water turns septic and smells horrible.)

5—Choose a sump pump with a vertical path float switch, where the float slides up and down a vertical pin passing through a vertical channel in the middle of the float, for level control. A tethered mercury-float switch can easily get caught on any part of the pipes, filter bag, or pump.

6—The float control(s) on the sump pump must be set to allow the pump's intake port to drain the tank as close to empty as possible—less than one inch is preferred. Thus, the least amount of GW is left behind to turn septic and create odors. Sump or sewage ejector pumps with intake ports above the pump's legs should not be used because they sit too far off the bottom of the tank.

7—The intake port's openings (the impeller housing) must be as large as possible. A vertically-slated impeller housing may be less likely to clog than perforated or mesh-type housing.

8—The pump must be rated for water heated up to 130° F.

9—The horsepower rating of the pump is the least important specification. The important ratings are the head (the number of feet the water can be lifted vertically) and flow, in gallons per minute (gpm) or gallons per hour (gph.)

10—To choose the right capacity/size sump pump, you'll need to know the flow rate at the desired head.

11—Typically, the head is the gross difference in elevation. As a safety factor, the head for a GWS is determined by adding the total changes, both up and down, in the elevation from the surge tank to the point of disposal. To this figure add at least 15% more feet of the total head. [Don't expect your pump to last long if it's always pumping at the uppermost limit of its rated capacity.] In other words, if the total change in the elevation from the tank to the landscape is 13 feet, then the sump pump must be rated at least a 15-foot head [a greater increase is better if you can afford the pump.]. Also account for the flow rate of the pump. [See Figure 72.] Check the manufacturer's chart of lift and flow rates to determine how much water can be pumped at the required head. Many pumps can discharge a huge volume of water when the point of release is level with the pump or only a foot or two higher; the gpm drops off rapidly with increased elevation. To prevent wasting GW via the surge tank's overflow port, make sure the sump pump can discharge enough water at your required elevation to keep up with the maximum input (in gpm) of GW as determined in Figure 72.

12—There must be a flapper check valve of the same diameter as the discharge pipe installed on the threaded discharge port of the sump pump. This will prevent any water from siphoning back into the surge tank and either turning on the pump again or leaving enough water to turn septic and smelly. Also note the one-way check valve that prevents the black water from filling the tank. [See Figure 68.]

13—Attached to the check valve is a discharge pipe. The discharge pipe up to the tank nipple on the wall of the surge tank should be PVC Sch 80 pipe or iron pipe. [Pipe on the outside of the tank nipple can be PVC Sch 40.]

14—Repair or cleaning of the pump will be facilitated if the discharge pipe has a union somewhere after the check valve and before the tank nipple. Use threaded fittings only within the surge tank.

15—Be vigilant in inspecting the surge tank and replacing or cleaning the filter bag.

Not as easy as some would expect. But remember, grey water is greyt for your garden. Drought or no drought.

The Drip Hardware

Now you know if setting up the hardware to get the GW to the drip assembly is right for you.

Assuming you want to plunge into the waters of drip irrigation with GW, here's the scoop:

More than regular city or well water, your system needs to be protected from clogging. A 200-mesh screen is a must. To get more protection, plumb the GW pipe to a one-inch filter and then step it down to a 3/4-inch pipe to the pressure regulator. A 1-inch filter has a much bigger surface area to last longer before it begins to get plugged and needs cleaning. Use the filter with the disks [See Figure 10] as they work better with dirty water. However, remember they take much longer to clean by hand. Or, just run them solo through the dishwasher to prevent germ and sediment problems. By avoiding the washing machine you're already reducing your risks.

It seems—but has not been proven—that some GW particles in suspension glob up together after passing through the filter, so an emitter with the shortest internal path and the largest exit hole is required. This would suggest an in-line emitter such as the Geoflow Wasteflow® PC 1/2- and 1-gph products. [With Treflan® embedded in the emitters.] This tubing is designed for effluent thst has more particulates than potable water. Also, consider the Netafim Bioline®, which is impregnated with Vinyzene to prevent the growth of microbial slime. [Both of these examples should not be used in an organic garden or lanscape.] The Techline PC tubing is designed to be buried [as are the two aboove] and has continous self-cleaning emitters, but no added chemicals. [My favorite of the three.] Keep the tubing ontop of the soil, but covered with an attractive mulch to avoid problems with gophers.

If clogging seems to be happening, the next step is to add a liquid fertilizer/proportioner to the system to flush the tubing and emitters with a mild acid after a rainy day. [See Chapter 12.]

To make it plug-proof, you could use the system invented by Larry Farwell. [See Figure 73.] By using upside-down flower pots and simple drip hose valves, it's possible to adjust each pot's flow to a reasonable rate. This is best used on flat land.

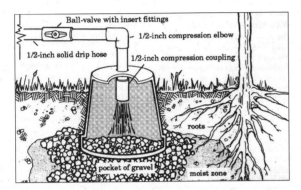

Figure 73 A simple, elegant way to distribute GW without the fear of clogging. Adjust the ball valves to even the flow.

CHAPTER 10

Drip Irrigation with Cisterns & Tanks?
(From Raindrops to Drip Drops)

Jean de Florette, a film by French director Claude Berri, is set in the scrubby, olive tree-covered hills of southern France. As the film begins, a severe drought has dried up a family's cistern—the underground stone storage tank that captures rain from their terra-cotta roof. A farmer, played by Gérard Depardieu (of *Green Card* and *Cyrano* fame), watches helplessly as his family's crops begin to wither and their cash crop of meat rabbits begins to die of thirst. Two peasant farmers plot to force the neighboring family into bankruptcy. Finally, the two conniving farmers manage to cause the early death of the Depardieu character, to destroy his family, and to acquire the farm for much less than the pre-drought price. All because the cistern was too small to store enough water for the driest years.

For better or worse, cisterns are used throughout the world to catch rainwater from the roof for drinking, washing, and irrigation. Tanks come in all shapes and sizes—rain barrels, round wooden tanks, stone wells, ugly black plastic drums, and nondescript gray concrete tanks. In the 1800s and early 1900s in America, cisterns were common, even in cities.

But the uses of cisterns and the reasons for building or buying your own have changed. Cisterns are experiencing a welcome and well-deserved revival, due to dwindling sources of clean water, erratic supplies during droughts, and a renewed interest in water independence.

Cistern systems are remarkably simple compared to many modern technologies such as wells, huge man-made lakes, and a complicated water infrastructure. Basically, the rain must be gathered, stored in a cistern [for the rest of the chapter, loosely defined as any tank in or above the ground] and drained or pumped to the landscape. In most cases, rainfall is collected from the roof of the home, barn, or garage. A typical gutter funnels the rain into a downspout, hose, or pipe that leads to the storage tank. A diverter valve is built in the downspout or pipe so the first rains after a dry spell, to flush all kinds of accumulated filth off the roof, can be turned away from the tanks until the roof is clean. Usually, a simple device or grate screens out any twig and leaf debris that may have gathered on the roof. [For the details of the construction of a diverter system, see the books in the Bibliography.] Commonly, the roof water drains into a tank made of concrete, fiberglass, or polyurethane.

Modern Reasons for a Cistern

Most gardeners will readily tell you their plants look and grow better with rainwater. Repeated use of municipal water, especially in arid climates with alkaline soils, does seem to have a mild adverse effect over time—browning of the leave's edges and, perhaps, yellowing.

Indoor plants can be a different story. The salts and minerals found in many water supplies, plus the chlorine, build up in the limited soil volume of the pot—they can be seen as a white crust on top of the soil. Over time municipal water can even kill sensitive houseplants. For this reason, a rain barrel under a home's downspout is a *must* for watering indoor plants.

Alas, unlike the romantic independence of bygone homestead days, I think tanks should not be used to collect drinking water. Some people have gotten permits for using rainwater as drinking water, but the cleaning process is very complicated, requires extra costs, needs vigilant maintenance, and won't work with certain roofs like composite shingles and wooden shakes. [See the Appendix for a list of books and web sites for more details on this important issue.]

In a study of water quality in tanks in Pennsylvania, they found that 70% of the 40 systems studied had, on at least one occasion, lead and cadmium levels in the tank's sediment, originally "as direct input (from) precipitation," which exceeded drinking water standards "with surprising frequency." Particulate filters for roof runoff reduced the lead input from 2610 ug/L to 102 ug/L. [The symbol ug/L is micrograms per liter or parts per billion. In this example, 2610 equals 0.02610 ppb.] The sediment from unfiltered water had 348 ug/L lead, and the filtered system's sediment was only 23 ug/L. Interestingly, due to rainfall, the corrosive action of the acid rainfall on the home's plumbing, and sediment in the water supply [either one or a combination of all three] led to 11% of the tap water samples exceeding the 50 ug/L [for lead in] drinking water limit for drinking water. In this study, the conclusion was "the presence of lead and cadmium in the tap water of tank water supplies in western PA was sufficient to constitute a hazard to users of such systems (and) users…were advised to discontinue use of the cistern…"

For drinking water, I agree. For landscape plants, it's a different story.

Drought-Proof Your Garden with a Cistern?—Maybe Yes, Maybe Not

Droughts are often the single source of inspiration for the installation of tanks throughout the Southwest, if not everywhere.

The recent changes in the climate seem to be making much of the Southwest more parched than in years past. The drought of the 1990s gave rise to the interest and need for water storage. During 1990, Michael Gould, a water entrepreneur from Santa Barbara, CA, found a direct corollary between drought and interest in water self-reliance. "In the third or fourth year of the drought, after Stage 3 [the third tier of water usage and the most expensive water] rationing was in place," Gould recalls, "our business for trucked-in water and tanks for landscape irrigation skyrocketed; we installed 220,000 gallons of storage tanks, most for the trucked-in water, and some were also connected to downspouts."

Ironically, tanks in regions with no summer rain whatsoever are expensive propositions. In such an area, you must store up enough water for as much as five to six months of landscape irrigation. Consider, for example, an anonymous two-acre estate in a wealthy neighborhood in Santa Barbara, California, planted with water-loving ornamentals, some drought-resistant plants, a large 1/2-acre lawn, and a vegetable garden. During the 1990 drought, such a grandiose and extravagant landscape, based upon the conservative figure of outdoor use equaling 60% of all water use, had a historical year-round usage of a staggering 500,000 gallons! A tank big enough to hold this much water would have to be a whopping 50 feet on each side and 27 feet tall! Try and hide that in your average backyard. Such a tank would also cause a severe drought in your cash flow.

Because construction costs usually limit their size, tanks for complete landscape irrigation are often more appropriate in places that get periodic, sporadic year-round or summer rains.

The Anatomy of a Tank

As technologies go, tanks are rather simple, but

they still require certain basic considerations and calculations, and some planning and attention to one's craft are important. [For details see the Bibliography.]

Rain Barrels

The simplest tank is a rain barrel connected to the end of one or more downspouts. The farm rain barrel was typically a used pickle or wine barrel or a 55-gallon drum with a lid. Such limited water was usually reserved for rinsing hair, washing delicate linens, or watering houseplants. Now, most gardeners use the spigot on the rain barrel to fill a sprinkling can to water plants both indoors and outside.

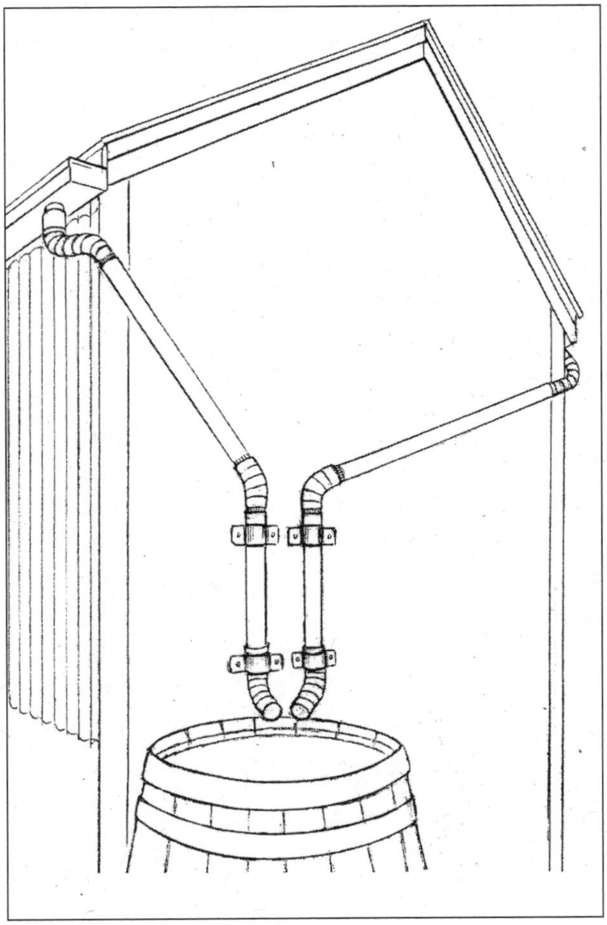

Mail order catalogs have begun to sell plastic versions of the ol'-fashioned rain barrel. Strangely, one plastic 42-gallon version has its spigot 13 inches from the ground to make it easy to slip a bucket or watering can underneath. This leaves one-third of the water in the barrel at all times–quite a waste. [The drum can be easily elevated so the spigot is near the base of the barrel. But in elevating the barrel, be sure to provide a solid base to support the drum's entire width and weight.]

Rain barrels, even moreso than other tanks with wire vents to help keep the water cool, may breed mosquitoes. Not so cool with the concern about West Nile disease. There is a simple solution—a product called Mosquito Dunks™. This is a gray, doughnut-shaped material impregnated with a naturally occurring insecticide known as *Bacillus thuringiensis* var. *israeliensis*, which attacks the mosquito larva and destroys its gut. One simply tosses the correct portion of a ring, or rings, into water, and the insecticide does all the work with no chemical poisons.

Figure 74 A view of a very simple rain-barrel catchment tank. Here the downspouts do not have filters or diverting devices. The barrel is used to fill hand-sprinkling cans with water to use inside the green-house. The lack of a lid means these people should be very vigilant about mosquito larvae and add *Bacillus thuringiensis* var. *israeliensis* as needed.

The Cost of Storing "Free" Rainfall

Homeowners who build their own tank systems usually link up a number of small recycled 50-gallon drums used for food or salvaged tanks, which are easy to move in place and save money. Such systems can end up storing an impressive amount of water but look like a Rube Goldberg contraption. Owner-builders can also use various sizes of plastic tanks that can be placed on compacted bare soil, a packed gravel base, or poured concrete slab—depending upon the type of plastic; be sure to ask your dealer for the specifics.

Prices for tanks vary across the country. The best

way to compare expenses is to convert all costs to the price per gallon of storage. For example, where I live, north of San Francisco, costs range from $0.40 per gallon for ugly above-ground storage to $1.00 or more per gallon for contractor-installed underground tanks.

This usually does not include fittings, valves, pipe, or installation fees. In some cases, a base or pad is an additional cost. Basically, the larger the tank, the less cost per gallon. Smaller tanks are easier for the do-it-yourselfer to work with, but this convenience will cost a bit more. Innovations in plastic tanks have made them competitive with concrete tanks—that can settle and crack or be damaged or ruined by earthquakes [a California certainty]. Spending a little more money for a polyurethane tank which can be set on compacted, level ground without the expensive of a concrete slab or gravel base will quickly be compensated for in the savings on the installation costs.

The location of the tank involves convenient proximity to the collector, aesthetics, and cost. Naturally, the closer a tank is to the roof, the more convenient. Systems that rely upon gravity to disperse the water to the garden usually have the tank above ground so some pressure is developed. [See Figure 75.]

Pumped tanks don't have to be above ground. Also, because most storage tanks are so bulky and ugly-looking, many people would rather bury them. But the cost of an underground tank can be quite high because it must be engineered to withstand compression of soil around its walls. Polyurethane or fiberglass tanks, which can be buried, cost $1.00 per gallon or more.

When considering a large tank, make sure it has a lid or hatch large enough to allow you to climb inside to clean or repair the tank. Aboveground tanks should have screen-covered air holes to help keep the water fresh but bug free. Every tank must have a large-diameter pipe with a ball valve for a bottom drain to flush accumulated sediment. In rural areas, use a quick knock-off fitting so firefighters can quickly use your water to fight fires.

Delivery

With a simple gravity system, one just needs a hose to reach the plants downhill from the tank. To protect the hose from sucking too much grunge off the bottom of the tank, make sure the discharge pipe is placed at least 12 inches above the bottom. This pipe should come through the side of the tank and have a standard hose bib.

Pumped systems require an electric centrifugal or sump pump. Sump pumps don't develop much pressure. A $100 to $200 sump pump usually won't develop more than 15 psi. Such pressure can power a limited drip irrigation system. Be sure to check the specifications on the sump pump's box to make sure it can lift the water out of the tank or pump it high enough uphill to meet your needs. This lifting capacity is called the "head" and is measured in feet as the vertical height of lift. Don't forget about friction loss. Add a factor of at least 15% more head than you'll need to compensate for friction loss. Or, ask your local irrigation supply house. Be sure to get a sump pump with as many metal parts as possible—not those wimpy garden pond pumps. And be sure the base of the pump is 12 inches above the bottom of the tank.

Centrifugal pumps are much more expensive than sump pumps but can pump more water, develop more head, and develop more pressure. Usually, they are connected to a small pressure tank to help maintain a constant pressure and to prolong the life of the pump. The pump is best mounted outside of the storage tank, in a frost-free shed, buried below the frost line, and level with its bottom. [Definitely the job of a plumber or very handy homeowner. You're messin' with 220 VAC and weatherproof housing.] The pump can draw water from a point below the pump, called the suction lift. With your pump dealer, double-check the centrifugal pump's head, suction lift, and total flow at different heads. A self-priming pump is much easier to operate. As

Figure 75 This ingenious gardener took a free-standing plastic tank, removed the entry cap, constructed a conical water catcher, and added it to the top of the tank like a funnel. The outlet and flushing pipes are on the back side. The ladder is used to clean the funnel as needed.

with sump pumps, remove the water not from the very bottom of the storage tank but from a slightly elevated discharge pipe.

How Much Water Can Your Roof Collect? Plenty!

During a recent drought, a winter's rainfall at my house varied between 35 to 45 inches, compared with an average precipitation closer to 60 inches. If I could afford the storage, I would be able to save from my 1000-square-foot roof anywhere from 21,000 to 27,000 gallons during a drought and up to 36,000 gallons in a "normal" year.

As an alternative to calculating runoff, multiply the roof's square footage by 0.6 to get the number of gallons of water your roof will collect for each inch of rain.

Picking the Size of Your Tank

Instead of building the tank to accommodate the maximum rainfall your roof can capture, there are two more practical approaches to determining size. First, you can simply store all the water you'll need to get through each dry spell. If you want to size your tank by this method and you live in the arid West, where the seasonal drought always lasts five to six months, money had better not be a limiting factor. Elsewhere, you'll need to know the average length of the dry spells in your area. Talk to the weather reporter for the local newspaper, radio station, or television station. Consult the weather records at the closest fire or forestry station or contact the Master Gardener program through your Cooperative Extension.

Next, estimate your landscape's irrigation needs. Look at past water bills and calculate the total water usage for the irrigation season. [Many bills list water use in HCFs, or hundreds of cubic feet; each HCF equals 748 gallons.] Now calculate how much of your total water use goes to the garden. In temperate climates with summer humidity, exterior plant use may account for only 30% to 50% of total water use. In the dry, hot summers of the West, the landscape may use 50% to 70% of the total. Check with your local water department's water conservation director for the average percentage for your climate.

Some landscapes were designed without water conservation in mind, and some gardens are so extensive that a tank large enough to irrigate the entire landscape is out of the question, such as the earlier example from Santa Barbara, CA. The second approach to sizing your tank is to build the biggest one you can afford, then replace plants with more water-thrifty types, reduce the amount of area in lawn, convert sprinklers to drip irrigation, use a broom instead of hosing off patios, transfer all container plants into the ground, use a car wash that recycles the wash water, and so on.

Caring for Your Tank

A periodic cleaning of the roof is helpful. With metal roofs, it's rather easy to scrub with a biodegradable detergent. Other surfaces will need a bit more scrubbing. Be sure to divert the wash water or the next rainfall from the tank until the water appears clean.

Cut back the limbs of surrounding trees to reduce the amount of tree litter that falls on the roof. This is especially important if you don't have wire screens over the gutters.

Ideally, the tank should be placed in a cool, shady spot where algae and scum won't easily form. If these moisture- and warmth-loving growths occur, you can often control them with a change in the water's pH.

To purchase a roll of pH test paper, which gives a visual indication of the pH, check with your local plant nurseries, pool supply stores, or aquarium stores. Avoid using toxic cleansers or chemicals inside the tank.

How to Experiment With Drip Irrigation

Water conservation in the garden should go hand in hand with any tank. Even though a tank gives you a measure of water independence, there's no sense in squandering this important resource.

Relative to drip irrigation, simple roof washers get rid of only the grossest stuff—only screening out everything above, say, 1/8-inch, depending upon the size of the wire mesh. [For the details on how to construct a water storage system, see the books listed in the Appendix.] Sprinklers and especially drip irrigation will quickly clog with particles as large as 1/8th-inch in the irrigation water. A simple polyester fabric filter, as mentioned before, cleans water far better than a wire mesh screen and can be added as needed. These bags can be found at suppliers of filter bags for making home-brew beer. Filter bags with finer mesh [200 and up] can be found at suppliers to aquarium stores or at the store. Tie the filter bag to a flange in a surge tank now used as a filter and pumping "station" for the tank-to-surge tank-to-garden drip system. See Figure 71 in the previous Chapter. Turn the filter bag inside-out as needed to flush accumulated detritus.

The irrigation filter should be after the pressure tank. Drip irrigation can be achieved when the tank's simple filters are followed by a typical, pressurized drip irrigation filter. A pump is required to force the tank's water through the last stage of filtration, just before the drip irrigation system. See the discussion earlier in this chapter on pump options.

To prevent clogging, use non-compensating in-line emitters that are self-cleaning.

Converting Mesh To Microns

Inches to	Mesh to	Microns
0.0625	70	210
0.0469	100	150
0.0308	140	104
0.0315	170	88
0.02	200	74
0.16	270	53

As an example, consider the Netafim 1/2-gph non-pressure compensating in-line emitter tubing. According to the manufacturer, the smallest internal passage is 0.043 by 0.046 inches, or about equal to a 100-mesh/150-micron filter bag. To avoid creating a new Pop Murphy's Law of Plumbing, choose a mesh that filters particulates to two-times smaller than the emitter's orifice. Multiply the inches, in decimals, by 0.5 for a 50% safety factor. In this example, 0.0469 X 0.5 = 0.02345, or approximately a 200-mesh/74-micron filter. This means the filter will take out everything down to particles one-half the size of the emitter's internal passage. Most emitters will need final filtration equal to at least a 200-mesh screen, or 75 microns. Using 1-gph non-compensating emitters will also reduce the risk of clogging.

As another example, the 2-gph DURA-FLO™ PC Dripperline [pressure-compensating] emitter made by Agrifim has a large orifice compared to other emitters. [In this example, the manufacturer of the 2-gph PC emitter recommends only an 80- mesh filter to protect the emitters. So the filter of 200 microns equals a safety factor of nearly three.]

Filtration lower than 75 microns usually requires a costly sand filter with automatic back flushing. The system I use for cleaning the iron out of the well's water has a sand filter with 1.5 cubic feet of sand to filter the water down to 3 microns. However, the filter automatically back-flushes once each night to discharge any sediment. The discharge uses 20 gallons. I use that water to irrigate some plants planted along a small swale.

But the loss of 20 gallons per day is a lot of water if there are no rains to replenish it.

A sand filter is a possibility where rains are sporadic but frequent. The total cost of materials alone is just under $900. And, such a system also requires a pressure tank like the ones used for household water. Not commton items for a cistern.

Also consider plumbing a larger filter than the typical 3/4-inch or one-inch filter that can have 28.5 square inches surface area. A 1.5-inch filter can have 60 square inches of cleaning area—more than double the 3/4- and 1-inch filters. A 2-inch filter can have 148 square inches. [Check with your local supplier about the square inches of filtration of the filter you're considering buying.] The larger the surface area, the less often you'll have to clean the filter.

If you get regular rainfall, give tanks.

CHAPTER 11

Controlling Your Drip Irrigation

It seems as if the new irrigation timers and controllers are being invented faster than the time it took Clark Kent to change clothes. Drip irrigation timers and controllers are like computers—the second you walk out of the store, it's already nearly obsolete. Pop Murphy was really thrown a curve ball when it comes to irrigation timers and controllers.

But don't award yourself the Degree in Dripology found in the Appendix yet. You must still master the Zen koan of drip irrigation—What is the sound of one valve turning? To control your drip system is to realize the art of refined simplicity. To fail means that your drip system will control you, or at least a lot of your free time as you scurry about troubleshooting electric valves, timers, and digital controllers. How to control this far-flung petrochemical octopus? The choices range from the merely manual to the electronically ingenious—or devious, if you don't like computerized gizmos. I will explain ways to time and control your drip system beginning with the easiest and ending with the most advanced—satellite real-time control of your irrigation. The choice is yours. But, at this point, my lawyers advise me to inform you that I cannot be held liable for the bizarre things that can go wrong once you cross over into the realm of microchip-controlled irrigation gadgetry. I will attempt to do three things in this chapter: Highlight some timers that are being used successfully in my area [Northern California, about 60 miles north of San Francisco]. Help you evaluate newer models and make an educated decision. I will also review some of the more reliable controllers.

[**NOTE**: I'm using timers to indicate the "ticking" part that tells when to start and stop a drip system. Controllers—aka, valves and/or manifolds and/or weather-based controllers—are, for this book, the devices that open and close the system's water supply. A bit like splitting hairs and some gizmos crossover into both categories.]

Your First Digital Timer

Your finger can tell you a lot about when to water and for how long. Just stick it in the soil and see how far down the soil is moist. If you just had a manicure, you can try a trowel. The Lamborghini of "digital" soil testers is a core sampler. It'll cost you about $70 [See Figure 76.]

A Twist of the Wrist

Throughout this book, I've discussed and presented drip irrigation systems with manual

ACTUAL LENGTH = 21 IN.

Figure 76 A simple but very useful tool. Insert the probe, twist gently clockwise. Remove the plug to inspect the soil horizons.

valves: sometimes faucets, at other times ball valves. There are three very good reasons for using such valves: simplicity, simplicity, and simplicity. Manual valves are a solution that is not overly engineered and is inexpensive, easy to operate, and elegant in its own way.

Most people don't need any instructions to turn on a manual valve. But the trick to manual valves is remembering to turn them off. I should know. I once gave some of my plantings some very deep watering when I failed to shut off the zone before I left town for the weekend [actually horizontal, since there's a clay pan less than 18 inches from the surface]. I quickly bought a digital kitchen timer with a liquid crystal display [LCD] as found in kitchenware catalogs, department stores, and grocery stores. I set the timer to the length of irrigation based upon the season's ET rate mentioned earlier. At last I began to go digital in the electronic sense of the word.

Manual-On, Automatic-Off Timers

The next gentle step up in complexity involves those timers that you attach to the faucet and turn on the gizmo and it turns off the water supply. Such a device gets rid of one-half of the equation of irrigation glitches—short-term memory loss. Gone is the task of remembering to set the kitchen timer after you've turned on the system.

But are these devices reliable? Alas, certain models are not really fail-safe. There are two very different versions of these ticking, self-closing timers—the commercial grade and the home gardener model. There is one popular European model marketed through many hardware stores and mail-order catalogs that is known by its distinctive orange and gray colors—the brand is Gardena™. The gauge on the knob is calibrated in minutes and ranges from

five minutes to two hours. I know many people who have had good results with this timer. However, I also know of a large commercial garden project that had purchased several dozen timers. The gardeners found that at least 30% of the timers broke at some time. Even though the company was very courteous and prompt in replacing the defective units, the hassle and time required to switch the broken models with new ones was considerable. Unfortunately, this type of timer was prone at the large landscape and commercial gardens to break while on—leading to an undetected trickle of uncontrolled water. Such timers are sold for about $30.

The next step up in quality costs an additional $40. You can purchase a rugged, sturdy landscape timer with controllers included called the Bermadon Automatic Metering Valve™, sold by the Bermadon Company for about $80. [See Figure 77.] The valve comes in three models, each with a different minimum flow rate and capacity. The lowest-flow valve operates between 0 and 2000 gph, between 7 and 85 psi. and 0.5–9 gpm. The numbers on the knob are calibrated at 100 gallons per notch. To irrigate, you simply twist to the total number of gallons desired and relax—the timer does the rest,

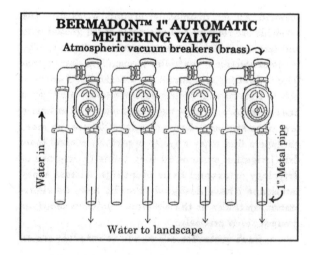

Figure 77 The Bermadon twist-and-set function helps keep the gardener in touch with how much water each zone needs. You must know the flow rate of each zone in gallons. Twist the knob in 100-gallon increments.

regardless of fluctuations in pressure. The mipt threads on both ends are one inch and must be stepped up and down to the more common 3/4-inch garden drip irrigation fittings.

Owen Dell of Santa Barbara, CA, one of the premier landscape designers in southern California, has long been dissatisfied with electronic controllers. Foremost, according to Dell, "The client doesn't grasp how to reprogram the controller and never adjusts the times from season to season. Plus, the controller is dumb—plants don't need water just because it's Tuesday and it's 6 A.M. Water need is a response to environmental factors, not just time." [More on how to avoid this problem later.] Dell is so impressed by the Bermadon controller that he has almost entirely given up on electronic digital timers, except for use in turf areas. He also favors the Bermadon because, in his words, "The homeowner maintains some active involvement with the landscape, can adjust the amount of water on a daily or weekly basis according to the weather, and can watch for any malfunctions or broken hoses." The assembly in Figure 77 shows a typical multistation setup as designed by Dell for his clients. **NOTE**: For sturdiness, all pipes to and from the controllers are made of galvanized metal.

Except for people who travel frequently, this system has a basic appeal. It is simple, sturdy, accessible, and easy to use. Plus, it keeps the gardener tuned in to the garden's watering needs.

Computerized, Digital Irrigation Timers

Another reason I favor manual timers and valves is that I hate digital appliances—especially automatic drip irrigation controllers. I have mastered my microwave oven, because my very survival is at stake, but don't ask me how to program a VCR. Luckily, DVD players have replaced VCRs and reduced my fear of digital appliances.

Yes, I have managed to learn to program several older makes of digital-readout automatic irrigation controllers, but I think the process was a living purgatory at best. I remind you of PMLP #12, and I quote: "Pop Murphy was temporarily diverted from plumbing devices with the start-up of the Star Wars defense program. But now that he has trained the Pentagon in all his best management techniques, he has returned to designing the all-digital, all-confusing, micro-chipped, controlling devices."

But new innovations in timers has all but relieved me of "digitalphobia".

Faucet-Mounted, Microchip Timers

Many gardeners first experiment with automatic electronic timers by purchasing one of the several models of stand-alone, battery-operated controllers that attach to the garden faucet. Some models use a 9VDC battery; others use AA batteries. In most cases, it's better to attach the controller to the faucet after both the atmospheric vacuum breaker and the filter and then the rest of the main assembly. Each timer is digitally controlled and must be programmed to turn the water on and off for a specific length of time, usually referred to as the "run" time. First, you set the current time on a clock, then you enter the day(s) and duration of irrigation into the microchip while viewing the LCD. A good example is the DIG™ hose-thread watering timer for single, four, or six zones, which costs about $100 depending on how many stations you want to irrigate. These DIG timers display the information on an LCD, but luckily use buttons to program the irrigation days and times.

NOTE: The DIG Model 7010 timers failed a study done in seven counties in New Mexico by a number of Master Gardeners as coordinated by the local County Extension agents. In the report they found "[that] it would not completely shut off." Be sure to research newer models. [The study was from 2001 to 2004.] As one reputable catalog [Drip Works] mentions "[we] will warranty DIG battery timers and valves for two years. DIG warranties them for one additional year, for a total of a three-year warranty. Valves are designed to operate correctly in the horizontal position. ALWAYS use a filter BEFORE these valves. Debris in the valve will void the warranty." So, the New Mexico study's problems may have been due to improper installation.

Various battery-powered controller models range in cost from $45 to $60.

There can be problems with some of these timers. First, although the language may be more readable than with many multistation controllers, while programming the device, one can feel "slow on the uptake" when trying to comprehend the owner's manual. Second, most of these controllers attach to one faucet and control only one zone. [DIG timers are an exception.] In other words, you can't irrigate hanging pots, which

require a very short daily run time, with the same controller used to water some fruit trees once a week for a long period of time. However, most models do allow you to program three different start times per day—which is also useful for short run times for sprinklers on a slope to avoid runoff. Finally, the reliability of these gizmos may not be as good as their visibility in mail-order catalogs or hardware stores would suggest. There are many new models on the market. Don't be bold and try out a new model without someone's recommendation. It is essential that you talk with other gardeners and get favorable testimonials about the model you're considering purchasing.

Although some models are designed to withstand freezing, the prudent gardener will protect his or her investment by bringing these timers indoors when fall's cold breath begins to nip at the blushing leaves.

Multistation, Truly "Digital" Timers

Fortunately, for LCD-impaired people like me, there are two styles of truly digital timers—meaning that you use your little digits to set the timer. Although I have achieved a measure of victory over the all-electronic, digital LCD timer, I've basically thrown in the towel and now demand an automatic timer that I can really get my hands on.

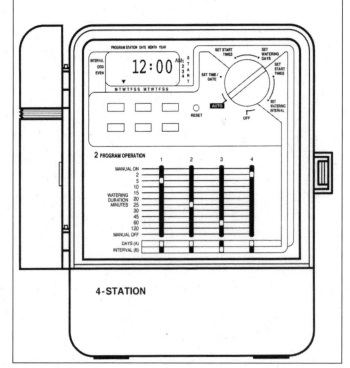

Figure 78 I like the easy-to-read settings for each zone. This model has sliding bars for four stations [zones]. They make 6-, 9-, and 12-station controllers.

Illustration used by permission of Orbit™ Irrigation Products.

One innovation is a modern electronic controller designed to actuate 24VAC valves but with sliding bars for each station. [See Figure 78.] The sliding bars on the Orbit® Irrigation Products Inc. timer are like those adjustable levers on fancy modern stereos, amplifiers, and radios by which the listener can fine-tune different frequencies of sound—often called graphic equalizers, even though no drawings are involved. The lever for each separate station is merely moved to the time indicated on the vertical axis. The irrigation settings on some of these clocks range from two minutes to two hours. [This may be a problem with a small number of containers and/or hanging pots.] This is my favorite style of controller because it's easy to see at a glance the setting for each station. Also, the length of irrigation can be reset almost effortlessly as frequently as the weather mandates. It does require digital programming for most functions, but you can easily adjust the time for each zone with slider bars. The web site [http://www.orbitirrigation.com/tutorials/6station.cfm] has a video that carefully explains how to initially program the timer. Although these units usually cost slightly more than the least expensive LCD controllers, the extra cost is quickly repaid in reduced aspirin consumption. The Orbit 62001 Digital Timer was selected when a Master Gardener and Cooperative Extension program in New Mexico studied four different timers from 2000 to 2004. Their experience was that this timer "was the most expensive timer but was also the most reliable. Not one of these timers failed over the three-year period." The cost is less than $100 for a six-station timer. They rated the readability of the manual at 3.8 with 4.0 being a perfect score—better than the Orbit 62015 and two other timers.

The second option is the Rain Bird® Company's new line of timers, which they describe as: "Simple-to-Program [STPi] timers are the easiest timers in the irrigation industry to program and operate. In fact, the STPi controller is so easy to operate you won't even need to read the instructions." And they're right. I got one from a big box store and found that pressing buttons does most of the work. You do have to use the LCD screen to set the date and time. A perfect match for the manifold controllers on the Orbit manifold system illustrated in Figure 81. These timers are the easiest non-Orbit indoor controller that comes in four, six, or nine zones. The most impressive newer feature to me is the "non-volatile memory," a fancy way to say no batteries are required to maintain the programming during power failures.

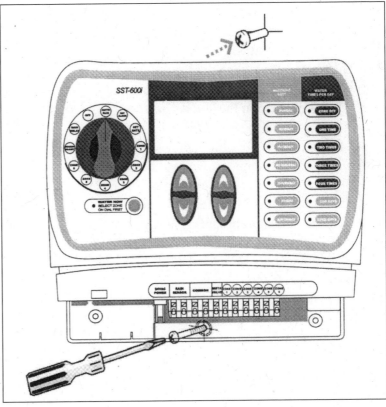

Figure 79 This Simple-to-Program timer [STPi] is very easy to program. You can look for it at your local big box stores. It has the convenient "non-volatile" memory. Costs around $70.

Illustration used by permission of Rain Bird Comppany.

Multistation Digital Timers

Now we can experience true gizmophobia. [See the Glossary in the Appendix.]

Foremost, choose the timer that is easiest for you to program. Simple programming is important in reducing your ulcer coefficient, in easily changing the duration of irrigation to reflect the seasonal changes in the ET rate, and in reprogramming if the power goes out and the electronic instructions are lost to the wind. Look for a timer with a non-volatile memory to avoid this problem altogether.

Multistation timers or controllers can turn on a number of different drip irrigation lines by activating a 24VAC solenoid valve controller. The least expensive models must be mounted indoors in a protected spot and near a 110VAC outlet. Wires can run as far as 1500 feet, depending on the wire's thickness or gauge, from the timer out to wherever the solenoid valves are located. Although the solenoid valves can be put anywhere in the landscape, most people cluster them together and place them as close to the timer as possible. This works fine with most home systems. However, check with the supplier or manufacturer about the friction loss for lengths greater than those found in the "Maximum Length of Tubing" chart in the Appendix. With supply pipes that reach beyond the limits in the chart, it would be better to have the solenoid located at the point of use in the landscape instead of the main assembly. [Add the wires underground in the trench you dug for laying the pipe.]

As with stand-alone timers, electronic multistation timers must first have the current time entered into the chip's memory. Once the correct time is displayed on the digital-readout panel, you will program the present day of the week, the length of irrigation, the days of the week for irrigation, and the number of start times per day.

Each computerized controller is rated as being able to control a specific number of "stations." Each station equals one solenoid valve. Usually, there is a strip across the bottom of the back of the timer where you screw down the station wire from each solenoid [valve]. All the common, or ground, wires from the solenoids are combined to one white-coded ground wire and screwed to the common terminal on the strip. The minimal electronic controller is usually a four-station "clock" [landscaping jargon for a timer], which is able to turn on and off four different solenoid-activated lines or stations. Always buy a timer with at least a few more stations than you expect to use, as most gardeners find more ways to accurately control their drip irrigation systems as they refine their grasp of dripology or expand their plantings.

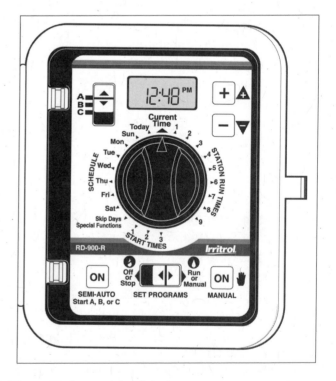

Figure 80 The Rain Dial® [by Irritrol] is the preference of some landscapers where I live. It represents a typical digital input with LCD screen timer.

Ilustration used by permission of Irritrol, Inc.

Almost every landscape I have designed takes at least an eight-station controller as the watering needs are zoned, or grouped, fairly precisely. Each timer allows you to schedule one or more "programs," those days when water comes on and the start and stop times for irrigation on those days. Less expensive timers may have only one option, or one program. Other inexpensive models have two separate programs but four or six stations. In the case of a six-station clock, the six different posts for the solenoid's station wires can be arbitrarily divided up between the two programs.

As an example, the timer used by Gary Miltenberger—who, for over 30 years has focused only on installing and repairing drip irrigation systems—is Irritrol's Rain Dial. The Rain Dial has three programs that can be divided among six stations. For example, Program A could run four lawn sprinkler systems every day for short periods, Program B may be set to irrigate for a very short period of time each day with potted plants, and Program C could be set to irrigate stations five and six for a long period of time, once a week. To encode the timer, you set the current time, enter the current day, choose the days you want the program to come on [from one to seven or by intervals, such as every third day], enter the length of the irrigation—the station or run time—and set the program's start time. Then all of the four solenoids [valves] wired to Program A come on in numerical sequence. With most, if not all, models, the timer cycles through each station during each program, one after another. Usually, the second station starts almost immediately after the first finishes; they can't overlap. For example, if lines one through four are set to start at 6 A.M. and run for 15 minutes each, they will stay on until 7:00 A.M.. The other two stations, Program C, can be set to start at 8 AM, run for two hours each, and shut off at noon. Make sure you don't overlap the start times, as a larger supply pipe may be required to service the simultaneous flow of all stations. With sequential start times, the supply pipe doesn't have to be as large since all of the stations won't be on at the same time. However, the valves are hydraulically controlled and need water pressure to close them. If more than one valve opens at a time, you need enough flow to close both. Otherwise, the valves will stick open. [Not a pretty picture.]

Some models allow each program to be set to start several or more times, with as many as 16 or more start times during the same day. This option is well-suited to short irrigation times with subsurface irrigation of lawns or misters in greenhouses but usually is not needed with drip irrigation. More advanced, and costly, timers allow each station to be programmed independently from all the other stations. This allows for the easiest and most specific programming, but at considerable expense: one eight-station version will set you back nearly $1,000.

The electronic timer can control the lines for a range of times. Some can be programmed for 1 to 99 minutes; others can be programmed for nearly six hours. Be sure you get a model which matches or exceeds the maximum run time you anticipate. Paying extra for a timer that has a longer run time will give you more flexibility and adaptability in the future. If you plan to irrigate container plants or hanging plants, double-check to make sure the clock can be set for times as short as one minute.

The Irritrol Jr. Max® timer has a program C that canbe used as a misting cycle. You can set the start time, end time, and run times in seconds and minutes apart. A four-station timer costs around $70.

Some timers are set up for a seven-day week. This makes programming awkward when planning to have the system come on every other day, because of the odd number of days in a week. Other timers allow a 14-day basis so you can easily set the program to alternate-day irrigation. Another option includes models that can be set independently of the days of the week to come on at any interval—every other day, every third day, every fourth day, etc.

In the "old days," if the power to the timer was shut off, the microchip with the program you've set lost its memory. Many controllers utilized a 9VDC alkaline or NiCad battery to supply enough current to maintain the memory until the power came back on. Most backup batteries preserve the programming for several days or more. If the power outage lasts any longer, the chip goes blank and you must reset the time and reprogram the irrigation cycle[s].

To me, the most impressive new feature in new timers is the "non-volatile memory," a fancy way to say no batteries are required to maintain the programming during power failures. Don't buy any timer that doesn't have the non-volatile memory feature. The Rain Dial utilizes a "non-volatile memory".

Virtually all timers have a manual override option. This allows you to turn on any station manually for extra spot irrigation or to inspect the lines. The difference from model to model is the ease with which you can start a manual cycle. Make sure the instructions for manual irrigation are printed inside the door of the timer or on the control panel.

When purchasing a digital controller, price should be the last consideration. Make sure you have the simplest-to-program model, not just the cheapest. To compare prices, divide the number of stations into the total cost. Sometimes it's less expensive to buy, for example, two quality six-station timers than a single, more costly, 12-station model.

In summary, before buying a digital irrigation timer, consider the following important points:

• What are the most popular timers in your area? Ask why? [One supply house recommends the Rain Dial timer. Another, 20 miles away, sells mostly the WeatherTRAK® ET to landscape contractors.]

• Is the handbook readable, or does it require a PhD in hieroglyphics?

• Are there enough stations to satisfy current and future irrigation needs?

• Can the clock be programmed for the longest anticipated irrigation run time?

• Can it be set to run for as short a time as you'll need for container plants?

• How many stations to each program?

• Is the programming on an odd- or even-day basis, or both?

• Finally, what is the cost per station?

Controlling the Flow of Water

The devices that actually let the irrigation water to pass are the controllers [aka valves]—usually 24-Volt Alternating Current [VAC] solenoids. A 24-VAC solenoid doesn't use only the AC power; it also relies on the pressure of the water. A tiny-diameter tube inside the valve utilizes the water pressure to assist in opening and closing the valve. This small diameter of the interior tube is prone to clogging, so many valves have an interior screen to protect the tubing. Still, a good filter upstream is a must. One of the workhorses of the irrigation valves for decades has been the 700 series of globe valves by Irritrol.

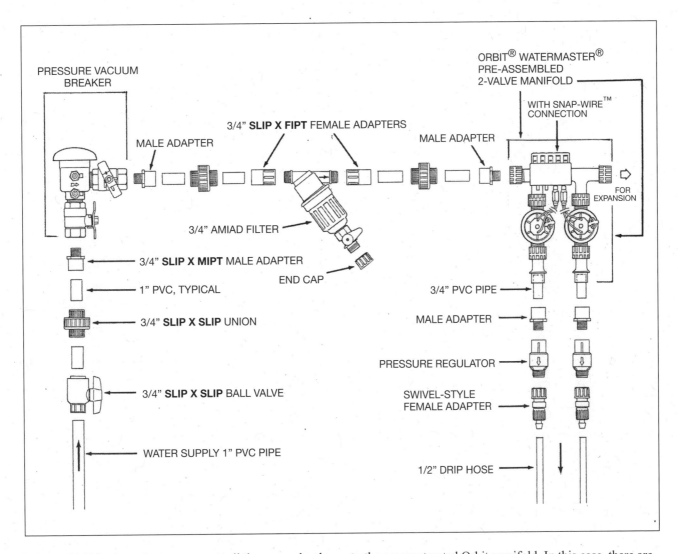

Figure 81 This shows how to connect all the proper hardware to the preconstructed Orbit manifold. In this case, there are two valves in the assembly in the upper right-hand side of the illustration. You can add in multiples of two or three by simply adding on to the outside fitting at the upper right in this illustration. The controller also features a quick snap-on wiring box located just above the manifold as seen here.

The Future of Controllers and Timers is Here and Coming

For the ambitious and financially endowed gardener, there are plenty more options for greater complexity, enhanced features, and a bigger dent in the budget. The following possibilities will remain dreams for most of us, things to consider in the future after our mastery of dripology has matured, and our lottery ticket

hits the big one. Some features available now and in the near future include those described below.

Periodic summer rains may temporarily negate the need for irrigation. Unfortunately, the clock on an automatic timer continues to tick. Normally, you'd have to remember to run out to the timer and throw the main switch from "automatic" to "rain" or "off." With a rain sensor wired to the timer, this troublesome task

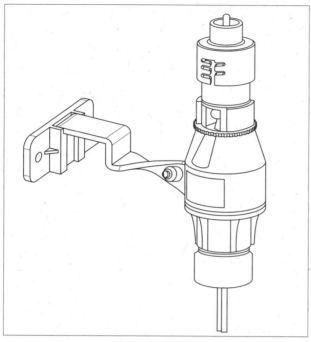

Figure 82 Where rains are sporadic during the irrigation season, a rain and freeze sensor is required.

Used with the permission of Orbit® Irrigation Products.

becomes automated. Since I live where the seasonal drought is continuous, I've never tried rain sensors. If you'll be needing one, be sure the controller you purchase has this capability. Much can go wrong with these widgets, so don't buy one without a referral. Ask friends, landscapers, and suppliers for their personal experience with specific models. The one pictured in Figure 82 is $18.

Soil water sensors, such as porous blocks or densitometers, can be buried at one or more depths in the soil to monitor the irrigation water's penetration and the soil's degree of moisture. A simple handheld gauge, costing $200 to $250, is connected to the porous block's [$5 to $6 each] wire leads where they come out of the ground, and the degree of soil moisture can be measured. Or, in the case of densitometers, a probe is buried to a specific level, and you visually read a calibrated meter. Densitometers cost between $35 and $70 for the standard agricultural models. These same soil water sensors can be used to prevent the automatic timer from irrigating an already wet soil. The sensor is wired to the timer so that the current can't pass to its corresponding solenoid if the soil is wetter than a predetermined level. When the soil dries more than the preset level, the automatic station current goes directly from the timer to the solenoid. To explore these options, contact Irrometer Company, at www.irrometer.com or write them at P.O. Box 2424, Riverside, CA 92516; or Soil Moisture Equipment Corporation, P.O. Box 30025, Santa Barbara, CA 93105 or www.soilmoisture.com.

Large estates may benefit from having the controller located outdoors, in the landscape itself. This provides straightforward access for reprogramming and direct observation when running each station using the manual mode. These weatherproof, metal-bodied housings always add to the cost of the controller—from as little as $15 extra for painted metal boxes to as much as $2000 for stainless steel pedestal models, which look like a preacher's pulpit. If the hassle of manually turning on a system and running across your yard to see the station come on and watch for leaks is too much, technology has the solution. At least one manufacturer sells an adapter for certain controllers which allows the use of a handheld remote control module. Much as with the remote controller for a VCR or television, you can stand just about anywhere [up to 300 feet] in the landscape and turn on any desired station. This time-saving feature will set you back $400-$500.

Since ET-based irrigation is the most accurate and efficient way to irrigate, why not adjust the irrigation time each day, as per the actual ET? You'll need a weather station, a PC computer, and some software. Since most ET data is based upon a few fairly scattered weather stations, chances are there isn't a facility near you. [Each state is different. In California, more than 60 weather stations provide computer modem transfer of data on a daily basis.] For the most accurate weather information for ET calculations, the fanatic gardener would need a personal weather station capable of recording temperature, wind speed, humidity and rainfall. Automatic weather stations with paper or digital recorders start at $350 and go as high as $1400. But to utilize this raw information, you'll need a computer and software to crunch the numbers into an ET-based recommendation. Unfortunately, the only programs available are geared toward agricultural applications—which means they're far more powerful and costly than is appropriate for the residential landscape. Prices for PC-based software start at $500.

Then there were the computer-controlled, ET-based drip irrigation systems in which weather data from satellites was automatically converted to adjust the duration of irrigation up or down. Such a robotic system was designed only for the landscape and golf course industries and originally came with a price tag of $5000 or more—until recently.

Weather-Based Controllers

With advances in computer technology, the price for a satellite-based automatic ET-based has brought the price for home landscape down to $400 or less as an add-on unit for some existing timers, such as the ET System by Hunter Irrigation added to an existing Hunter Smart-Port® controller.

The City of Santa Monica is one of the most proactive cities when it comes to irrigation water conservation. They require any plant from a one-gallon container or bigger to be irrigated solely by drip irrigation. [They also limit lawns in new homes to 20% or less of the property.] They are one of the municipal pioneers that require Weather Based Irrigation Controllers [WBIC].

WBICs are rapidly carving away at the cost of such controllers while, at the same time,

adding more refinements for precision irrigation based on your yard—not even relying on a governmental weather stations such as the 60 widely scattered weather stations with daily reporting capability and managed, for example, by the state of California.

The irrigation industry's organization for the country is, simply put, the Irrigation Association. They have developed standards for testing irrigation controllers and timers called Smart controllers. Smart irrigation controllers are defined by the Irrigation Association as "… controllers [that] estimate or measure depletion of available plant soil moisture in order to operate an irrigation system, replenishing water as needed while minimizing excess water use. A properly programmed smart controller requires initial site specific set-up and will make irrigation schedule adjustments, including run times and required cycles, throughout the irrigation season without human intervention."

Such controllers help deal with the fact that 30%–300% of irrigation water is wasted in residential landscapes. [Outdoor watering uses up to 60% of the total household water usage.] Not all Smart controllers are the same. Some are much more efficient than others. Through independent testing the Irrigation Association has come up with a higher standard. The official standard of excellence uses what is called a SWAT controller—Smart Water Application Technologies™. Not all WIBCs pass the test. The list below shows some of the WBICs that have passed the SWAT test.

Manufacturer	Model
Alex-Tronix	Enercon Plus 4-24
Alex-Tronix	Smart Clock SMC6
Aqua Conserve	Aqua ET-9
Calsense	ET2000e
Cyber-Rain	XCI System
ET water Systems	ETwater Smart
Controller Residental	

Hunter Industries	ET System
Hydrosaver,	ETIC
Irritrol	Smart Dial [Not a Rain Dial as mentioned earlier.]
Rain Bird	ET Manager
Rain Master	RME Eagle
SMG Superior Controls	Sterling 8
Toro	Intelli-Sense
Weathermatic	SL 1600
Hydropoint	WeatherTRAK ET

Santa Monica requires a WIBC on all new landscape installations. The debate is which of the more than 15 WIBCs on the market does the best job. For advice I turned to Bob Galbreath of Garden Technology, Inc. He was formerly the Water Resources Specialist, for the Office of Sustainability and the Environment for the city of Santa Monica for five years.

Galbreath's favorite SWAT-tested controller is the ET System by Hunter® Irrigation. In his words: "I like the fact that I can see what any given controller has done for the last 30 days [including adjustments for rainfall] from any internet-connected PC. ET System is the only one that has this capability in a residential model. ET System controllers communicate with 'headquarters' via toll-free telephone call. If my controller doesn't call in or someone alters the program or suspends operation of the timer, I get an e-mail alert. Having said all that, it is a $400+ timer. All the WBICs are better than a conventional timer from a water-saving standpoint. So everybody should have one. Hunter's new Solar Sync retails for about $140." As described by Hunter: "The Solar Sync® continually gathers on-site solar and temperature data used in the calculation of evapotranspiration [ET], then determines watering requirements." It's like having a simple weather station in your backyard to measure the irrigation water very precisely. The sensor must be within 200 feet of the controller.

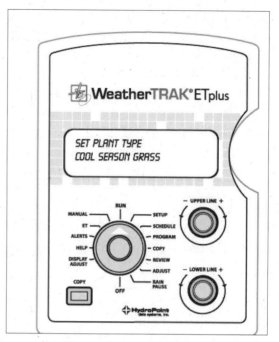

Figure 83 According to the product information— "Weather TRAK® ET Plus reliably delivers sustained savings and optimal plant health by eliminating overwatering. With its unique combination of precise irrigation scheduling, daily, [and] local ET updates." Real-world savings have ranged from 33–59%. A local store for the "trade" sells mostly this controller. The timer is sold for 9–24 stations.

Illustration used by permission of HydroPoint Data Systems.

Another in "distant second" is, in Galbreath's experience, a WBIC called the WeatherTRAK ET Plus from HydroPoint Systems, Petaluma, CA. As with the Hunter ET System, these WIBC are actually more like a controller than a timer. You can adjust your irrigation from anywhere in the world via an Internet connection using either a PC or a MacIntosh computer. It has a chip inside the controllers that runs the scheduling as entered, downloads weather from a satellite "feed," and can be adjusted to 11 types of plants—such as native shrubs, lawns, etc. The monthly cost for the Internet connection is $48 per year after the first year. A six-station model will cost you about $400.

Until George Lucas has his people at Industrial Light and Magic turn to irrigation systems programmed by three-dimensional, virtual reality animated software that allows you to merely voice your commands, we'll just have to make do with the above list. In the interim, there are plenty of gizmos and widgets to satisfy every gardener.

New Vistas in Drip Tubing, Perhaps

Out of Israel, where most drip parts were originally designed, comes an exciting new development—"Ultra Low Drip Irrigation" [ULDI].

ULDI uses emitters with very low distribution rates compared to our current 1/2-gph emitters [really 0.4 gph or 0.6 gph, depending on the manufacturer.] ULDI uses only about 0.2 liters per hour, an amazing 0.05-gph emitter. All these contribute to great system cost savings because you can run far more tubing per valve. This also cuts down on the cost of main assemblies in large applications, reduces the number of subsystems, and reduces the cost of pumping. The three main drawbacks are that it is not yet available to home gardeners, it's only been used in soilless greenhouse applications, and you can only use it in straight rows.

Like the history of in-line emitter tubing, which started out as a product only for commercial farmers, ULDI tubing may become available to gardeners sometime in the not-too-distant [I hope] future.

UniRam

Another agricultural in-line drip irrigation tubing that is in the wings and may also make it into the gardener's yard, it is Netafim's UniRam. This is a heavy-gauge tubing with in-line emitters that have been "developed for extremely poor water quality and rolling terrain."

Sounds like a candidate for grey water applications. We'll see.

NETAFIM UNIRAM	12" centers	45 psi	0.6 gph	███████████████		387'	
18mm, 700 series, blue ring	18" centers	45 psi	0.6 gph	██████████████████████			548'
				200'	300'	400'	500'	600'

CHAPTER 12

Keep Your Drip Together

All your investment in time, sweat, profanity, and money will be for nothing if you don't perform a little routine maintenance on your new drip irrigation system. Unlike a regular garden hose, drip irrigation requires some periodic attention. This slight extra effort will be repaid many times over.

Flush Your Troubles Away

The first three rules of drip maintenance are flush, flush, and flush. As mentioned earlier, the drip irrigation hose should be flushed when it's first laid out in the garden, again after any emitters or smaller-diameter tubing are punched into the 1/2-inch hosing. and before the ends of each line are capped. [This is if you don't heed my recommendation of using in-line emitter tubing.] Once your drip irrigation is installed, the more you open the ends of the lines and flush the 1/2-inch hosing, the safer you'll be from conjuring up some new Pop Murphy's Law of Plumbing. Each line in the system should be flushed at the beginning of every growing season and at least once during the season.

At one time, I thought dripology researchers had licked this problem of renegade filth and was led to experiment with a gizmo called a "flushing line valve." The concept sounded great. Each time the system was turned on, the lines would run the water for several minutes before the bladder sealed shut.

Even with a quality Y-filter, some sediment and crud may slip through the line flushing valve would remain open for a short period of time to allow some water, and its sedimental contraband, to escape. As the pressure in the line built up, over a minute or two, the line flushing valve's bladder would shut off and the emitters could get to work irrigating the landscape. In the real world, things went awry. First, the little springs didn't always do their job and the flushing end caps kept flushing the entire time the system was on. Second, people with well water (unchlorinated) occasionally found bits of

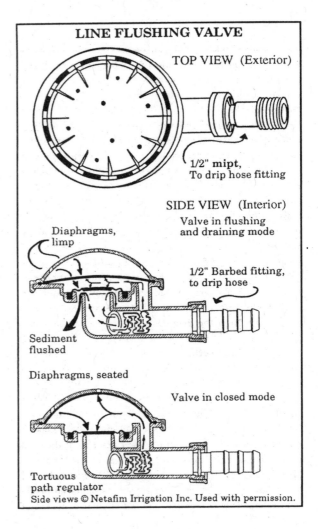

Figure 84 The line flushing valve purges sediment, insects, and other contaiminates out each time the water is turned on. Install it with the dome facing up over a small gravel sump.

slime clogging the end cap and preventing proper sealing under pressure. And finally, an open end cap was an open invitation to slugs, earwigs, and pill bugs to set up house. These pesty critters can cause far more havoc than any amount of sediment suspended in the water. So my flushing end caps are safely stored in the box marked "Sounded Like a Great Idea, but Doesn't Work." Another "great" idea bites the dust.

Fortunately, dripology researchers continued to experiment with and redesign flushing end caps. One newer model which looks very promising is called a line flushing valve. [See Figure 84.] This particular automatic flushing device utilizes, in part, the same tortuous path technology used with in-line emitter tubing. The tortuous path helps keep insects out. When the system turns on, any sediment or insects are flushed out. Before the drip system is turned on, a diaphragm covering the valve is limp [open]. Each time the drip system is turned on, about a gallon or more of water is allowed to pass through the valve's tortuous path, then the diaphragm inflates [fills] to close the small ports used to allow for the flushing of accumulated sediment.

After the drip system is turned off, the line flushing valve allows water to drain out of the lines, again removing any wayward sediment. The lack of standing water in the lines helps to prevent the buildup of algae scums and iron-water bacterial slimes—both of which can clog emitters, especially with unchlorinated well water. The line flushing valve is best placed inside a purchased or homemade valve box over a large pocket of 3/4- to 1-inch round river rock. [Not crushed and washed gravel, as it will settle and fill up the "pore" space.] If you use the version with the 1/2-inch mipt fitting, add a fipt fitting to the end so the line flushing valve can be easily removed for a more lengthy manual flushing.

A Filthy Filter Is a Terrible Waste

A properly designed drip irrigation filter insures clog-free emitters and adequate flow for even distribution of water. The Y-valve with a ball valve, as recommended earlier, makes it easy

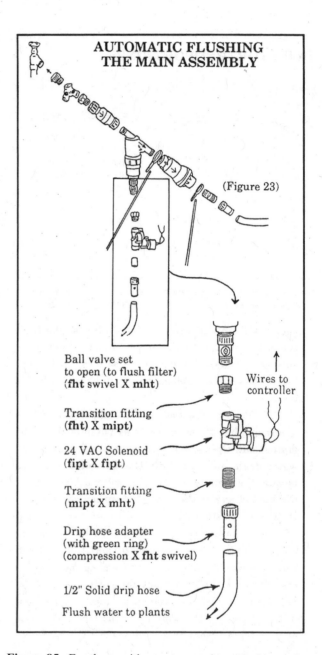

AUTOMATIC FLUSHING
THE MAIN ASSEMBLY

(Figure 23)

Ball valve set
to open (to flush filter)
(fht swivel X mht)

Wires to
controller

Transition fitting
(fht) X mipt)

24 VAC Solenoid
(fipt X fipt)

Transition fitting
(mipt X mht)

Drip hose adapter
(with green ring)
(compression X fht swivel)

1/2" Solid drip hose

Flush water to plants

Figure 85. For those with poor memories or lacking calendar scheduling [garden tracking impaired], an automatic flush helps some during the growing season. It still does not replace a thorough scrubbing with a toothbrush and bleach.

to flush the filter cartridge regularly. You should flush each Y-filter at least once a month to prevent laser tubing or porous tubing from getting blocked with sand, silt, or sediment. The filter may stop all the filth, but if it is left uncleaned, the flow of water to your emitters is greatly reduced. Gardeners with well water may find even a weekly flushing is required.

If you install an electronic irrigation clock to control 24VAC solenoid valves, there is a sneaky way to flush your filter automatically. At the end of the filter's flush ball valve, install an irrigation solenoid. [See Figure 85.] Leave the filter's flushing ball valve in the open position. Wire the solenoid to your electronic irrigation timer, but to a separate "program" from the irrigation zones so as to automatically flush the filter of everything off the metal screen, except algae and other unrecognizable slimy stuff. So, at the beginning of every irrigation season and at least once each summer, take the Y-filter apart, remove the metal screen cylinder and scrub well

with an old toothbrush and a strong solution of bleach. Then you can set the controller to turn on that program once a week for one or two minutes to flush the filter automatically. No matter how much you flush your Y-filter, the water streaming by will still have the possibility to clog emitters other than in-line tubing.

Give Your System Some Acid

Despite all these precautions and tidy compulsions, some buildup may occur on the emitters. This is especially true where the water supply is high in minerals, such as soluble iron or calcium. Most filters can't clean these soluble minerals out of the water while they are in solution. As the minerals tumble along the dark labyrinth of your drip system, the agitation and contact with oxygen will precipitate some of them—especially iron—into solids. These particles can build up on the interior surfaces of the emitter, as in hardening of the arteries. Sometimes the soluble minerals don't get enough

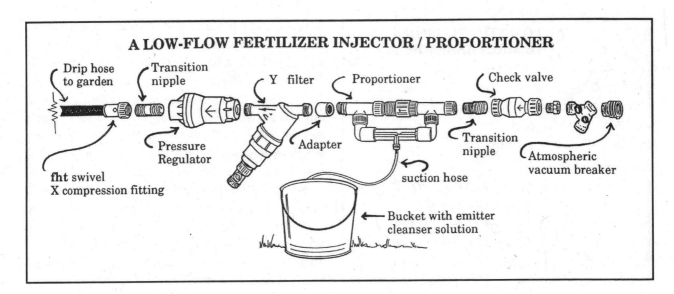

Figure 86 A Mazzei™ injector works only with large drip systems as the minimum flow rate for a 3/4-inch model is 126 gph up to 610 gph. If you don't want to fertilize every time you irrigate, plumb a shut-off vave in the suction hose. Expect to pay nearly $100. An Add-It Fertilizer Injector™, not pictured here, holds one pint and works at a minimum flow of 30 gph. It will be empty after 35 gallons have passed through the system at a 280:1 ratio. It's around $25.

exposure to air to precipitate until they reach the opening of the emitter, in which case you'll see a buildup of minerals around the orifice of each emitter.

In either case there is, so to speak, a solution. Once a year, or as needed, you can dissolve mineral buildup by pumping a dilute solution of acid through your drip irrigation system. Sounds gruesome, but it's not too difficult or risky. First, you'll need to plumb into your system a special gizmo called an injector, or proportioner. This device draws [suctions] a concentrated solution from a pail or bucket while the drip system is running a low-volume type of injector/proportioner. These are available from a number of the mail-order companies in the Suppliers and Resources listing in the Appendix. Be sure to use a low-volume proportioner. [This device can also be used, with thorough filtering, to inject a dilution of liquid fertilizer into the drip system for automatic feeding.]

You must purchase the proper proportioner, one that requires enough low-flow to suction the concentrated solution from the bucket . The inexpensive proportioners sold at many hardware stores are designed to function with the flow of a regular garden hose and oscillating sprinkler [five gpm] and will not work at the low flow rates of a typical drip irrigation system. Each proportioner requires a minimum flow rate to begin the suction of liquid concentrate into the system. Check the box or instructions to make sure the proportioner will operate at the flow rate, in gpm or gph, of your drip system. Also check for operating pressure, some units need to have a pressure regulator to protect the drip system's fittings.

For example, one model of a proportioner called the Dosatron™ works at a flow rate between 0.02 and 3.00 gpm [1.20 gph and

180 gph, respectively, while another Dosatron model functions between 5.40 and 420 gph [respectively]. A Mazzei injector works only with large drip systems as the minimum flow rate for a 3/4-inch model is 126 gph up to 610 gph. [See Figure 86.] The EZ-FLO Fertilizing System™, functions at as little as 2.5 gph flow at only 5 PSI water pressure.

Total up the number of emitters in your system and divide by the flow rate to get

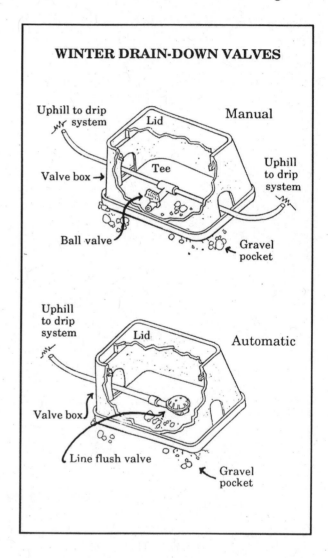

Figure 87 Two ways to drain the tubing for the winter. The ball valve is the easiest to use and guarantees a full drainage. Or, remove the line flush valve to drain all the water out. Then thread it back on the drip hose adapter. Each spring, check for insects that may have moved in over the winter.

the flow in gph. For example, a series of lines of in-line tubing with 1/2-gph emitters every 12 inches totals 224 feet. This equals 224 emitters times 1/2 gph, or 112 gph. Thus, both Dosatrons would work properly but not the Mazzei . But if you had a series of hanging plants with a total of fifteen 1/2-gph emitters, for a flow of 7.50 gph, both Dosatrons would barely be able to function. But the EZ-FLO is well within the range of flow.

The proportioner must be plumbed in between the backflow preventer(s) and the filter and pressure regulator. [See Figure 86.] Placing the proportioner before the filter [upstream] allows the filter's screen to catch any wayward dirt, sediment or undissolved chemicals or fertilizers. The fittings required to plumb the proportioner into the main assembly will vary with the model.

To begin, wear a long-sleeve shirt and pants. Use acid-resistant gloves and protective eye goggles. Pour the acid solution into the water, not water into the acid, to avoid splashing. To flush your drip system, you simply mix up a solution of any one of the emitter cleaners on the market, pour the solution into the bucket and turn on the drip system. Follow the manufacturer's instructions for both the dilution rate and the length of flushing. This is best done during the dormant season or during a heavy rain to mitigate the effect of the acids on the soil. Commercial orchardists in the Central Valley of California have been routinely flushing their drip systems for years with no deleterious effects.

One emitter-cleansing product, Drip-A-Tron Cleaner™, purportedly cleans and lubricates the drip irrigation system with a solution of 5% hydrochloric acid, 10% phosphoric acid and 2% copper sulfate, among other chemicals. Obviously this material doesn't qualify for use on a certified organic farm because the chemicals are processed with fossil fuels. For all but the certified organic farmers, these chemicals are represented by the manufacturer

as biodegradable and nonpolluting. The manufacturer says "[It] clean[s] plugged emitters of all mineral deposits carried by water and intermittent use allowing water to flow freely throughout the system for the season."

Winterize Your Drip System

A proper drip irrigation system is too valuable to leave neglected like an abandoned garden hose at each winter's nippy return. Shut off your system's water supply at a point inside the house where the water supply is protected from freezing. Loosen all unions at each main assembly to drain all water out of the pipes, filters, pressure regulators, and check valves. Make sure you don't loose the O-ring which seals each union. Be sure to open the flush ball valve on the Y-filter so the filter chamber doesn't crack. Better yet, bring the filter or the entire main assembly indoors. Also bring inside any battery-powered controllers which you have attached to faucets.

The drip irrigation hose can stay in place in the landscape, but as much water as possible should be drained out. Open the end-closures on all lines, let all water drain out, and close. Start at the highest elevation and work downhill. Use threaded end caps because the Figure 8 end closures will quickly wear out the kinked end of the hose. It's essential that the water is drained from every low point of the system.

A deep mulch will help protect in cold winter climates. You don't want anyone stepping on cold plastic tubing, but since many drip systems are primarily located in perennial plantings, the risk of trampling the tubing is low. Some compulsive people do lift out the entire assembly of header and lateral lines, roll up the tubing and store it in the garage for the winter. Porous pipe and in-line emitter tubing make this a lot easier than hose with emitters punched in or hose with,

God forbid, spaghetti tubing with emitters. If possible, lay out your drip irrigation lines so they can all be drained from the low ends. Otherwise, install your drip lines so they naturally drain to various low spots, install an access box at the lowest spot in each line of the system for the winter. Install a manual drain-down valve a simple ball valve. Each fall, the metal drip irrigation ball valve should be opened to fully drain the line.

Lonnie Zamora, a former rooftop-gardener and irrigation designer in New York City, used in-line emitter tubing for over four years on most of his jobs, even in the flower boxes for a penthouse on the 27th floor of a Manhattan apartment building. To winterize his client's drip irrigation systems each fall, he would:

- Drain the pressure regulator.

- Close the faucet at the home's wall.

- Attach a 110VAC air compressor with the necessary fittings to the fht at the beginning of the drip system.

- Set the timer to run each line or zone for five to seven minutes.

- Run the air compressor pumps at 25–40 psi to blow out all the lines.

- Manually drain all lines on multilevel, terraced gardens.

- Open the Y-filter's ball valve to drain the filter cartridge chamber.

Tidy Tips for Your Drip System

Every piece of rigid PVC pipe which shows aboveground should have been painted with a quality exterior latex paint right after installation to protect the pipe from the degrading effects of sunlight. If you haven't done this, do it! Occasionally, some of the paint may flake off the pipe. Repaint as needed. Besides protecting the pipe, you'll help disguise it. Choose a color which matches your house paint or an earthy brown which blends into the background better than green.

Keeping Your Drip Stuff Together

No matter how much time you spent planning and installing your system, it will need some attention. Some boxes used for other "stuff" will handily manage your drip parts.

I got this idea from Sidney Ocean, when she was the head landscape gardener at the Esalen Institute in Big Sur, CA. She has all her small miscellaneous drip irrigation parts neatly arranged in a sewing box. The box, like some fishing tackle boxes, has lots of small divided chambers and a clear lid so you can see what is stored in your drip irrigation system repair kit, because you'll think of new ways to improve and change it, or there'll be the occasional repair. For

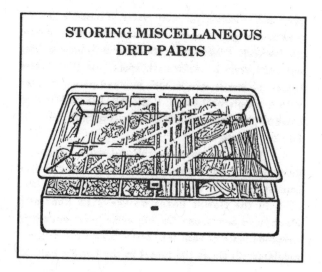

STORING MISCELLANEOUS DRIP PARTS

Figure 88 A simple and elegant way to store all the left over parts. Or, have a small battalion of parts to readily fix any drip system meltdown.

such occasions, the drip irrigation emergency
repair kit comes in handy. [See Figure 88.] This
is where goof plugs, various single emitters,
transfer barbs, mister heads, and hose punches
can all be neatly stored and easily located
when repairing or improving your container
and hanging plant drip systems. Include some
compression couplings to repair the occasional
split with in-line emitter tubing.

No longer will you have to rummage among
various paper bags or coffee cans to find the
parts you want to schlep out into the landscape—
only to find, once you start, that PMLP #1 has
insured you're missing a part.

Cut here to have the PMLP availble to refer to as you read the book. It'll make the book more fun to read.

The Offical List of Pop Murphy's Laws of [PMLP]

Numero Uno—No matter how small the job, you will be missing one part—but only when the hardware store is closed.

#2. The thought, "Just one more twist," instantly produces a cracked pipe or leaky thread.

#3. Whenever a job calls for two pipe wrenches, only one is to be found.

#4. Leaks will always wait for the most inopportune times—like just after you've put on your tux.

#5. When you drop a threaded metal pipe, the pipe always manages to turn around in midair and land directly on the threads—damaging them beyond use.

#6. With any part that has an arrow clearly marking the direction of the flow of water, you will install it backwards at least once.

#7. Even though you know PVC glue is toxic and should not touch skin, you will decide to "skip the gloves just this once and be extra careful." Before you finish the word "careful," a dribble of glue will already be drying on your ungloved hand.

#8. Pipe dope is the only correctly named plumbing part.

#9. When a plastic pipe breaks, it will always break where the threads meet an expensive fitting so that the fitting is rendered useless.

#10. Pipes are just the *Titanic* and water turned inside out. [Think about it!]

#11. Be forewarned: Pop Murphy is, at this very moment, perfecting a gopher capable of gnawing through plastic PVC pipe; metal-chewing gophers will take a bit longer.

#12. Pop Murphy was temporarily diverted from plumbing devices with consulting on the start-up of numerous wars. But now that he has trained the Pentagon in all his best management techniques, he has returned to designing the all-digital, all-confusing, microchipped, maxi-priced irrigation-controlling devices.

❧ APPENDIX #2 ❧

Subsurface Drip Irrigation [SDI]—Putting it all Together

During geopolitical upheavals, going "underground" can be an important means of survival. Subsurface drip irrigation [SDI] is primed to take its place in the upcoming geopolitical issue of water rights and distribution, and will no doubt have more and more influence on how we water our lawns, shrubs, trees, or plantings in narrow spots. The future is subterranean. Out of sight!

Start With a Main Assembly

SDI can start at the faucet or any other plumbed connection to the water supply as seen in Figure 88.

There are three main producers of in-line drip irrigation tubing in the USA. They are all in California but market to distributors all over the country. They are: Geoflow™, which features Treflan-impregnated emitters [more on this later], Agrifim™, and Netafim™. Both have pressure- and non-pressure-compensating emitters. Use the pressure-compensating ones if your total elevation change, both up and down, is greater than five feet or if you want to make sure your garden or lawn gets reliable, even distribution of water. I always use the pressure-compensating emitter tubing.

The single most important aspect of this type of watering system is the proper placement of the in-line drip tubing. Consistent irrigation of the entire root system is a must to ensure even, healthy turf or perennial plant growth and to prevent roots from invading the buried emitters. Two important horizontal criteria are the distance between emitters along the tubing and the measurement between the laterals [lengths of tubing]. Usually, these two distances are the same. Generalized spacing guidelines vary considerably, depending on the tubing manufacturer or designer. For example, Geoflow recommends equal lateral and emitter spacings, with a 12- to 18-inch spacing in sandy soils, 18-inch intervals in clayey soils, and 24 inches for clay-loams. The apparent anomaly of the narrower interval for clayey soils is due to the inherent mechanical resistance of clay to horizontal water movement. In clay soils, the lines and emitters must be closer so that not too much water is lost downwards to gravity beneath the root zone before the water begins to bulge sideways.

At the Center for Irrigation Technology at the California State University at Fresno, Field Research Manager Greg Jorgensen has installed Geoflow non-compensating 1/2-gph tubing on an 18-inch-lateral-distance-by-15-inch-emitter-interval on one acre of the University's high-traffic lawn. [Geoflow no longer makes the 15-inch interval tubing but sells it with 12-, 18- and 24-inch emitter intervals.]

Netafim's recommendations are 18-by-18-inch emitter spacings in clay, 12-by-18-inch spacing in loam, and 12-by-12-inch intervals in sand. Dennis Hansen, a landscape architect located in Sausalito, CA, has accumulated over 30 years' experience with subsurface irrigation. He generally keeps his line and emitter spacings at 18 inches for lawns.

The Tubing Layout

Since the soil texture ultimately determines these important measurements, you'll have to test your soil in various areas. To do so:

• Lay out some in-line emitter tubing next to the tubing in an area that seems to represent your yard's typical soil, connect it to a water source, and run water through it for a half-hour.

• Dig a shallow trench to see how deep and wide some of the wet spots have spread beneath each of several emitters.

• Run the water for another half-hour.

• Repeat digging the trench to follow the range of the wet spots. Shave away at the sides of the trench to see how wide the moist spot is getting.

This will give you an idea of the appropriate interval along the length of the tubing needed for emitters to maintain efficient irrigation, that is [as mentioned above], to create bulbous underground moist spots that converge beneath the surface of the soil.

Tubing Depth

This is a project for a new lawn and can't be done with existing residential lawns. For lawns, the depth at which the emitter tubing is placed is a very important factor. Regardless of the choice of spacing between emitters, the tubing in the best lawn drip systems is laid out at a level six to ten inches below the soil surface. According to Geoflow, a 6-inch depth is best for lawns, shrubs, and trees in home landscapes. Dennis Hansen has found that four inches deep—plus or minus one inch—is best. **NOTE**: If you use a lawn aerator, be sure to set the tubing below the level of the aerator's piercing spikes.

Not for Gophers!

If your garden is plagued by gophers, do not use buried irrigation as the pesty rodents will just chew through the tubing to get a free drink of water. However, in the over 20 years I've placed the tubing on the soil's surface and then heavily mulched the area, gophers have not eaten any of my tubing—cross my fingers! At the Center for Irrigation Technology, tubing was buried five inches deep [+/-] and suffered no gopher damage. BUT, when they installed the SDI 16–18 inches deep in a new vineyard where alfalfa had been grown, they "had significant damage." Also, if squirrels live in your neighborhood, you might want to try a small test plot to see if they dig down to chew on the tubing.

The Air Vacuum Relief Valve

According to the manufactures, once your tubing is in place there are two more very important gizmos to assist the emitters in remaining unclogged. An air vacuum relief valve is a must for a successful subsurface drip system. [See Figure 88.] This simple and inexpensive part is placed at the highest point of the tubing in each zone [also called a subassembly] attached to one valve. When the water comes on, the pressure quickly shuts this valve—it acts much like a check valve. An air vacuum relief valve must be placed at every high point in an undulating or bermed landscape [a berm is a bank of earth often used as a retaining wall or hilly landscape feature]. On the other hand, in talking with Dennis Hansen, he finds no need for this component as long as the system is on level ground and there's a flushing mechanism at the end of each subassembly. "The designers of air release valves," he cautions, "have not figured out how to keep out earwigs and other insects, which can clog the device." He notes that a new in-line product from Netafim has anti-backflow emitters built into the tubing, and is well adapted to slopes.

The importance of the air vacuum relief valve becomes evident when the system shuts off; as the pressure drops, the valve opens and air rushes into the tubing, helping to dry it out while also relieving the pressure on water draining out at the end of the line. The drier the inside of the tubing is between irrigations, the harder it is for searching root hairs to find a way inside, and the bloom of emitter-clogging algae is also reduced. The air vacuum relief valve should be 6–12 inches higher than the tubing, or at least 6 inches above the soil surface, whichever is higher. For its protection, this valve is usually placed inside a standard circular valve box.

Or, use a line flushing valve [as seen in Figure 88, page 145] at the lowest point of the system. This gizmo is also prone to failure due to insects and other critters. Check both the air vacuum relief valve and the line flushing valve often for "bugs" clogging the valve[s].

Winterize

In really cold climates, it's safer at the end of the growing season to flush the above ground main assembly, drain it, and store it in the garage or basement. Remove the line-flushing cap and drain the drip hosing. There are also fittings available that allow small air compressors to purge the drip hose before winter. Or, simply open the valve at the lowest point of the system to drain out any remaining water. [This same valve is used to flush the lines in the spring and as needed through the growing season.]

How Much Water?

It's nice to know, according to literature provided by Toro Company [the manufacturer and distributor of lawn mowers, lawn equipment, and irrigation products] that SDI systems make a "46% larger wetted volume of soil than a surface drip system. This decreases the saturation point of the soil, which not only leaves room for more air…[but] decreases the water lost to deep percolation."

Use the chart entitled *Daily Water Use* in Figure 35 on page 52. This converts the monthly ET rate from inches-per-month into gallons-per-day for one-square foot of lawn or garden space up to one full acre.

Timing is Everything

Subsurface lawn systems require short, frequent daily irrigations. One irrigation cycle per day is the minimum interval at the Center for Irrigation Technology, but multiple start times are preferred. Landscaper Dennis Hansen suggests "unlimited *very* brief start times, actually up to 40 times per day, run by a controller with independent stations [programs] to have control over separate zones."

Geoflow recommends a single daily watering, but because it's impregnated with a substance they call Rootguard [the chemical Treflan], every-other-day irrigations will work, with no root intrusion.

The duration of each application is calculated by dividing by the number of start times per day into the total length of irrigation needed each day. The length of each of Hansen's irrigation cycles, however, is based upon achieving "no dry zones beneath the surface; I run the drip system until there is a solid, thin blanket of water across the surface." No long run times are required because the feeding root hairs of lawns, trees, and shrubs occupy only the upper 12 to 24 inches of soil.

Treflan, *Not* for Organic Gardeners

Treflan is a relatively benign, but by no means "organic," chemical that's been around for 30-plus years and acts as a growth inhibitor by arresting cell division [it stops the apical root bud from dividing]. Applied in a granular form, Treflan can control the sprouting of annual seeds. According to DowElanco, Treflan doesn't dissolve in water and doesn't leach into the soil because it adheres to the clay.

In-Line Drip Hose Resources

You may have to look around for a supplier of in-line tubing. Check in the Yellow Pages under Irrigation Systems and Equipment. Or, contact the following manufacturers:

Nano-ROOTGUARD® [pressure compensating emitters, with Treflan] is distributed to the trade by: Geoflow, 506 Tamal Plaza, Corte Madera, CA 94925 800-828–3388 or 415-927–6000. [http://www.geoflow.com] Call or go to their web site to find out about a distributor and contractor[s] in your area if you are too nervous about doing it yourself. There is a PDF about design, installation, and maintenance

Toro Company [http://www.toroag.com] sells their pressure-compensating in-line tubing with Rootguard [Treflan] to landscapers as "DL2000". [However, the city of Santa Monica will not approve the use of this product for contractors.] Toro also makes a tubing called Drip In® Classic [with Rootguard, Treflan], which is marketed

to farmers but will work for homeowners. Toro Company doesn't offer tubing with a 12-inch emitter spacing, only 18 inches and up. You can get a detailed design "manual" for SDI by going to http://www.toroag.com and print the PDF file.

Check first your local irrigation suppliers for Netafim and Agrifim products.

The Natural Gardening Company is a mail-order source for [Internet only] Techline 12" spacing with 1/2-gpm emitters. [See other suppliers in the Appendix.]

Studies by the Center for Irrigation Technology confirm the effectiveness of the root-excluding properties of Geoflow's emitters embedded with Treflan®. According to CIT Field Research Manager Greg Jorgensen, "In 1990, after three years of use with tall fescue grass, there was a root-free sphere the size of a golf ball around each emitter." Later studies found large, malformed roots alongside the emitter, but no intrusion. All this would seem to indicate that the Treflan does, in fact, dissolve a bit. It does not, however, translocate into plant stems, leaves, fruits, or flowers.

The compound has a low LD_{50} (a controversial way to rank chemical toxicity) of 10,000 mg/kg—the smaller the number, the more toxic the compound; the LD_{50} of a very strong organic pesticide such as nicotine sulfate is 50–91 mg/kg. Testing in 1977–78 showed Treflan-related patacellular carcinoma (cancer) in female mice, but the Treflan formula used was contaminated by nitrosamines, which are now kept, according to DowElanco, "well below 0.5 ppm." According to a DowElanco spokesperson, out of eight subsequent tests, only one, at the relatively high rate of >4000 ppm dermal exposure for rats, "showed a possible cancer potential for people."

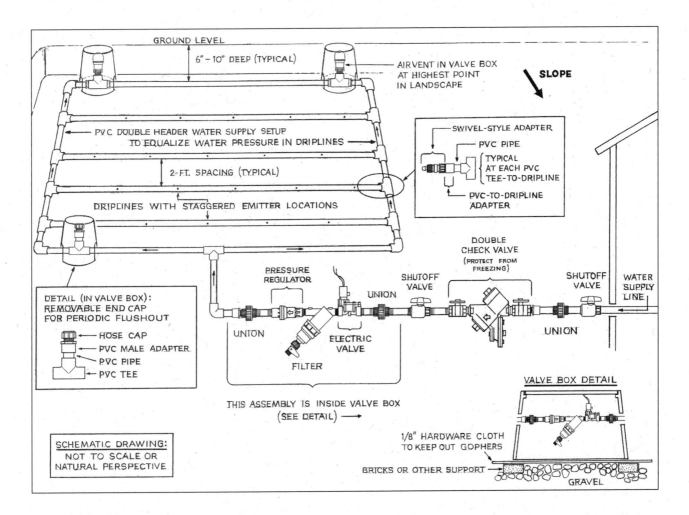

Figure 89 Subsurface drip irrigation demands careful placement of the in-line tubing—the distance between emitters along the laterals (lengths of tubing) and the measurement between the laterals—to ensure even irrigation. Soil texture determines these important measurements. Guidelines vary, from 24-inch-by-24-inch emitter spacing in clay, 12-inch emitter and 18-inch lateral spacing in loam and 12-inch-by-12-inch intervals in sand. A tubing depth of 6 to 10 inches is the common recommendation. A double check valve is required when any of the tubing in the landscape is 12 inches or more above the source of the water so siphoning of the irrigation water doesn't contaminate the home's water. The double check valve must be installed only by a licensed contractor. [This is a schematic of an installation. The actual parts and specific adapters will vary with each installation. Read the in-line tubing manufacturer's web site installation manual carefully or hire a landscape irrigation contractor.]

APPENDIX #3
Maximum Length of Tubing

The following two charts are perhaps the most important illustrations in the book. I've put together a listing of various drip irrigation tubing and pipes in a chart form to compare how long one product can be used on flat ground. The first column is a listing of the manufacturer's name brand. The next column designates the spacing between emitters. [The 1/8" and 1/4" rating for solid "spaghetti" is for the solid length of each— 5 feet to 15 feet respectively.] Some in-line emitter tubing [hose] are listed. This is followed by the recommended highest level of psi. [Even though solid PVC can take a much greater psi, it is sized here to reduce the pressure enough to prevent the drip hose fittings from blowing apart.] The gph is in the following column. Next comes a visual aid showing the maximum run on flat ground for each product. A "fudge factor" has been added to compensate for pressure lost due to the friction of tees, elbows, and other parts.

Instead of using complicated formulas, this chart will work quite nicely in small-to medium-sized landscape or garden. You can simply look up the pipe or hose that you want to use and follow the arrows to determine a safe number for the total of each assembly. Consider the 1/2-inch supply PVC pipe which can pass no more than 250 gph. As an example, you might have drip tubing totaling 350 gph. Since you've exceeded the 250 gph flow rate of the 1/2-inch solid pipe to supply the drip system, you'll have to break the water into two subassemblies [each turned on at a separate time] or use the 3/4-inch PVC that is rated for 480 gph. As another example, using in-line emitter tubing

with 0.62-gph emitters installed every 12 inches, allows for a maximum run of total of 369 feet of Techline CV tubing. This provides a flow rate of 228 gph [0.62 gph x 369]. Now, you simply total all your emitters to see if a length of Techline CV works off of one valve or the main assembly. A large garden with a thousand feet of this tubing might need a number of subsystems but will require that only one valve can be open at a time to supply numerous subassemblies.

Try sketching a map of your yard to scale. Draw your first idea of an irrigation scheme. Double check the number of total irrigation hoses. Be sure to size the PVC pipe to match the flow rates of the tubing. This just a divide and conquer approach to sizing your systems. Increase the supply pipe where need.

It's safer to put the pressure regulator and valve out in the yard inside one of the green boxes made for hiding drip hardware. If you trench to get to a distant control valve, be sure to add the wires for opening and closing the valve[s]. Use Sch 125 PVC if the gophers are a problem. It is a good idea to fill the trench half way with sand so someone digging near a pipe may be clued by the sand that pipes are under the sand.

MAXIMUM LENGTH ON FLAT GROUND
DO NOT DESIGN FOR BOTH MAXIMUM FLOW AND LENGTH

TUBING/PIPE		PSI	GPH	Maximum Length
"SPAGHETTI" TUBING	1/8"	20	15	(5')
TUBING	1/4"	20	30	(15')
1/4" IN-LINE TUBING	6"centers	25	1 gph/ft.	(20')
	12" centers	25	2 gph/ft.	(30')
SOLID DRIP HOSE	12" I.D.	25	110	(240')
	3/8" I.D.	25	110	(120')
SOLID SCH 40 PVC	1/2"	40	250	(200')
	3/4"	40	480	(300')
	1"	40	780	(300')
	1-1/4"	40	1200	(300')
TECHLINE CV	12" centers	45	0.26	(618')
1/2" pressure-compensating	18" centers	45	0.26	(877')
in-line tubing	12" centers	45	0.6	(369')
with a check	18" centers	45	0.6	(523')
valve in each	12" centers	45	0.9	(280')
emitter (self cleaning)	18" centers	45	0.9	(397')
TECHLINE RW	12" centers	45	0.6	(369')
RW = reclaimed	18" centers	45	0.9	(280')
water, 17mm	24" centers	45	0.6	(666')
blue series	24" centers	45	0.9	(506')
POROUS PIPE (HOSE)	0.38" O.D.	45	54gph/100'	(100') each lateral
Mr. SoakerHose	0.58" O.D.	45	54gph/100'	(150') each lateral
	0.70" O.D.	45	54gph/100'	(150') each lateral
	0.82" O.D.	45	54gph/100'	(250') each lateral
POROUS PIPE (HOSE)	0.25" O.D.	25	varies	(10')
The Drip Store	0.58" O.D.	25	varies	(75')

Length scale: 10' | 20' | 30' | 40' | 50' | 100' | 200' | 300' | 400' | 500' | 600'

600' total from one hose bib

I.D. = Inside Diameter   O.D. = Outside Diameter   16mm = 600 series uses green compression adapters   18mm = 700 series uses blue compression adapters.   Porous pipe should never exceed a 2' change in elevation.

MAXIMUM LENGTH ON FLAT GROUND
DO NOT DESIGN FOR BOTH MAXIMUM FLOW AND LENGTH

TUBING/PIPE		PSI	GPH	Maximum Length
AGRIFIM DURA-FLO PC	12" centers	45	0.5	(430')
	18" centers	45	0.5	(610')
	24" centers	45	0.5	(775')
pressure compensating	12" centers	45	1.0	(315')
700 series	18" centers	45	1.0	(450')
18mm, blue ring	24" centers	45	1.0	(570')
GEOFLOW Wasteflow PC	12" centers	45	0.53	(354')
	24" centers	45	0.53	(501')
	12" centers	45	1.02	(222')
	24" centers	45	1.02	(321')

Scale: 10' 20' 30' 40' 50' 100' 200' 300' 400' 500' 600'

❧ Glossary ☙

A

actinomycetes — Soil inhabitants that resemble molds and fall between true molds and bacteria in classification. Their filaments, that are much smaller than a mushroom's, permeate the soil and form fruiting bodies. Actinomycetes thrive in moist, well-aerated soil. They assist in the digestion of organic matter and lignin, and in the liberation of nutrients.

adapter — Generally speaking, any plumbing or drip irrigation part that connects one size of pipe or part to another. Often used to refer to the female fitting, whether glued or threaded, that joins different parts together. For example, an fht [female hose thread] x [by] fipt [female iron pipe thread] adapter converts hose threads to pipe threads. The male versions are often called transition nipples. [See transition nipple.]

aerobic soil — A well-drained soil with sufficient pore space to allow plenty of air to circulate in and out of the ground. The pore space is usually dependent upon a reasonable amount of organic matter and humus, both of which hold onto nutrients and keep the pore structure open. A healthy soil doesn't have to move nearly as fast as Jane Fonda to remain aerobic.

atmospheric vacuum breaker — This linguistic mouthful is actually a simple device that uses air to break any reverse siphon of water from the yard's irrigation system back into the home's water supply. Helps keep the home's water supply pure and disease-free.

B

backflow preventer — A device that keeps irrigation water from siphoning back into the house and contaminating the home's drinking water supply. There are three major types of backflow preventer: check valves, atmospheric vacuum breakers, and reduced-pressure backflow preventers. Always check with your local building or water department to determine that a backflow prevention device is code-approved for your area.

ball valve — A valve that has a globe-shaped, rotating interior. The solid globe has a circular tunnel through one axis. When the handle of the valve is rotated, the solid portion of the ball cuts off the flow of water. Another rotation lines up the tunnel with the inside of the hose, and water flows through the valve. Ball valves are often found at the discharge ports of quality Y-filters. Because ball valves shear off any contaminants and because they don't easily wear out, as gate valves do, they are the preferred valve for manual irrigation systems.

barb — Not at all related to the famous stoic, anatomically incorrect child's doll. Rather, any fitting with an arrow-like flange that allows the fitting to be inserted, like a fishhook in some poor catfish's throat, in only one direction. Barbed parts allow emitters to be inserted into the wall of solid drip hose and insert fittings to be placed inside the drip hose itself.

C

check valve — A backflow preventer with an internal spring around a plunger rod and a gasketed disk, that stops any water siphoning back toward the house. Often not legal as the only backflow preventer in a drip system; must be coupled with some form of atmospheric vacuum breaker.

close nipple — A short, 3/4-inch pipe nipple

[see nipple]. Because the length is so short, close nipples are completely covered with male iron pipe threads. You'll never see one of these in the *Sports Illustrated* swimsuit issue!

combination stake — Used to hold up misters and spaghetti tubing in the landscape and containers.

complex path emitter — See tortuous path emitter. [See, it wasn't that complex, was it?]

compression fitting — A type of fitting used to join two pieces of drip irrigation hose. The hose is forced inside a circular opening that has a barbed, ringed opening. Once inserted, the hose can't be easily pulled back out because of the circular barb. Unlike other types of fittings, this fitting seals better, up to a point, as the water pressure increases because the swelling hose squeezes tightly against the compression ring.

compression ring — A single compression barbed ring that can be glued into the slip [unthreaded] opening of a 1/2-inch PVC fitting to convert it to a drip irrigation compression fitting.

controller — An electronic device used to turn irrigation valves on and off automatically. Plugs into the home's 110VAC power and steps the power down to 24VAC to control the solenoid valves. Unlike timers, controllers usually service more than one irrigation line or zone. Most modern controllers are operated by computer chips and have digital readouts. As scientific as this sounds, controllers have a way of messin' up, which remains unexplained, sporadic, and very irritating. Besides, it takes a rocket scientist fluent in Gibberish to understand most of the manuals and to program the darn gizmo. [See also timer.]

coupler — Also called a coupling. Used to join two pieces of drip irrigation hose. Best done in the privacy of your own home.

crown rot — See *Phytophthora*.

D

diaphragm — Drip irrigation parts, in spite of their male and female names, don't need birth control. But some emitters use an internal diaphragm, usually made from some type of rubber, to modulate the flow of water and to help purge the emitter of any built-up sediment.

drain header — The drip hose, whether solid or with in-line emitters, that collects all the water at the end of the laterals farthest from the supply header. Like a supply header in that it's connected to one or more laterals. Usually a flushing end cap or a threaded end cap is added to the drain header to make it easy to flush the hose and drain out water for winterization.

drip — [1] An unwanted droplet of water at the base of your water heater, which means a multi hundred-dollar visit from the plumber. [2] The tiny dribble of water passing from an emitter. [3] That ugly oaf who sat behind you in ninth grade science class. [4] A style or technology of irrigation in that a tiny trickle of water is slowly applied to every plant.

drip hose adapter — The first fitting at the beginning of a drip irrigation system. Almost always an fht [female hose thread] swivel x [by] drip hose adapter. The female hose threads of the swivel go onto the male hose threads of a faucet or a transition nipple. The swivel action makes it easy to add or remove this fitting quickly. The other side of the adapter is either a slip [glue], compression, insert or Spin-Loc part, depending upon the system.

drip line— A length of solid drip hose. Sometimes used as a way to describe dripper line or even the edge of a plant's canopy. [See below.]

dripline — The width of a tree or shrub's foliage, where water would drip off the edge of the canopy. Not an indicator of the width of the root system—roots grow from one-half to three times wider than the drip line.

dripology — The modern, albeit inexact, science of drip irrigation. The only recognized school of higher learning for students of dripology is the School of Hard Knocks.

dripper line — Also known as in-line drip hose or line. See tortuous path emitter.

drought — Practically speaking, not a clearly defined word. The dictionary defines it as "a prolonged period of dry weather; lack of rain." But drought is certainly a relative term. A 5-week dry spell in the humid South may be devastating to certain unirrigated plants, while five months of no rain whatsoever is routine in California.

dweeb — An accurate description of some plumbers—looks sort of like the school nerd and acts as if he or she has been around too much pipe dope; a certified klutz. [See klutz.]

E

elbow — As amazing as it may seem, this has nothing to do with that joint halfway between your wrist and shoulder. An elbow is actually a fitting that allows drip hose or pipe to make a 90° turn. Also informally called a "90." Nobody knows what the joint in the middle of your arm is really called.

elbow grease — My grandfather, "Popper," always told me, "A little elbow grease'll make the job go faster." I looked for years in his garage for a can or jar of this important compound, but to no avail. If you know where to get some, let me know.

emitter — [1] The little gizmos attached to, or built within, solid drip irrigation hose that control the flow of water to the landscape or plant[s]. There are many name-brand versions of emitters, but they basically fall into four generic styles or technologies: single diaphragm, double dia-

phragm, tortuous [or complex] path, and simple orifice. [2] A New Age self-help and personal-growth addict who is always emitting his or her feelings.

end cap — The fitting added at the end of a drip hose lateral to make it easy to open the tubing for drainage or flushing. Has a female hose thread cap with a washer that threads onto the male hose thread fitting. The other end will be a compression, insert or Spin-Loc opening, depending upon what system you have.

evapotranspiration — Loss of water from a plant or crop via transpiration from the foliage and evaporation from the soil's surface. The ET [evapotranspiration] rate is influenced by humidity, rainfall, wind speed, temperature, and mulch.

F

faucet — The standard gizmo on the end of the pipe sticking out of the house's exterior wall or on top of a metal water pipe in the yard onto which the garden hose is attached.

fertilizer injector — See proportioner.

fht — Plumbing moniker for a female hose thread.

figure 8 end closure — A simple end closure that involves threading the end of the drip hose through one side of the Figure 8, bending the end of a drip hose over and securing the bent end inside the other half of the Figure 8 end closure.

filter — A device with a metal screen [cheap, poor-quality models have plastic screens] that is used to trap any particulates, dirt, or scum before it can clog the emitters. An essential component of all drip irrigation systems.

fipt — Plumbing moniker for a female iron pipe thread.

free lunch — No such thing.

G

gate valve — A valve where the internal mechanism is a vertical-closing panel [gate]. Because the gate rubs against its vertical channel, this type of valve is more likely to start leaking than a ball valve. Usually has a round handle perpendicular to the valve's shaft.

gizmophobia — A recently defined modern illness. Symptoms include: refusing to program the clock on your VCR; making coffee the old-fashioned way, with boiled water from the stove top; the reluctant ownership of an answering machine [severe gizmophobia involves refusal to purchase an answering machine and refusal to talk to such devices]; and avoidance of all ATMs. Thought to be due to a virulent form of computer virus. No known cure.

goof plug — No dripologist should be without a set of goof plugs. This essential part is merely a solid barbed plug or barbed cap that is used to patch holes where emitters have been removed. The goof plug is inserted into the hole and left there permanently.

green manure — A cover crop that is tilled into the soil to improve its tilth and to act as a mild fertilizer. Has nothing to do with the color of any animal's feces.

H

hardware cloth — Not a cloth at all but a mesh of galvanized metal wire. Good for excluding gophers from plantings or lining the bottoms of irrigation main assembly boxes so the gopher or mole throws [piles of dug-up tunnel dirt] don't fill up the enclosures. Comes in a mesh with 1/8-inch to 1-inch or larger square holes.

hose bib — See faucet.

hose shut-off valve — A small ball valve that can be added at the end of a hose to control water without you having to run back and forth to the faucet. With a few extra parts, this valve can be spliced into any drip hose, allowing the gardener to exclude water from portions of a system. Often used with a drip irrigation system for vegetables.

I

in-line emitter hose — A more recent and effective type of drip irrigation hose in that the emitters are placed inside the hose at regular intervals by the manufacturer. The pre-spaced emitters use a tortuous path technology for water regulation without clogging. Water can be distributed at 1/2-, 1- and 2-gph rates at many separate intervals ranging from 12 to 72 inches.

insert fitting — These fittings have male-shaped parts with barbed exteriors that insert inside the drip irrigation hose. As the water pressure increases, up to a point, the fitting is more likely to fail because the swelling drip hose can bloat away from the barbed posts. A ring clamp must be used to secure the hose against too much pressure.

IPS flex PVC — A thick-walled, flexible tubing that can be glued directly into 3/4-inch PVC slip fittings. The flexibility of the "pipe" makes it ideal for situations in that a riser coming out of the ground is likely to be knocked around or disturbed.

J

J-stake — A landscape pin used to secure drip irrigation hose, landscape netting, and 12VDC wiring. Made like an upside-down version of the letter "J." Not as sturdy as the best U-stakes.

K

klutz — A cross between a twitching schlemiel and a stumbling politician. Someone who has plenty of coordination problems but no corporeal medical problem to blame them on. The modern word for a spaz.

Kourik — A bohemian name of obscure origin. The author and publisher is the last of the species. Not related to Katie Couric of television fame…yet.

L

labyrinth — A complex, tortuous path inside certain emitters. The labyrinth of passages keeps any sediment in the water in suspension so that it will pass through the emitter's orifice. All in-line emitter tubing uses some form of labyrinth to allow for a relatively large emitter orifice and to keep the emitter from clogging.

Laser tubing — Resembles 1/4-inch or 3/8-inch spaghetti tubing but has a small cut every 6 or 12 inches, depending upon the type. Much cheaper than in-line drip hose but will clog easily, is not pressure compensating, and can't be used for very long runs.Has been replaced by in-line 1/4-inch emitter tubing [spaghetti].

lateral — A lateral is a water-bearing pipe or hose that originates as an offshoot of a main supply pipe. Laterals are usually attached to the supply line via a tee.

M

main assembly — The collection of parts at the main water supply [often a faucet] that keeps the home's drinking water pure, filters the water supply to the emitters, and regulates the water pressure to keep the drip system intact. The main assembly is usually composed of a backflow preventer, filter, and pressure regulator—plus the miscellaneous part needed to connect everything.

mesh — Most irrigation filters are rated by mesh size. The larger the mesh number, the better the filtration—smaller particles are trapped. Many metal screen filters are either 60 mesh [254 microns, or 0.01 inch], 100 mesh [152 microns, or 0.006 inch], 140 mesh [104 microns, or 0.004 inch], or 200 mesh [75 microns, or 0.003 inch].

mht — Plumbing moniker for a male hose thread.

micron —A common measurement for irrigation parts. The bigger the micron number, the bigger the opening. A single micron equals one-millionth of a meter. Two hundred fifty-four microns equals 0.01 inch and equals a 60-mesh screen.

mipt — Plumbing moniker for a male iron pipe thread.

N

nipple — Actually, not as sexy as it might sound. Plumbing nipples come in plastic and iron versions, with male iron pipe threads on each end. Unlike people's, the plumbing nipple ranges in size from 3/4 inch [See close nipple.] to 48 inches in length. Used to join two female iron pipe threads.

Numero Uno — The first, most frequently occurring cosmic plumbing law. See PMLP.

O

O-ring — Not a zero ring but a circular rubber gasket. Used in a union fitting to seal the joint where the two flush plates of each side of the union meet. Not attached to the union. Don't let the O-ring fall out or disappear.

P

Perma-Loc — Another name brand for the same type of screw together fitting such as a Spin-Loc.

Phytophthora — The crown of the root system is the upper 6 to 12 inches of the root system. This is the zone most vulnerable to crown rot [*Phytophthora* spp.]. The genus name for various species of fungal diseases [spp.] that attack the upper portion of the roots to destroy the bark's active layers of transport. Often called crown rot.

pipe dope — The sticky, gooey stuff you spread on pipe threads to make sure there are no leaks. Pipe dope has a magical magnetic attraction to all clean clothes, rugs and expensive suits. Other than the mess, any dope can use the stuff.

PMLP — Pop Murphy's Laws of Plumbing. A list of the seven most annoying, yet universally common, plumbing problems, as inscribed on a pair of galvanized tablets. Developed and inflicted by Pop Murphy. These rare tablets were uncovered at a secret, undisclosed site at a large urban hardware store beneath an enormous pile of old, corroding, and rusting special-order plumbing parts that were never delivered. [See also Pop Murphy.]

Pop Murphy — The inventor of devious, cunning and irritating plumbing gizmos. Also the perpetrator of all leaks, broken fittings and plumbing problems. Honored in the recently found tablets titled "Pop Murphy's Laws of Plumbing." [See PMLP.]

pressure-compensating emitter — A special type of emitter that is engineered so that the flow rate stays the same regardless of the length of the line [up to a point] and any change in elevation. Required when irrigating landscapes with a total elevation change of 20 feet or more. Has nothing to do with stress reduction—you're on your own.

pressure gauge — A handy device that is attached to a faucet or to the end of a drip line to check on the operating psi [water pressure, in pounds per square inch].

pressure regulator — A gizmo that magically reduces the water pressure in the city or home's plumbing to 25 psi or lower to protect the subsequent drip irrigation fittings. Put one in with every main assembly. Don't ask how it works; just do it.

proportioner — A special device that draws a proportioned amount of a concentrated solution out of a tank and mixes it with the irrigation water going through the drip system. Can be used to apply soluble fertilizers or to clean out the tubing and emitters with dilutions of acids.

psi — Pounds per square inch; the unit of measure for water pressure. Typical home water pressure is 40 to 80 psi. Drip irrigation systems generally operate at 10 to 25 psi.

punch — A hand held device used to poke a small hole in solid drip hose so an emitter can be added to the hose. Not required with in-line emitter tubing.

PVC — A type of semi-rigid plastic made from polyvinyl chloride [PVC], that is often used for garden plumbing. Some of the more common grades of this pipe are [from sturdiest to weakest walls] Schedule 80, Schedule 40, class 200 and class 120, that resist bursting, in 1/2-inch to 1-inch pipe, up to, respectively, 620–850, 370–480, 200, and 120 pounds per square inch.

R

reduced pressure backflow preventer — The best and most expensive type of backflow preventer. Best plumbed in at one location to protect the home's water supply from all of the exterior irrigation lines. Must be installed by a professional plumber or landscape contractor.

riser — The vertical pipe coming out of the ground to a faucet. Actually a very long nipple. [See also nipple.]

S

Sch — Stands for the word "schedule." Used to denote the type or grade of PVC pipe and fittings—Sch 40 or Sch 80.

shrubbery — Plants that are smaller than most trees [and dumber] and bigger than ground covers [but slower, in every way] but refuse to get a real life. Also known as one of the prerequisite offerings for travelers who wish to appease the guardians of the Dark Forest of Evening—the Knights-Who-Say-Kneek—and pass through those enchanted woods unharmed. [See the movie *In Search of the Holy Grail*, featuring Monty Python.]

sinker roots — Those tree roots that grow straight down and help anchor the tree against wind, snow and ice. Not the same as taproots. Sinker roots descend into the ground from all areas of the root system.

slip — It would be nice if this word meant that your garden [or mine, for that matter] were littered with lots of skimpy underclothing. Alas, it just means a PVC fitting with an opening that requires glue, as opposed to threads with pipe dope, to "weld" the two parts together. Usually, the end of the hard, rigid PVC irrigation pipe and the fitting are moistened with PVC glue and the pipe is slipped into the wet, round opening of the waiting fitting.

solenoid — The electrical valves used to control drip irrigation systems. The wires to the electrical valve usually carry 24 volts of AC power. The irrigation controller has a transformer to step down the house current to 24VAC. These valves are dependent upon the static line pressure of the water supply to assist in the opening and closing of the valve.

spaghetti stake — Either a slotted stake that holds the spaghetti tubing in place in the landscape or a plastic stake with a post onto that the spaghetti is slipped, turning the stake into a form of emitter.

spaghetti tubing — Don't try to eat this stuff at home. Actually, a tiny or slender type of polyethylene tubing that can be used to distribute water to emitters or plants. Comes in 1/4- and 1/8-inch diameters. Because of this tubing's propensity to knot up, twist around itself and—it appears to be breeding and will most surely make a tangled mess of itself. Only a severely masochistic person would use this stuff out in the landscape. It can be controlled by its use in container plantings.

speed coupling — A fitting used with garden hoses and devices with hose threads that allows for the quick insertion [coupling] of two parts instead of the tedious process of screwing the parts together. The coupling mechanism resembles the male and female fittings found on an air compressor hose at the gas station. [Although, with the status of the modern American filling station, you're lucky to find an operating version.]

Spin-Loc — A series of fittings that allow for easy connection of drip irrigation hose. Utilizes a male post that the drip hose fits over and a threaded ring that tightens down over the outside of the hose.

spot emitter — Not a true emitter because it makes a spray. A plastic stake used with spaghetti tubing. The spaghetti is inserted onto a post at the top of the stake; the depth and width of the V-cut in the post control both the flow rate and the spray pattern.

sprinkler — A soon-to-be-antique method of irrigation that pisses a large amount of the irrigation water into the wind.

stabilizing leg — For people who drink and irrigate. Not really. Metal legs attached to a main assembly so it isn't stressed as it hangs off the faucet and won't be broken if bumped into.

subsystem — A branched system of laterals originating from a main supply line. Unlike a single lateral, a subsystem, also called a submain, usually has several subordinate lines all connected by tees in a pattern similar to a candelabra.

supply header — The solid or in-line drip irrigation hose that supplies one or more laterals.

swivel — A rotating fitting that can be screwed onto another fitting. Usually refers to a female hose thread [fht] that is threaded onto the end of a hose, faucet, or drip irrigation part. Usually requires a rubber gasket in the swivel to prevent leaks.

T

tee — A fitting that joins a lateral line [solid PVC pipe, in-line emitter tubing, or solid drip hose] to another water supply line. Tees come in compression, slip [glued], barbed-insert or Spin-Loc models. In this book, a device that has nothing to do with getting a tiny ball to disappear into a hole in the ground.

timer — A battery-powered controller that controls one irrigation line. Attaches to the faucet and controls the flow of water to a hose or drip irrigation system.

tortuous path emitter — Emitter that contains a complex path or labyrinth, that allows larger particles to flow through it without causing clogging. This type of emitter stays virtually clog-free, even when used with well water or filtered water that remains high in sediments and suspended solids, or when iron oxides, dissolved calcium and other minerals are present in the water supply. One of the more recent developments in drip irrigation technology, and one that has virtually eliminated the chance of clogging—the Achilles heel of the older types of emitters.

transfer barb — A plastic part usually used to connect spaghetti tubing or Laser tubing to solid drip hose. The drip hose is first pierced with a punch to make a hole. Then, one of the rigid posts with a barb is inserted to keep the hole from squeezing shut around the spaghetti or Laser tubing. The other barbed post secures the spaghetti or Laser tubing. [See also Laser tubing adapter.]

transition nipple — A plastic or metal fitting with a male hose thread [mht] and a male iron pipe thread [mipt] that is often used to connect conventional garden plumbing to drip irrigation fittings.

U

union — Actually, somewhat related to a coupling. A union is a plumbing part that, after the locking ring is unthreaded, separates into two pieces and allows you to take a portion of any irrigation system [providing there is a union on each end of the section] out for repairs without having to cut the pipe. The use of unions allows for the quick reinstallation of the repaired section without having to reglue with extra fittings.

U-stake — A landscape pin used to secure drip irrigation hose, landscape netting, and 12VDC wiring. Shaped like an inverted letter "U." Much sturdier than a J-stake.

V

variable spaghetti stake — A plastic landscape stake with a V-shaped opening to adapt to various sizes of spaghetti tubing or Laser tubing. Ideally, it attempts to hold the tubing in place, but it is often unsuccessful in a real landscape. Best used with container plants.

W

wet spot —The wet spot in drip irrigation, unlike other wet spots, has both depth and breadth—the extent of that is dependent upon the rate of the dribble [in gph], the duration of the trickle [in hours], the soil type, the slope of the land, and the climate.

X

x — In spite of the lascivious nature of male and female plumbing fittings, there are no X-rated plumbing parts. Actually, a plumbing symbol for the word "by," used to denote a fitting's specifications. The notation "mipt x mht" reads "male iron pipe thread by male hose thread"—that is a transition nipple. [See also transition nipple.]

Y

Y-filter — Because. Actually, the best type of filter for a drip irrigation system. Easily identified by the filter chamber, that is integrated into the filter at an obtuse angle. The best Y-filters have a metal screen filter within the filter chamber and a ball valve at the end of the chamber to make it easy to flush the screen.

Y-valve — A valve that has two hose hookups. It allows two hoses or irrigation devices to be attached to one faucet. Usually has a small ball valve on each of the two male hose thread [mht] hookups.

Z
z end.

❧ Suppliers ❧

I always recommend finding a local drip irrigation hardware supplier over a mail-order company. Find a local landscape contractor's drip irrigation supplier that you can ask any-and-all questions. Unfortunately, quality drip irrigation hardware, especially in-line emitter technology, is still hard to find in many towns, big box stores, and cities around the country. Hence, this listing of mail-order sources for drip irrigation widgets.

What follows is a basic listing of those companies that offer irrigation gizmos. Some carry in-line emitter tubing. This listing is not meant to be exhaustive, but even the most ambitious dripologist will be able to satisfy his or her drip techno-fix.

Dripworks
190 Sanhedrin Circle
Willits, CA 95490-8753
800-522-3747
www.dripworks.com

An excellent full-color mail-order catalog. They feature 1/2-inch and 1/4-inch in-line emitter tubing among a very extensive selection of hardware for any place that needs to be irrigated. They offer several manifold systems. Source for T-Tape®. Among the listings of timers is the Orbit Control Star Timer. Support service is excellent.

The Drip Store
980 Park Center, Drive Ste. E
Vista, CA 92081
760-597-1669
www.dripirrigation.com

This catalog feature various kits, not individual parts. No in-line tubing, sells solid drip hose and 50' and 100' rolls of 0.25" and 0.58" tubing. Low lateral runs.

The Gardener's Supply Company
128 Intervale Rd.
Burlington, VT 05401
802 -863-1700
www.gardeners.com

Offers several downspout rain barrels and an English-style diverter, with no screen.

Harmony Farm Supply
P.O. Box 460
Graton, CA 95444
Store: 3244 Gravenstein Hwy. North
Sebastopol, CA 95472
707-823-9125
www.harmonyfarm.com

Don't let the word "Farm" deceive you. Harmony Farm Supply has a very large number of drip irrigation gadgets and widgets for gardeners. It carries various types of in-line emitter tubing, but these are not listed on their web site. The offerings via their site are very small compared to the vast number of options at the "brick and mortar" store. Perhaps the most comprehensive catalog, it is best suited to those with some previous irrigation experience, but everyone will benefit from reading this catalog. Also, it includes organic gardening supplies, seed, books, and tools. The large spacious retail store is located in Sebastopol in Sonoma County wine country. Catalog is free.

The Natural Gardening Company
www.naturalgardening.com
707-766-9303

A mail-order [internet only] source for Techline™ CV [Check Valve] tubing along with all the fittings and accessories. They sell Techline 12" spacing with 1/2-gpm emitters.

The Urban Farmer Store
2833 Vicente St.
San Francisco, CA 94116
415 661-2204
800-753-3747 questions and order line
www.urbanfarmerstore.com

A comprehensive offering of automatic and manual drip irrigation systems. Carries in-line emitter tubing from several manufacturers and all the required fittings. Ask for the special sheet listing the in-line emitter tubing. Oriented to the urban and suburban gardener, not the commercial farmer. Has a 6000-square-foot retail store near Golden Gate Park, San Francisco, CA. They now have stores in Mill Valley [Marin County, CA] and Richmond [Contra Costa County, CA]. Paper catalog is free. Web site has an extensive listing of parts.

The Irrigation Mart
300 South Service Road
Rustin, LA 71270
800-729-7246
www.irrigation-mart.com

A good cross section of what a homeowner usually needs. Also carries irrigation tapes only appropriate to farmers.

In-Line Drip Tubing

In-line tubing to look for in irrigation stores, hardware stores, and big box stores now and in the coming years:

Netafim's —Techline CV® [Check Valve] and Techline®
www.netafim-usa-landscape.com/Landscape/landscape-products.php

Agrifim's —Dura-Flo™ and Dora-Flo PC™ [Pressure Compensating]
www.ndspro.com/cms/

Rain Bird's —Rain Bird Landscape Dripline PC [Pressure Compensating]
www.rainbird.com/DIY/products/drip/index.htm

Geoflow's —Geoflow Subsurface Tubing: nano-ROOTGUARD® and
Geoshield™ [Both with Treflan®]
www.geoflow.com/landscape.html

Salco Products Drip Irrigation's —SMARTInline® PC [Pressure Compensating]
www.weathermatic.com/index.php?key=smartline

Toro's —Blue Strip Drip™ DL2000 subsurface irrigation [with ROOTGUARD® (Treflan®)], but not recommended by the 2008 Santa Monica guidelines for "professional landscape use".
www.toro.com/irrigation/res/lowvolume/dl2000/index.html

GoDrip—A great source of many makes of in-line emitter tubing including the new 0.26-gph in-line drip tubing.
www.godrip.com/browse/?coil-length=100FT&cat=dripperline%2Ftechline-cv%2F

Raindrip—I typed in www.raindrip.com and was led to this page.
http://66.241.193.42/cms/
A basic set of kits and rolls of porous hose (pipe). Kits are often seen in the big box stores.

Irrigation Direct, Inc.—Makes their own in-line tubing, Comes in 100- or 400-foot rolls, either 1/2-gph and 1-gph.
www.irrigationdirect.com

✿ Web Sites to Explore ✿

Search this site for a handbook on making and using cisterns in Texas.
www.twdb.state.tx.us/home/index.asp

A very good site for a PDF file that links to other drip irrigation sites, for both residential and farm applications.
mtngrv.missouristate.edu/publications/Drip_Irrigation_&_Watering_Web_Links.pdf

An excellent place to find links to many of the manufacturers of timers [controllers].
www.irrigationtutorials.com/links/controllermanf.htm

You can use the search feature to find suppliers in all states. Some have mail-order catalogs, retail stores, and retail web sites.
www.giyp.com/results.asp?cc=GIYP&catID=125&cgID=6273&b=&biz=1&srg=C

Provides the test results in PDF format of a large number of timers that passed the SMART guidelines. As defined by the national Irrigation Association: "'Smart' controllers estimate or measure depletion of available plant soil moisture in order to operate an irrigation system, replenishing water as needed while minimizing excess water use. A properly programmed 'smart' controller requires initial site specific setup and will make irrigation schedule adjustments, including run times and required cycles, throughout the irrigation season without human intervention."
www.irrigation.org/SWAT/Industry/default.aspx?pg=tested_climate.asp

Lists WBICs [Weather-Based Irrigation Controllers] that are approved for a rebate program. While written in 2008 for Southern California water districts, it is a good model for what other cities could [should] be implementing.
www.conservationrebates.com/programs/mwd/pdfs/List_WBICs.pdf

Another way to find many links related to all types of irrigation. Includes long lists of manufacturers of products for drip irrigation.
www.lwd.com/personal/irrigationlinks.htm

How to find the report on how yields of chilies increased even though less water was applied via drip irrigation. Includes other trials for more economic crops.
http://books.google.com/books?id=rUcioPHBAN8C&pg=PA236&lpg=PA236&dq=yields+of+chilies+drip+irrigation++India&source=web&ots=7AFMYz7Wn1&sig=VFughtQOrp3yNUSj3sWSxzONXng&hl=en&ei=XzyXSarwFJHItQP8ysmRAQ&sa=X&oi=book_result&resnum=2&ct=result#PPA236,M1%00

Or, try a search for: "**Performance of Chilli Under Drip-Irrigation with Mulch.**" Annals of the Sri Lanka Department of Agriculture.

Brochure with guidelines from the Arizona Department of Environmental Quality for grey water use. Search the site with these words: grey water.

www.azdeq.gov/environ/water/permits/download/graybro.pdf

A simple review [brochure] of the 2006 guidelines from the New Mexico Environment Department for the use of gray water.

An interesting list of cistern regulations from the Virgin Islands to various places "on the mainland". Good list of references.

www.bvsde.paho.org/bvsacd/cd47/texas/cap5.pdf

An excellent listing of Web sites in Canada and the U.S. for cistern, fog drip collection, and grey water information.

www.birdcrossstitch.com/Family_Focus/Rainwater_Collection.html

Best place to learn about cisterns for potable water. They produced a book and video, and stock all the hardware you'd ever need. They are located in Texas where there are periodic rains all spring, summer, and fall.

www.rainwatercollection.com

The best site on the Internet about grey water. Lots of free content. Art Ludwig publishes the two best books on grey water systems—and more. Also, a book on building and using tanks and cisterns.

www.oasisdesign.net

QWEL stands for Qualified Water-Efficient Landscaper. Landscaping in the arid West can use 50–80% of a homeownwer's entire water usage. This is an innovative program to enhance the knowledge of commercial landscapers to help the water conserve water. Should be a model for all water districts.

www.qweltraining.com

The American Rainwater Catchment Systems Association. Great "portal" to many other sites via their extensive Links page. The links include listings of governmental regulations for rainwater catchment systems in various towns and states.

www.arcsa.org

Texas Rainwater Catchment Guidelines. An 88-page document entitled: *The Texas Manual on Rainwater Harvesting,* Third Edition. 2005.

www.twdb.state.tx.us/publications/reports/RainwaterHarvestingManual_3rdedition.pdf

Jandy® Valve. The Web page describing the Jandy® 3-way valve [Neverlube]. You must find a local swimming pool or spa retail store to purchase one. You can search for a pool contractor using your zip code.

www.jandy.com/html/products/valves/neverlube.php

MicroIrrigation Forum. The most extensive listing of Links for every aspect of water use for farms and some information for gardeners. Has an active Trickle-L discussion group and archives of past discussions.
www.microirrigationforum.com

Water SWAT Testing List. A listing of those timers that passed testing as Weather-Based Water SWAT Testing List. A listing of those timers that passed testing as Weather-Based Irrigation Controllers from the industry's nonprofit, the Irrigation Association.
www.microirrigationforum.com/index.html

Explanation and Graphics About How a UniRam In-line Emitters Works
www.netafim-usa-agriculture.com/Agriculture/p-heavywall/p-hw-UniRam.php

***Weather and Soil Moisture-Based Landscape Irrigation Scheduling Devices, Technical Review Report*—2nd Edition. Southern California Area Office, 2007.** The most comprehensive listing of timers and hardware related to Weather-Based Irrigation Controllers. Available for free [at least in 2008] from 951-695-5310 or download at:
www.usbr.gov/waterconservation/docs/SmartController.pdf

University of Missouri Extension, Drip Irrigation & Watering Web Links. Another good PDF file with listings of Web sites about drip irrigation.
mtngrv.missouristate.edu/publications/Drip_Irrigation_&_Watering_Web_Links.pdf

Irrigation Controller Manufacturer Links. Exactly what the title suggests.
www.irrigationtutorials.com/links/controllermanf.htm

Listings for Drip Irrigation Supplies in California [I live in California, so I'm prejudiced. But many other state's mail-order companies are listed. You just have to search a bit.]
www.giyp.com/results.asp?cc=GIYP&catID=125&cgID=6273&b=&biz=1&srg=CA

City of Santa Monica's Ordinances. A great source of information about drip irrigation, grey water, cistern guidelines, and rebates. A model more U.S. cities should adopt.
www.smgov.net/epd/residents/water/landscape_index.htm

Bibliography

Banks, Suzy. *Rainwater Collection for the Mechanically Challenged*. Dripping Springs, Texas: Tank Town Publishing: 1997. 2nd edition 2004. 3rd edition 2008.

Buckman, Harry O., and Nyle C. Brady. *The Nature and Properties of Soils*. New York: The Macmillan Company, 1963.

Dickerson, George W. *Evaluation of User Friendly Drip Irrigation/Mulch Systems for Urban and Small Farm Speciality Crop Production (2001–2004)*. Cooperative State Research Education, and Extension Service, USDA: New Mexico State University, Water Task Force, Report #6, 2006.

Drip Irrigation Specification Binder. Agrifim - Quality Products by NDS. Fresno, CA: Agrifim, May 2008.

City of Los Angeles, Office of Water Reclamation. *Gray Water Pilot Project Final Report*. Los Angeles, CA: November 1992.

Harris, Richard W., James R. Clark, and Nelda P. Matheny. *Arboriculture-Integrated Management of Landscape Trees, Shrubs, and Vines*. Upper Saddle River, NJ: Prentice-Hall, 1999.

Jeavons, John. *How to Grow More Vegetables —Than You Ever Thought Possible on Less Land Than You Can Imagine.* Willits, CA: Ten Speed Press, 2007.

Kolsnikov, V.A. *The Root System of Fruit Trees*. 2nd edition. The University Press of the Pacific. Honolulu, HA: 2003.

Kourik, Robert. *Designing and Maintaining Your Edible Landscape—Naturally*. Occidental, CA: Metamorphic Press, 1986. [Reprinted: East Meon, Hampshire, UK: Permanent Publications, 2004.]

- - -. *Drip Irrigation, For Every Landscape and All Climates*. Occidental, CA: Metamorphic Press, 1992.

- - -. *The Lavender Garden*. San Francisco: Chronicle Books, 1998.

- - -. *Pruning, Clipping with Confidence*. New York: Workman Publishing Company, 1997.

- - -. *The Tree & Shrub Finder*. Newtown, CT: Taunton Press, 2000.

- - -. *Roots Demystified, Change Your Gardening Habits to Help Roots Thrive*. Occidental, CA: Metamorphic Press, 2008.

Krasilnikov, N.A. *Soil Microorganisms and Higher Plants*. Academy of Sciences of the USSR, Institute of Microbiology. Moscow: 1958. Reprinted for The National Science Foundation, Washington, DC and The Department of Agriculture, Jerusalem: Israel Program for Scientific Translations, 1961.

Lancaster, Brad. *Rainwater Harvesting for Drylands and Beyond*. Tucson, AZ: Rainsource Press, 2008.

Ludwig, Art. *The New Create an Oasis with Greywater—Choosing, Building and Using Greywater Systems — Includes Branched Drains Revised and Expanded 5th Edition*. Santa Barbara: CA, Oasis Design, 2007.

- - -. *Builder's Greywater Guide / Installation of Greywater Systems in New Construction and Remodeling*. Santa Barbara, CA: Oasis Design, 2006.

Nijamudeen, M.S. and P.B. Dharmasena. "**Performance of Chilli Under Drip-Irrigation with Mulch.**" Annals of the Sri Lanka Department of Agriculture, 26-27, September 2002, Plant Genetic Resource Centre [PGRC], Gannoruwa, Peradeniya, Sri Lanka. 4: 89–94.

Russell, E.W. *Soils Conditions and Plant Growth*, 10th edition. New York: Longman Group, Inc., 1973.

U.S. Department of the Interior, Bureau of Reclamation, Southern California Area Office, "**Weather and Soil Moisture Based Landscape Irrigation Scheduling Devices, Technical Review Report—2nd Edition.**" Temecula, CA: August 2007.

Weaver, John, and William Bruner. *Root Development of Vegetable Crops*. New York: McGraw-Hill Book Company, 1927.

Whitney, Alison, Richard Bennett, Carlos Arturo Carvajal, and Marsha Prillwitz. "**Monitoring Graywater Use: Three Case Studies in California.**" The California Department of Water Resources (DWR) with the City of Santa Barbara and East Bay Municipal Utilities District, January 1999.

ℰ𝒞 Index 𝒞ℛ

Note: Page numbers in *italic type* refer to information in illustrations, graphs, tables, or captions.

transition nipples, 158
Male iron pipe threads (mipt), 38, 40, 61, 151
    defined, 155
    transition nipples, 158
Master Garden Program, Germone Demonstration Orchard, 79–80
Mesh size, for filters, 155
Mice. *See* Rodents
MicroIrrigation Forum, web site, 167
Miltenberger, Gary, 123
Minerals
    acidifying system to remove, 133
    in cistern water, 110
    emitters clogged by, 36
    in water supply, 36, 133–135
Moles. *See* Rodents
Mono- and Bi-wall tubing, for vegetable beds, 87–88, *87*
Mosquitoes, in rain barrels, 111, *111*
Mounting brackets, installing, 40, 41
Mulch
    drip systems hidden by, 8, 14, 47, 80, 99
    grey water applied beneath, 99
    for landscape trees, 80
    newspaper, 14
    to protect tubing in winter, 135
    for raised beds, 89
    for weed control, 7, 14

N

The Natural Gardening Company, 144, 162
Netafim (UniRam) tubing
    for grey water systems, 129
    for SDI systems, 141, 143
    suppliers, 31, 163
    web site, 167
Nipples
    close, 151–152
    defined, 155
    transition, 158
"Non-volatile memory", for automatic timers and controllers, 124
Numero Uno, defined, 155
Nutrient absorption
    by deep roots, 14, 49
    soil structure and, 16
    wet and dry soil cycles and, 15–16, 49–50
Nutrients, released by soil microbes, 15, 49

O

Ocean, Sidney, 136
O-rings, defined, 155

P

Pathogens (human)
    survival time in soil, 97–98
    transmitted in grey water, 98, 99
Perennial plants
    grey water used for, 98, 106
    See also Trees and shrubs
Perma-Loc fittings, defined, 155
Phytophthora crown rot, defined, 155
Pipe dope
    defined, 155–156
    Teflon, 39, 61
Pipe tape, Teflon, 39

Pipe threads
    adapters, 39
    fipt, 38, 40, *60*, 151, 153
    mipt, 38, 40, 61, 151, 155, 158
    transition nipples, 158
Plant factor chart, ET efficiency rates, *53*
Plant growth
    benefits of drip irrigation, 2, 5–6, 16–17
    evapotranspiration rate, 17
    wet and dry cycles, 15–16, 49–50
    See also Root systems
Plantings, new, 46–47
Plumbers, professional
    to design/install grey water systems, *101*
    dweebs, 153
    to install cistern pumps, 112–113
    to install reduced pressure backflow preventers, 156
Plumbing
    collection pipes for grey water systems, 100
    fear of, 9, 17
    getting to know plumbing parts, 2
    for proportioners, 135
    reality-based, 10
Point-source drip irrigation, defined, 27
Pop Murphy, defined, 156
Pop Murphy's Laws of Plumbing (PMLP), 2, 9, 9–10, 139
    cheap system components and, 19
    defined, 156
    digital irrigation timers and, 119
Porous blocks, soil water sensors, 125–126
Pots, for container plantings, 72
Pressure gauges, 35, *36*
Pressure regulators, 23–24, *23*
    for containers, 71
    defined, 156
    installing, 40
    limit of, 46
    location of, 147
    for multiple-station systems, 67–69
    for porous hose, 25
    ratings, 23
    Senninger, 23–24
Preston Vineyards, raised vegetable beds, 89–91, *90*
Proportioners. *See* Fertilizer injectors and proportioners
Psi (pounds per square inch), defined, 156
Pumps. *See* Sump pumps, for cisterns; Sump pumps, for grey water systems
PVC glue
    for rigid PVC pipe, 67, 93–94
    for slip fittings, 38
    toxicity of, 10, 38
PVC pipe, rigid
    attaching fittings, 61, 93–94
    cross-threading, 61
    defined, 156
    flow rates and size of, 147
    IPS Flex-PVC, 93–94, 154
    maximum length for flat ground, *148*
    for multiple-station systems, 65, 67–69, *69*
    to prevent gopher damage, 42, 147
    schedule nomenclature, 156
    slip fittings for, 157
    for unframed garden beds, 93–94, *93*

The

SCHOOL OF HARD KNOCKS

DEPARTMENT OF DRIPOLOGY

This prestigious piece of paper verifies that

_____

has, by virtue of reading this esteemed training manual, attained the highest honors in the study of the trickle-down theory of irrigation and is hereby annointed a certified

BIG DRIP
(aka, Dripologist)

In witness thereof, my signature is affixed on this day

in Occidental, CA.

Murphy

Certified Biggest Drip and Instructor